I0147132

PARADOX

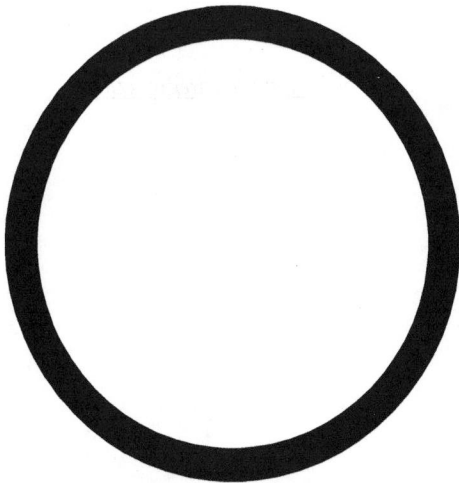

PARADOX: EXISTENCE UNVEILED

NE Publishing, Santa Rosa, CA

Copyright © 2022 by James Bond

For contact information, visit www.neparadox.com

ISBN: 979-8-9869139-0-2

First Edition: October 2022

For the second MOE, who supported my efforts and kept our young children from breaking down the office door. — J.B.

CONTENTS

PREFACE

W e live in a time of shift. A digitally connected humanity is fighting wars of culture, ideology and survival. Meanwhile, our population has reached a tipping point and many of us are fighting for our livelihoods while the natural resources on which we rely are diminishing. If our fellow man doesn't vanquish us, the collapsing environment surely will. Though the previous sentence would have rung true eighty, five hundred or even three thousand years ago, it does seem that another long peace is coming to an end. In our lifetimes, human technology and other circumstances may lead to our destruction, rebirth or both. Before one of those scenarios occurs, the most important knowledge available to mankind must be conveyed. Now and in the future, it should be used to further our causes, quell our quest for meaning and give us motivation to overcome challenges. It must also be recorded durably in our memories and physical media to be passed on to future civilizations – human or otherwise.

Having been fortunate enough to live in a time and place when beliefs could be analyzed without persecution, worldwide travel could be made via jet aircraft and many were afforded time to ponder existence, you'd think this knowledge materialized exclusively out of contented introspection. To an extent, that's accurate. Having the time and freedom to contemplate existence is of paramount importance in discovering the meaning of life. Truth be told, though, such knowledge could not have materialized from a wholly positive and pain-free perspective. It was time spent in dark realms of thought, emotion and conflict that supplemented my journey to the Paradox. Simply living exposes each of us to amazement and joy as well as sorrow and darkness. Everyone experiences a full spectrum of emotions, even the most fortunate of us. I had to put meaning to darkness to reconcile its presence in such a glorious world. In my case, the only way to understand it was to consider it without preconception. When I did, I discovered something astonishing.

This book has been written in fits and starts. The writing began in 1999. I had theorized the Paradox just two years prior while I was under immense pressure as an engineering student and my family was suffering the catastrophic results of my younger sister's drug addiction. Mentally exhausted and in emotional agony, I was grasping for meaning. Encountering the Paradox is all that separated me from the destruction of my life and some others in my path. It wasn't until I had a moment to reflect that I decided that I should write about it. The writing was started, but within only a few pages, it was shelved. Though the Paradox was a life-changing principle, I was quite novice in life. A recurring case of writer's block and my early life's adventures sidelined the writing process. Fate would take me on journey after journey over the subsequent decades. Every few years I'd pick it back up, having new life experience and ideas for its application, but fate would intervene yet again.

Although I couldn't yet fully articulate the workings of the Paradox during those times, I was able to benefit from its fundamental truths in confronting the many enigmas and difficult challenges life threw at me. It has brought an aura of kinship in times of isolation, forgiveness of the wicked, swift action in times of necessity and absolute control over my path. Twenty-five years since its revelation to me, I've experienced the power and rigidity of the Paradox as the founding principle of existence and the driving force behind it. The years of hard charging through life with all its heartbreak and wonder helped me formulate a more expansive picture than I could have illustrated previously. The act of writing this has caused me to explore facets of the Paradox that I hadn't considered before. Some subjects are better understood only after arranging them for public consumption. I've applied the Paradox in countless situations but outlining its application to specific subject matter was surprisingly educational. Over the years, I had become accustomed to automatically deploying it to the particular situation at hand without further thought. The writing process forced me to investigate its specific role in various facets of life and brought its obscure silhouette into crystal-clear focus. On some level, I had worried of discovering an aspect of it that didn't pass the test of logical scrutiny or would completely invalidate it. I also dreaded the thought that I'd come across some group of enlightened people that have possessed and disseminated the same knowledge decades or centuries ago. Like anyone with a seemingly novel concept, I wanted mine to be unique. Nonetheless, I am ready to learn otherwise and be satisfied merely by the reward of valuable insight. I'm sure someone is out there, but thus far, I haven't learned of or encountered them. Perhaps this book will bring them forward.

Throughout the book, references are made to cosmology, quantum physics, religion, psychology, historical events and figures. My knowledge of these subjects is limited to what can be gained through rudimentary research. I do not claim to be an expert in any of these areas, nor am I proclaiming scientific or historical findings. I am proclaiming the truth behind existence which, by extension, affects all aspects of reality. The purpose of discussing these subjects is to briefly examine each of them in context of the Paradox. Through these examinations, many of life's mysteries can be clarified, simplified, redefined, and even answered. Regardless of how well you understand or apply it, there is always more to learn of the Paradox as each scenario unfolds a new key map of its landscape.

Though acting as a conduit of the most important information in existence, I am man – subject to all the nuances, emotions, impulses, miscalculations, and other shortcomings of modern people. As you'll see in the coming chapters, there are two parts of our being. One resides within the animal, supporting the life that makes this perspective possible. The other resides in the continuum, delighted by limitless contemplation. To this day, I do what I must to survive and to further the cause of this animal and his offspring. I play this role with as much fervor and determination as any other role in the universe. Still, another part of my being looks on, offering vast possibility and humor while I entertain the ins and outs of being human. The viewpoints and observations on each topic are made from the perspective of a man and further analyzed in terms of the Paradox.

As mentioned, the fundamentals of the Paradox may be acquired quickly, but its specifics will reveal themselves only when applied to challenging situations or quandaries. By proceeding to read this, the Paradox will be yours to apply to your unique perspective. Approach with an open mind, as you may read revelations that shock, insult and frighten as well as some that inspire, encourage and comfort you. In the end, it'll be up to you to interpret it and either wield its power or succumb to it. At the time of this writing, a pandemic has descended upon humanity, forcing separation and isolation and a long peace has revealed its infirmity. I stand in an empty, shuttered warehouse with a laptop and precious time. Fate no longer leads elsewhere and, at last, I will complete the delivery of this precious knowledge.

HERE IT IS

Understanding the Paradox means knowing the meaning of existence. Not all who read this will fully grasp the concepts herein, but this book's mere presence offers you the opportunity to decrypt, master and enjoy your perspective in this world and beyond. If you fully comprehend what is written on the next few pages, you'll have obtained a license to make unobstructed quantum jumps toward the realities of your making. You will join the ranks of the vanishingly few people who have deciphered existence and have shone its glory unto their lives and those around them. Today may be the day you vastly alter your perspective. Then again, maybe not. If the timing for a major change in your perception of existence is not right, heed the upcoming warning.

The Paradox will inspire you to experience reality on both macro and micro levels. You will find that your emotions and needs are products of your location in the spacetime continuum and are neither to be feared nor circumvented. It will become impossible for you to hate, yet you'll bask in the catharses so often brought about by well-directed force. Oneness will be the foremost emotion you feel concerning those who share your spacetime vicinity. You will prevail in physical and metaphysical matters, for you will understand the inception and objective of all earthly and spiritual occurrences. In the natural realm you will have the ability to excel, charging forth with a passion to sample the magnificence of a rare time and place. In the spiritual realm, you will have peace in knowing your path and its reason. You will be at harmony with both life and death. Once the Paradox sets in, four personality traits that people will associate with you are: tranquil, loving, humorous and powerful. If you understand the Paradox, your environment will be one of self-creation, complete ownership and, if you choose - happiness.

On the following pages, the answers to every question you can fathom will be revealed. This accounts for all time, space and occurrence. No longer will you be forced to choose between spiritual and physical realities, for knowing this will consolidate the natural and supernatural. Upon first comprehension of it, your perspective will be reconfigured permanently. It will function much like an executable software program, automatically changing your interface with the world and your ability to control your experience. As the author, I am asking for your permission to install the Paradox into your memory. If permission is not granted, read no further. **This is a genuine warning. If your life is in balance and you do not wish to make a quantum jump or disrupt your surroundings, stop reading. After reading the Paradox, the only way to annul the knowledge is through traumatic brain injury, dementia or death.** It is possible you may die shortly after learning the Paradox as your life's mission may be completed. This likely occurred in two separate instances over the past few years. In both instances, the deceased had been introduced, one agreeably and the other not so, to the Paradox. Within months of learning the Paradox, they both died unexpectedly. It may have been coincidence. If not, the completion of life's mission is to be celebrated and not lamented.

One of the more noticeable effects the Paradox will have on you is a decreased aversion to risk, which comes with reduction of or complete loss of fear. The boldness may transpire socially, professionally, or physically and you may experience changes in your surroundings or in the people you know. You will insert yourself into places and situations that you previously would have sidestepped or avoided. And why wouldn't you if you were in control? Knowing the Paradox will increase your courage, but it will also test the limits of your valor as the intensity of your life involvement increases. You will notice people reacting to your unusual gravity – sometimes through imitation, other times with jealousy or contempt, but mostly with twinkling positivity. Negative reactions from people will be due to confusion, as you'll be less predictable and to most people that signifies danger. It will be your responsibility to offer the Paradox to all those who would benefit from it – especially those who are displaying negativity or fear. Their comprehension of it may not be immediate, but at least you will be at peace knowing it was offered. Many times, the Paradox will take months or even years to set in, but planting the seed is a good investment into your community and society in general.

Initially, the boundless possibilities and implications of finding yourself in comprehensive command may feel overwhelming. Your mind may swirl and you may feel disoriented as you attempt to select the proper heading to complete your journey. You may feel like you're piloting an airplane without having had a flying lesson. Distilling infinite possibility into a single human life would be unconceivable, but thankfully won't be necessary. After reading this, you'll be comfortable in knowing you have ample time to do everything and that no time is wasted. This world and the great beyond will reveal themselves as the blank slates and playing fields for your manifestation. You'll harness unique perspectives and the multiplicity of possibilities therein. Mastering your specific spacetime circumstance will require enormous creativity and perseverance, but it will be rewarding. While the Paradox is available to you, it is important to apply it to your situation as often as possible to maintain your masterful perspective.

As animals with traits evolved over thousands of years, we are sometimes driven by forces of habit over empirical insight. After your illumination, you must resist returning to the habitual way of dealing with life and love. You must knock down all uncertainty, fear and shame with this knowledge. Any presence of negative emotions from this point forward shall be an indication you have veered off the path and need to recall and apply the Paradox. As someone who's observed it for over two decades, I can tell you that forgetting or disregarding it in favor of succumbing to tidal waves of emotion is a hard-wired tendency. The keys to managing that tendency lie in your readiness to apply the Paradox. Just as in self-defense, presence of mind and quickness of action make the difference between success and failure. The path to success here, as in so many other endeavors, is gaining knowledge and applying it regularly. With practice, the Paradox will become your center of power, affirming that your actions are natural, justified and imminent. Without further ado, here it is -

PARADOX

Nothing is. For Nothing to be, all possibility must be counteracted. Thus, Everything transpires as an infinite contemplation of what would be. Everything is possibility. We are Everything. We are all possible matter, space, time and occurrence in all dimensions. We exist in all spacetime and at no spacetime. Existence is both an illusion and the ultimate reality. As Everything, we will see, do and be all.

The symbol of reckoning for this is a circle, wherein Nothing, represented by the circle, encapsulates all possibility in the form of Everything, represented by the interior of the circle.

This is a critical moment. You've just been reminded of the makeup of existence. It was conveyed early and concisely so that if your reading is stopped or interrupted, you'll have already been exposed to it. Don't let the reference to Nothing or the admission of its being alarm you. Its opposing core, Everything, is your infinite reality. Within Nothing, Everything is contemplated. Everything is a condition of Nothing and vice-versa. Both exist such that neither does. Understand that observing the Paradox does not make you a nihilist. Quite contrarily, it makes you an omnist due to the unavoidable inclusion of Everything as a condition of Nothing. Comprehending this paradoxical relationship is key to mastering existence.

You may have noticed that Nothing and Everything are capitalized. This has been done to differentiate between the subjects of this book, Nothing and Everything, and the commonly used non-specific words, nothing and everything; "I said nothing", "it's nothing like I imagined" or "how's everything?" The subjects Nothing and Everything are specific and singular. It is necessary to write in those terms when describing the cause and reasoning of existence. Nothing refers to *absolute* non-existence, as opposed to nothing, which refers to *relative* non-existence. The Nothing characterized in this book has no real sum, dimension or position. It is so elusive that it ceases to occur. Yet, it prevails and all else occurs only as counteracted possibility. As such, Nothing is capitalized to differentiate it from nothing. Similarly, "everything", used in our daily vocabulary, refers to our immediate surroundings. What we see as everything is contained in our proximate environment, a group of people, a space or a number of objects. In that sense, "everything" is useful in describing anything within *relative* existence. The Everything that will be presented to you in this book is vastly different. It is positive infinity. It is a collection of what is, was, and will be. It includes all dimensions and is unfathomably immense. Everything encapsulates its common meaning yet surpasses it infinitely. Consequently, Everything is capitalized to differentiate it from everything.

Although we're its perpetual subjects, we're only aware of the Paradox under the rarest of circumstances. If we were always consciously aware of it, it would interfere with other manifestations and experiences in the infinite continuum of possibility. Reading this is an exceedingly rare opportunity to comprehend and enjoy the benefits of the Paradox, hereafter referred to as *NE (pronounced like the word 'any', short for Nothing and Everything)*. Once realized, it can be applied immediately in all areas of life. You may employ it internally or externally. It can be used to mend emotional wounds or settle internal conflicts. It may be administered to people and matters that you cherish as well as those you detest or disagree with. Above all, it can act as a point of reference for your being and confirmation that all is as it should be.

The upcoming chapters will provide examples of how NE applies to our objective as well as intangible realities. I will attempt to convey the vastness of reality. Be warned that illustrating reasoning of NE requires deviation from common reason. We'll explore finding a balance between our finite lives and infinite existence. We'll investigate our perceptions of positive, negative, living and otherwise, how they define our paths and how a fluid understanding of them can unlock untold potential. Other chapters will offer insights into the practical application of NE and how the reader may successfully articulate and exemplify it to others in philosophical and physical terms. The aim of this book is to help you to harness the power of NE and use it to enhance your reality and that of those around you.

This is your key to understanding the workings of the universe and discovering the power that you already have. Signs from many creative minds and an increasingly connected human consciousness point to mankind's readiness to embrace NE. In the grand scheme of the cosmos, our organic life spans are mere sparks lasting nanoseconds compared to those of celestial bodies. Odds are that your spark is partially expended, but if you're reading this, it's still burning bright. Having the knowledge of NE, you now have more potential energy than ever before. It's time to use the spark to ignite the kindling that surrounds you into a blaze that can be seen across the galaxy.

MOE

All potentials already exist and lie waiting to be initiated.

As an awakened ***Master of Existence (hereafter referred to as MOE)***, you will find yourself in the same position as before, but with a revised perspective. This new perspective will reveal untapped power. You'll apply it to your life to either change or preserve it, but the latter is doubtful. Do not despair if you find that life remains challenging after discovering NE. All will be experienced, including challenges. Do not deny your struggles their rightful place in the tapestry of life. As you know, triumph over struggle is a source of motivation and happiness for people. NE will inspire you to welcome challenges with zeal.

As mentioned in the prologue, it will be your duty as MOE to impart NE to your fellow person. The most important metaphysical knowledge mankind can possess is simple to convey if done properly. One method is to recite the Paradox from the previous page. It consists of a few short sentences and fully encapsulates the fundamentals of NE. You may even draw the reckoning circle as a visual aide or a finishing touch. Of course, in the wrong setting you may be taken out of context or appear that you're reciting your allegiance to a cult or losing your mind. A less abrupt way to convey the NE paradox can be found in applying its fundamentals to everyday situations or topics of discussion. Perhaps a friend is angry about a confrontation they had with someone. You could offer your friend some NE logic to tug them out of their state of mind. You could remind them that the only thing separating them from the person they're angry at is time. Ask them why they're angry at themselves in a different spacetime location. The proposition is so outrageous to most that it may induce laughter but will also exemplify an undeniable cornerstone of NE – true oneness. Your friend may be amused and pass it off as a pun, but your elegantly zoomed-out viewpoint will eventually make an indelible impression. Let them laugh and move on, seed planted. The NE Paradox is so simple that when described, it may be overlooked as an overt absurdity. Nonetheless, when regularly applied to conversations, it naturally promotes benevolence and is the opposite of absurd. NE has a calming effect when applied because it forges an immediate kinship with all those around you. It is already part of our natural intrinsic knowledge, but much like firmware on a computer, it works in the background and most of us generally ignore it.

The absence of restriction, exclusion, hierarchy, historical incongruities and other contradictions found in other belief systems liquidates many of the rehearsed defenses and shouting-match triggers that most people may offer in opposition to this perspective. It is impossible to formulate a defensible argument against NE, but even groundless arguments may easily be defused by applying its principles to the matters referenced by your philosophical opponent. NE proves and disproves all occurrences and beliefs. By nature, people are emphatic about having their beliefs and observations acknowledged. When speaking to a MOE, that need will be met quickly. As hard as one might try, there is no argument when both parties are correct. Most people are flattered to the point of blushing and will offer no arguments for fear of displaying hubris as the creators of reality. Do not expect, however, for everyone to comprehend it easily or immediately. You may find yourself toe to toe with someone who holds their beliefs sacred and won't hear anything in addition or to the contrary. Some ideologies even rely on violence and suppression of other viewpoints for survival. Fortunately, those principles are obsoleted by and will accede to the inclusivity of NE over time. Simply convey the Paradox once. Thereafter, any attempted counterpoints may be validated in context of NE and therefore considered correct, however insignificant. You may let them validate their points and move on having planted a seed of more significance.

The void of impossible singularity and countless worlds that Nothing and Everything reveal are enough to drive anyone to psychological extremes. The entire book is based on a contradiction that will hopefully resolve once the reader begins to practice NE in their journey to becoming MOE. You now have the elegant solution sought by countless physicists, cosmologists, religions and civilizations throughout the millennia. If you comprehend what the circle means, you know Everything and are free to enjoy it. If, after reading this, you feel anything other than blissful, understand that its part of being human and recenter by recalling the Paradox. As simplistic and minimalist as it is, it requires proper application to achieve its full potential. You've already made the ultimate commitment, nonexistence and therefore infinite virtual existence. Herein you'll find great examples of how to apply NE to your everyday life. At this point, it will be beneficial to make a list of what you want to know, what you want to resolve and what you want to experience. As you develop into MOE, the questions will be answered definitively, resolutions will ensue and countless experiences will come to pass on the journey through all possibility.

Before we delve into more concrete applications of the Paradox to our lives, it'll be beneficial to understand the concepts of its two primary components, Nothing and Everything. The next sections will examine both from an extremely panoramic perspective and describe some of science's most important discoveries pertaining to existence as we know it. Though many abstract theories are covered, a basic understanding of the foremost concepts of how our universe works will expedite your journey to mastering existence. The subsequent section, 'Being Human' narrows the focus from cosmic to terrestrial as we examine the origins, current reality and possible fate of humanity. Again, a lot of academic topics are covered, but a general grasp of these topics will prove beneficial.

NOTHING

"It's my fault. Everything is my fault." – Nothing

Nothing is. To the average observer, this is an overtly ominous and lonely statement. To MOE, it is the most liberating declaration one can make. If Nothing is, then nothing is of consequence. If it never happens, we can free ourselves from worry and rejoice all the possibilities of virtual existence. Whereas Everything is the ultimate permission, Nothing is the ultimate forgiveness. So, where is Nothing and how does it relate to us? Nothing isn't the vacuum of space that separates celestial objects. It isn't the void inside of a black hole. It isn't absence of space or time. It isn't even absence itself, for absence implies the prospect of presence. The only conclusion one can make about Nothing is that it doesn't materialize in the realm of possibility. Even the number zero is something, but Nothing eludes even that sliver of tangibility. The majority of this book is about Everything and why *it* happens, but to truly embrace Everything, you must first understand and respect Nothing. In the realm of Everything you will never interface with Nothing, yet knowledge of it can provide a life-altering change in perspective. Nothing is the key to clarity amongst infinite possibility. It is a force of emotional peace and centering. In meditation, Nothing is what we aspire to. It can be summoned to dampen complexity, cultivate courage and ease the mind. If you harness the perspective of existence within Nothing, you'll discover the calm, comfort and forgiveness that only it can offer.

The origins of creation have been envisaged in mythology, folklore and religious scripture over many millennia. There is a broad spectrum of myths and theories about the creation of the universe. Generally, creation theories can be separated into two distinct groups: *'creatio ex nihilo'* (creation from nothing) and *'ex nihilo, nihilo fit'* (from nothing, nothing comes). '*Creatio ex nihilo*' subscribers believe that the universe was created from nothing by a deity or spontaneous manifestation at an initial cosmic moment. Three major religions of the world, Christianity, Islam and Judaism share the *creatio ex nihilo* stance that God is the absolute Creator and did not create the world from pre-existing matter. Interestingly, some scholars recognize that Genesis 1:1 describes the pre-existence of matter to which God gives form. Who could blame the author(s) of Genesis for failing to envision Nothing before God? In the 5th and 6th centuries B.C., as today, the concept of true nothingness was nearly unfathomable. Still, God was eventually reenvisaged at the very beginning, before matter itself.

'*Ex nihilo, nihilo fit*' subscribers maintain that only nothing comes from Nothing and therefore the Everything must have always existed as a dark and primordial ocean of chaos which God entered and reconfigured. Sumerian, Babylonian, ancient Egyptian and ancient Greek myths characterize the primordial chaos as gods, elements and celestial objects. Hindus and Buddhists see the universe as beginningless and reject any notion of an absolute beginning of time. It is interesting to note that most ancient religions took the *ex nihilo, nihilo fit* viewpoint and more recent religions adopted the *creatio ex nihilo* stance. Perhaps it had something to do with the transition from polytheism, where many gods had different powers to monotheism, where one God is considered the all-powerful Creator. Pre-existing matter, whether chaotic or tranquil, would suggest that the universe does not depend on God for its existence and therefore the *creatio ex nihilo* is the prevalent view of the major monotheistic religions today. The paradoxical boundary between most creation myths is one of 'chicken or egg' and, as in all paradoxical conundrums, there is more than one correct answer and both are less than satisfactory. The root question is, "Did reality always exist or was it created from something?" If your answer is that it always existed, then you'd be implying that existence itself is divinity and that God didn't always occupy it. If your answer is that nothing existed before God, then you'd be implying that God is existence.

From the NE perspective, there are two fundamental laws of creation. The first is that it starts and ends with Nothing (sometimes referred to as God). The second is that for Nothing to be, all possibility must be contemplated and countered, thus creating the infinite virtual existence we know as Everything (sometimes referred to as creation). This perspective combines '*ex nihilo, nihilo fit*' and '*creatio ex nihilo*' creation theories to form *'Nihil intus, omnia contemplari'* (within Nothing, Everything is contemplated). This permits Everything to transpire while remaining firmly rooted in non-existence. The competing ideologies about the root of existence are components of the same truth. Nothing comes from Nothing and Everything transpires as contemplation within Nothing. Nothing and Everything are one, making the distinction between Creator and creation illusory. We are the Creator experiencing creation.

NOT ZERO

Nothing and zero have some things in common, but they are not equivalent. The symbol of reckoning for the Paradox closely resembles the ovular symbol for zero, but that is more of a coincidence than anything. Zero would have remained a large dot had it not settled into a more space and ink-efficient written form. The Paradox circle symbolizes Everything within Nothing. For that, only a perfect circle will do. If you ask someone what zero means, they'll confidently tell you, "nothing". In so doing, they'd be referring to the relative non-existence implied by zero and they'd be correct. Zero symbolizes three specific things. Firstly, it represents *relative* absence - something that exists but is not there. Secondly, it represents a column placeholder; 'nothing in the hundreds' column, the thousands' column, etc.' Lastly, it represents transition between positive and negative. Interestingly, zero is the only numeral that can be neither positive nor negative. As versatile and important zero is, it fails to describe the *absolute* non-existence of Nothing. Zero's five-thousand-year quest for recognition is complete. Given that, it's still worth looking into the fascinating history of the numeral to understand the twists and turns of logic that eventually led to its acceptance and its matchless contributions to the advancement of humanity. With zero's convoluted journey complete, perhaps our comprehension of Nothing will be less precarious.

The first evidence we have of the mathematical idea of zero is from the Sumerian culture in Mesopotamia (currently part of Iraq) around 5000 years ago. They had devised a system for counting and number grouping. They used reeds and styli to inscribe wedge-shaped symbols (cuneiform) in pyramid-like patterns to signify grouped quantities of 10 or 60. The Sumerians yielded to the Akkadians around 2500 B.C. but passed on their system of decimal and sexagesimal counting to them. The Babylonian Empire inherited the counting system from the collapsed Akkadian Empire and made their own modifications to it. Somewhere between the sixth and third centuries B.C., some unnamed person in the Neo-Babylonian Empire created the first known symbol for zero. They used two slanted cuneiform wedges to signify 'no number in this column'. Much like the '0' in the number 503 means 'no tens', but still holds the place for tens as opposed to letting 503 mean 53. The double wedge was not yet circular and was used as a placeholder only and differentiated between magnitudes like the decimal we use today. Perhaps the concept existed in the human imagination before then, but this is the oldest surviving evidence of it.

Ancient Greeks were unsure about the status of zero. They asked themselves, "How can nothing be something?" This led to philosophical arguments about the existence of something within the vacuum of nothing, but the subject was generally avoided due to the looping and paradoxical nature of it. The usefulness of zero in mathematics was left virtually unrecognized until the time of Alexander the Great. After invading the Babylonian Empire in 331 B.C, Greeks under Alexander discovered the crucial role that numerical zero played in counting. Greek astronomical papyri used the symbol 'O' for zero by the third century B.C. The reason for the transition from two slanted cuneiform wedges to the astonishingly tidy circle to represent zero is unknown. One theory is that 'O' symbolized the letter of the word 'ouden' from the Greek omicron, meaning 'nothing'. Another theory is that the circle was just a more elegant depiction of a void than the cuneiform wedges. This seems logical, given that nature is full of hollow circular voids like ponds, caves and craters. The true reason for it may never be known.

By 150 A.D. the astronomer Ptolemy, influenced by the Babylonians, was using a symbol for zero (ō) in his work on mathematical astronomy called Syntaxis Mathematica. In spite of its accounting potential, zero was scarcely used by the Greeks outside of astronomy. Strangely, in spite of the influences from Greek culture and contact with Hellenistic countries, the Romans never adopted a symbol for zero. In the yet-to-be-discovered New World, the Mayans devised numerical zero circa 350 A.D. as a placeholder in their elaborate calendar systems. They symbolized it as an empty seashell-like character. The Mayan capital of Tikal in modern-day Guatemala is 6,600 miles from Greece. It's safe to say that the concept of zero evolved separately in the case of the Mayans (1). The Mayan example is compelling evidence of groups of Homo Sapiens gaining characteristic knowledge nearly simultaneously (in an evolutionary sense) in spite of being isolated from each other. It suggests that such knowledge was imminent in people. Although usually passed from one society to another, the concept of zero was also an intrinsic part of evolution as human populations reached the critical masses of agriculturally supported city-states.

Back in the Eastern Hemisphere, Alexander's invasion path and later the routes of commerce to and from Alexandria had brought the gift of zero to India. It was there that humanity's full grasp of zero's meaning would finally be had. Although there is speculation of it being used as early as the fifth century A.D., less ambiguous evidence comes from around 650 A.D. wherein mathematician Brahmagupta and others used dots under numbers as placeholders. Brahmagupta also demonstrated how to arrive at zero through subtraction. Even more importantly, the Indians depicted the dot as having a null value, called "*śūnya*". (1) To them, the dot symbolized both zero and the unknown. Nothingness (śūnya) played a central role very early on in Hindu thought, and as mentioned, we find speculation of it in many creation myths. For the Hindus, there is no unqualified nothingness. Substance for them cannot disappear or be added to but can only change form. According to them, this fullness, brahman, pervades the universe and cannot be subtracted from or added to. At first glance interpretation of *śūnya* is 'void' or 'empty'. On closer examination, the meaning isn't so much vacancy as receptive womb-like hollow ready to swell. The numeric definitions of zero as a placeholder and null were finally understood but also nothingness as potential – somewhere where something might be.

Zero spread to Cambodia near the end of the seventh century and into China and the Islamic countries at the end of the eighth. The Chinese had a system of counting rods to perform decimal calculations as early as the fifth century but didn't use zero as a number until much later on. In 690, Empress Wū promulgated Zetian characters, one of which was 'O', but the oldest surviving example of a Chinese mathematical text using a round symbol for zero comes from the 1247 Mathematical Treatise in Nine Sections by Qin Jiūshao. (2) Chinese authors had been familiar with the idea of negative numbers by the second century A.D., as seen in the Nine Chapters on the Mathematical Art. (3) Arabian merchants brought the zero they found in India to the Middle East along with spices and other exotic items. By 773 A.D. zero had returned to the once Sumerian Iraq and was further developed from the Indian system. In the ninth century, equations that equaled zero (later to be known as algebra) were devised by Mohammed al-Khowarizmi. He also developed quick methods of multiplying and dividing numbers known as algorithms (after a rough interpretation of the name Khowarizimi). He called zero 'sifr'. By 879 A.D., zero was written almost as we know it – an oval, albeit much smaller than other numbers. (4)

Thanks to the conquest of Spain by the Moors, zero made its way into Europe. In 1202, Italian mathematician Fibonacci built on al-Khowarizmi's algorithms in his book, Liber Abaci (Abacus Book). Italian merchants and German bankers quickly took notice of the ease at which they could balance their books by the use of zero, negative and positive numbers. Governments were suspicious of Arabic numerals due to the ability to change positive and negative with a mere dash, so they were banned. Though outlawed, merchants continued to use zero, or 'sifr', in encrypted messages known as ciphers. Adding, subtracting and multiplying by zero was understood relatively well, but division by zero confused even great minds. How many times does zero go into ten? How can a non-quantity divide a quantity? Much later, this question was the key to the creation of calculus by Gottfried Leibniz and Isaac Newton in the 1600s. Consider a continually changing variable, like speed, volume or magnitude. If you want to know it's value at a specific point in time, you can divide its various values by increments so small that they approach zero and thus have a very close approximation to the correct answer. This is the essence of calculus and the physics of movement. Nothing truly arrives at zero, it only approaches it. The symbol we use today was gradually accepted and the concept has since flourished.

Zero is such an integral part of our lives that it seems an obvious concept. It's important to understand the journey it took to be widely accepted and utilized. Its history was outlined here both because it is fascinating and to show how long it took humanity to fully comprehend in spite of our mastery of seemingly more complex subjects. Zero embodies man's highest thought. In modernity, it has led to countless technological innovations, the most prevalent being binary code wherein a unit, or 'bit' is either true '1' or false '0'. A string of eight bits forms a 'byte' and we have the foundation of modern software and computing. In the numerical sense, we have a valuable place holder and transitional point between positive and negative and an origin from which all other points can be referenced. It is astonishing that the symbol the world has settled on to represent zero is an enclosed oval. It just as easily could have been a dot, a line or an 'x'. It has elongated from a circle to an oval over the years because it was easier to draw with split quills and took up less space on precious paper (5). The only difference between the symbol for numerical zero and the symbol for its progenitor, Nothing, is a slight change in curvature. Zero depicts an origin surrounded by possibility whereas Nothing is the origin of possibility. Zero is a symbol with several meanings while Nothing embodies and envelops all meaning. Nothing contains zero, but it doesn't equate to zero. A perfect circle summarizes the concept of Nothing very well, "Within Nothing, Everything is contemplated". We are fortunate to live in a time where zero is a mature and broadly utilized concept. Nothing is on a similar journey in the human psyche. While its meaning is still elusive for most, we can benefit from our understanding of Nothing and the inner peace and strength that comes with it.

THE BIG CONTEMPLATION

Within Nothing, Everything is contemplated.

What eventually became the universe expanded from a singularity 13.8 billion years ago and, as far as we can tell, came from Nothing. In 1927, Belgian astrophysicist and Catholic priest Georges Lemaítre theorized that the universe expanded from a single point or "primeval atom". Soon after, observations made by Edwin Hubble showed that other galaxies are moving away from ours at a rate proportional to their distance from us. This became known as Hubble's law, though it was later acknowledged that Lemaítre was the first to provide an estimate of the Hubble constant. If you look to the cosmos from any vantage point in any galaxy, other galaxies would be receding in all directions proportional to their distance from that vantage point. This suggests that all matter in the universe once occupied the same location. In 1949, the concept of the universe expanding from a singular point with zero volume was pejoratively referred to as 'a big bang' by Fred Hoyle, a cosmologist who was in opposition to the theory. The nickname stuck but took a couple decades more to catch on. In 1964, two American radio astronomers, Arno Penzias and Robert Wilson, picked up an inexplicable 'hiss' in the radio wave spectrum on a research antenna in New Jersey. Later, they discovered that they had stumbled on the echo of the universe's birth, or cosmic microwave background radiation (CMB). CMB was very uniform and came from all parts of the sky at all times. Its remarkable uniformity of both temperature and dispersion was puzzling. It would later be concluded that uniform radiation arriving from all directions meant that light from one side of the universe hadn't yet made it to the other side. This lent support to the theory of cosmic inflation from a single point. The Big Bang theory was finally on solid footing, as it is the only theory that explains the phenomenon of uniform CMB.

According to the now mainstream Big Bang theory, a singularity rapidly expanded into a superheated micro universe and has expanded and cooled ever since. When we picture the first moments of the Big Bang, we imagine the universe exploding from a single point and emanating forward in a parabolic bloom. That's partially because many of the visual aids depicting the universe are really timelines depicting a bell-like cross-section of its expansion over time. But was the Big Bang really an explosion? Although it sounds straight-forward, the way most of us imagine the expansion is fundamentally flawed. The birth of the universe was a different kind of event. The universe isn't expanding because preexisting mass is being flung apart like bomb fragments. It's expanding because the space between galaxies is growing while the galaxies themselves remain like spots glued to the surface of a swelling balloon at eternally fixed points of latitude and longitude. All points in the universe remain stationary while space dilates between them. Nevertheless, posterboard and theatrical depictions of the universe portray it as more of a firework display, presumably because it's difficult to illustrate what's actually happening. Nevertheless, it was not an explosion. For an explosion to occur, there are a few requirements: There must be a pre-existing mass to explode, a pre-existing time at which the explosion happens, pre-existing three-dimensional space into which the exploded fragments of mass will be projected, and something must trigger the explosion. Another deviation from the explosion paradigm is that explosions originate from a central origin and radiate outward normal to the origin. The surface of an enclosed membrane like a balloon has no discernable center as it expands. This is also true of the universe. The center is not a point in space but a point in time. From the beginning of time, all points in the universe occupy equivalent positions. Its center is not on the fabric, but alongside it in the fourth dimension. We can't see time, but we can look back through time at ancient images from distant objects in space. We see the early history of the universe in these images - the farther away, the older the image. So, you can think of us as living in the present surrounded by spherical shells of the past - the bigger the shell, the farther back in time (6).

The mathematics of the General Theory of Relativity require that three-dimensional spacetime and mass be created at "Time Zero" after the Big Bang and there is no pre-existing space, time nor mass. Some theoretical physicists believe that the universe may have existed in a state of zero dimensions before the Big Bang. In other words, it was in a state of zero spacetime. The late Steven Hawking examined the mathematics of the nothing-state using the physics of quantum gravity theory and concluded that at the start of the Big Bang time emerged from something utterly different and may have been created from another "timeless" dimension of space. If the universe is expanding, where do the brand-new billions of cubic light years of spacetime come from? This is where NE diverges from astrophysical explanations. The Paradox dictates that spacetime occurs as contemplated within Nothing. Our consciousness witnesses spacetime in segmented events with beginnings and ends, prompting us to perceive 'new' spacetime as the universe reveals itself over the fourth dimension. Spacetime is eternally contemplated, yet it is only as the contemplation is processed through infinite perspectives that the full shape and size of the contemplation is revealed. Everything has no age and doesn't come from any single event. The universe is an instantaneous consideration of possibility and it is one of many. Thus, a better name for the Big Bang would be the Big Contemplation.

HINTS FROM HEISENBERG AND DIRAC

While Lemaître was proposing that an expanding universe could be traced back to a single point, other theoretical physicists were considering ways to predict the movement of quantum particles. An inescapable reality in the quantum world is that we cannot know both the position and the momentum of a particle, such as a photon or electron, with absolute precision. The more we know about one value, the less we know about the other and vice versa. This is known as Heisenberg's uncertainty principle. Introduced in a 1927 paper by Werner Heisenberg, it arises in quantum mechanics due to the wave-particle duality of all matter. The same principle can be applied between the quantities of energy and time. If we took a small volume of space and tried to analyze its energy content over a small enough time, the uncertainty about the energy contained in that time could be such that it might be great enough to manifest particles from nothingness, provided that they were returned very quickly (7). This suggests that even in the tiniest volumes of vacuous space, something can truly be put forth by Nothing, at least virtually.

A possible path for the coexistence of quantum physics and special relativity was uncovered in 1928 by Paul Dirac. He developed a new way to describe the movement of electrons. Dirac published a paper that mathematically predicted the presence of an anti-electron that would have the same mass as an electron but a *positive* charge. Upon interaction, the negatively charged electron and positively charged anti-electron would mutually annihilate. In principle, an anti-electron, or positron, could be part of an anti-atom, or antimatter. It would also mean that for every reality, there could be an anti-reality. This provided a possible mechanism by which matter could be created in empty space and just as quickly disappear again (7). It would rank as one of the greatest triumphs of the 20th century in theoretical physics. Dirac's ideas were developed into quantum field theory. The strange, fleeting quantum fluctuations in empty space became known as virtual particles. The vacuum of space is full of virtual particles popping in and out of existence trillions of times per second at a submicroscopic scale. In 1947, scientists Willis Lamb and Robert Retherford created an experiment using microwave techniques to stimulate hydrogen atoms. It was hypothesized that if quantum fluctuations were occurring, then it would cause electrons to wobble slightly. The experiment proved Dirac's predictions to one part in one million. This conclusively showed fluctuation in apparently vacuous spaces. This experiment and its subsequent explanation by Hans Bethe of "Lamb shift" in the hydrogen spectrum laid the foundation for the development of modern quantum electrodynamics.

For every billion particles annihilated in the Big Contemplation, only one became part of what now makes up the universe. We are the debris from that unimaginably colossal event. The only remaining evidence of the annihilated particles exists as cosmic radiation. Launched in 2001, NASA's Wilkinson Microwave Anisotropy Probe (WMAP) mapped a full-sky thermal image of the CMB over 9 years. The resulting final image of the first light released after the Big Bang could be compared to the photo of a two-week-old embryo vs. a 50-yr-old universe of today. The full-sky CMB image was a revelation. From it, astronomers were able to work out the ratios of the three types of matter (5% atoms, 25% dark matter, 70% dark energy). Yet there was an even more profound discovery. Instead of a uniform distribution of light, tiny areas of temperature variation were visible. It was apparent that the differences were scars left by quantum fluctuations early in the development of the universe. Those fluctuations would go on to form the irregular clumps that would become individual galaxies (7). This means that, at the earliest stages, Galaxies were affected at sub-microscopic scales by exchanges between Nothing and Everything. Spacetime is contemplated and exists virtually. It has always existed in full form and in all dimensions within Nothing. This universe is one possible structure within it.

Now that we know Everything is a contemplation intrinsic to Nothing, one might inquire whether an infinitely powerful void that envisages existence only to ensure its negation defines God. From the NE perspective, Nothing is certainly the source of all possibility. Yet the word 'God' evokes all the imagery and illogicality of the deity we've imagined over millennia. The God typically envisaged is an ancient grand paternal spirit who is predominantly concerned with mankind. He watches over, loves and disciplines us. He longs for us to believe in him, constantly inventing scenarios to prove his existence. The God we know is separate from man. He discerns between good and evil and makes trades with the negative deity, Satan. He takes requests if they are sincere, even if those requests come at the peril of other people or creatures. He takes sides. That version of God exists as well as his counterpart, Satan, but perhaps just in the vicinity of Earth. Though it may sound a mockery, understand that this view of God isn't being disputed because, within Everything, all deities exist because all realities are definite.

By contrast to the prototypical image of God that most of us have, Nothing has no form, yet defines all. Nothing isn't a distant theory or concept. Everything occurs within Nothing, but it's not a relationship with definable boundaries. Nothing permeates Everything, continually exchanging particles for anti-particles, contemplating and counteracting possibility. Nothing is everywhere. Although we are merely contemplated by Nothing, we are one with it. To analogize, if Nothing were a body, Everything would be its internal organs. The external body makes it possible for the organs to exist and the organs return the favor. Each operate on different levels while working independently. Both are components of a combined master assembly – the body of NE. Unlike belief in God, belief in NE is never in question, nor is it of concern to any deity. Existence is believing. Although we may make heartfelt prayers and requests, they are redundant. Our prayers remain important visualizations to guide our actions, but all realities have already been granted.

Though we've put a face on Nothing to explain it in terms we can fathom, understand that Nothing has no position, no face and no reason. It never happens. It remains by virtue of the contemplation of what would be *if* anything was. And within that contemplation, Everything emerges.

EVERYTHING

"There are more things in heaven and earth, Horatio, than are dreamt of in your philosophy." – William Shakespeare, Hamlet

Now, let's take a brief tour of Everything. Although it transpires in the confines of Nothing, it is where we truly reside and what we interact with. Everything is an exhibition of limitless and timeless possibility. It is the known, unknown, true, false, possible, impossible and imagined in all dimensions. Many of us draw the border of reality around planet Earth, while others draw it at the outer limits of the Milky Way galaxy and yet others draw it at the edge of our ever-expanding universe. Everything encapsulates an infinite number of universes, making it unquestionably boundless. The revelation that you are part of such an incredible continuum is the greatest gift one can receive. It brings a sense of permanence without monotony, hope without doubt, and invincibility without regret.

If you're seeking something that exceeds the beliefs we're accustomed to, you'll find it in Everything. Everything is the eternal caretaker of existence and all therein, including Earth and mankind. Within it lies another possible characterization of God. Everything is a contemplation that we interact with. It can appear anywhere and as anything. It is immediately accessible, reacts to our needs and offers shelter within chaos. Not only does Everything reside in objective reality, it *is* objective reality. In this sense, there is no separation between man and God because Everything is God. One notable difference between Everything and the more familiar gods offered by religion is that in the eyes of Everything, there is no distinction between 'good', 'bad', 'correct' or 'incorrect'. These indications are perspective-dependent and therefore subjective. Within Everything, all paths and their accompanying experiences are imminent and therefore acceptable. With two seemingly contradictory concepts (Nothing and Everything) defining existence, what are we to believe? Though Nothing and Everything are two parts of the same whole, I find it best to relate to and participate in Everything while acknowledging its basis within Nothing. This allows life to be fully experienced with the option of using nonexistence as a way to reboot if things get shaky or out of hand.

You may have noticed 'theories of everything' emerging in the realms of theoretical physics and even in major motion pictures over the past decade. Science is one area where collective human thought has merged paths with NE, but the scientific community's embezzlement of the word 'everything' is difficult to overstate. Historically, it had been rare to name specific theories grandiose terms like 'ultimate', 'complete' or 'everything', but in the era of celebrity physicists like the late Stephen Hawking, Neal deGrasse Tyson and Michio Kaku (who also has a book by the eye-catching title, 'The God Equation'), it is understood that alluding to major breakthroughs in the titles of books and movies helps them sell. When Stephen Hawking's biographical movie, "A Theory of Everything" was released to theaters, the title had me believing Hawking had finally constructed his theory of existence. I couldn't wait to see it visually illuminated in Dolby surround-sound. Upon closer inspection, I was disappointed to learn that it was mainly about his personal life with hints of his quest to find a unified theory of physics. Still, had the movie been given a more accurate title, fewer people would have gone to see it. The benefit of grandiose titles and grand visual effects like those seen in deGrasse Tyson's series "Cosmos: A Spacetime Odyssey" is the popularization of theoretical and astrophysics. This benefits those areas of research by inviting a wider audience to take an interest in them.

If the various physics theories could be linked, the resulting congruent 'theory of everything' would verifiably explain all the phenomena in the universe. It would act as a patchwork to unify the quantum world, gravity and electromagnetism. That would be mankind's biggest triumph to date and possibly provide the keys to boundless energy, resources and mobility in our universe. Although incredible progress continues to be made on that front, science is still very far from definitively explaining much of the universe. For a "God equation" to prevail, multiple unifications would have to occur between particle and gravitational physics. And that would be just the tip of the iceberg in an infinite multiverse. The more scientists learn, the more unknowns they discover. One unification may lead to the discovery of more unexplained relationships that require further research. Although the journey they're on is endless, their work is important because many of the discoveries have practical uses. In a sense though, it's like watching a kayaker row upstream. They're dealing with an infinitely complex subject and insisting on decoding all its internal workings before declaring an overall understanding of it. While the complete workings of Everything are too complex to ever decipher completely, the elegant explanation for *why* it happens hides in plain sight. As theoretical physicists and scientists continue their fascinating and important work, the true explanation of Everything awaits our engagement.

The missing variable in science's 'Everything Theory' is Nothing. With Nothing included in the concept of creation, the Paradox emerges as both an elegant and irrefutable solution to existence. It both validates and falsifies all other hypotheses and propositions. The Paradox proves all occurrences by disproving them. While all phenomena within our universe must be further deciphered to understand their meaning in the context of virtual spacetime, Everything within Nothing is the ultimate answer. Although NE is ineffective at explaining the specific workings of physical phenomena, we can continue using science to further our understanding of our surroundings and to enhance our ability to manipulate it.

We're only scratching the surface when we ponder the vastness of Everything. It's an overwhelming prospect. On one hand, as components of infinite contemplation, we no longer need to strive for permission to experience any aspect of existence, for all is forthcoming. On the other hand, we are obliged to experience all, regardless of the circumstances in our current lives. That means every scenario, imaginable and unimaginable, will come to pass. The prospect is spectacular, frightening, beautiful and daunting. We are on an instantaneous tour of infinite possibility exploring each atom and molecule in every possible configuration at high resolution. We imagine ourselves as solitary beings, but we are part of a grand singularity. Within this singularity, quadrillions of possibilities occur in even the smallest of volumes. There are billions of versions of each of us, exploring various manifestations of being. Some are working in slow motion, while others are moving at warp speed. Some are on Earth, while others are on asymmetrical versions of Earth with different species, landscapes and languages. Some occupy the same time as us but in different locations, while others occupy the same locations at different times. We must experience the universe as it unfolds from a human's perspective but understand that the individual perspective is one of an infinite number within.

EARTH, THE SUN AND THE MOON

There are infinite stars, celestial bodies and occurrences to consider in the multiverse but our tour of Everything must begin somewhere, so we'll start with three celestial bodies that we interact with directly – Earth, the Sun and our moon. Other than the occasional asteroid or comet that rings Earth's bell from time to time, nothing really affects earthly life other than those three.

EARTH

Within the vast contemplation, it is necessary and refreshing to appreciate our immediate surroundings. It goes without saying that existing as humans on Earth is extraordinary. Here we are in this beautiful and tangible world, the prevalent species amongst millions on a planet so far from other habitable planets that it would take light-years to travel to another. We happen to be at the apex of human achievement during a time of technological renaissance and vast individual freedom. When considering all the daily needs, conflicts and complexities of being a modern human, one fact should also stand out: we live on a planet. Even the word 'live' implies that near impossible odds have fallen in our favor – not once, but millions of times. The sun and moon effect Earth and, by extension, us, yet we interact solely with Earth. As astronauts have observed, she's all we have. When astronaut Bill Anders first took the famous "Earthrise" picture of the Earth from the lifeless, desolate orbit of the moon, one of his prominent thoughts was how alone and beautiful Earth appeared from that perspective. He said the moon was like "dirty beach sand and quickly became boring" and that Earth "seemed to provide the only color in the universe".

Conditions on Earth are rare. We're locked in an elliptical orbit around a star that happens to be at its most stable phase of life. In orbit, we never get too close or too far away from it. Not only is the temperature relatively stable ($\pm130°F$ at the extremes), but the average temperature lands between the freezing and boiling points of water, allowing the presence of liquid water on its surface. The amount of water on Earth is precisely tuned. There's not so much that it covers the land, and not so little that it's a desert like Venus or Mars, our sister planets. A system of plate tectonics moves the Earth's crust, allowing a carbon-silicate cycle to regulate the levels of carbon in the atmosphere, keeping the surface temperature around that of liquid water. Water returns the favor, percolating into the lithosphere and allowing plate tectonics to remain ductile. Earth has a captive atmosphere protected from the stripping effects of solar winds by magnetic fields created by a liquid core dynamo. Another aspect to consider is Earth's size. If it was much smaller, the magnetic field would be weak and Earth wouldn't be able to retain its atmosphere. Any larger and gravity would greatly hinder life and space travel.

We are presented with four distinct seasons during our annual orbit of the sun. There are plants to nurture and shelter us and animals to hunt and domesticate for complete sustenance. For humans, Earth is as close to perfect as one could imagine. Our planet and the peaceful time in which we live are so rare and precious that it is difficult to fathom an alternative. Given this, job number one should be the preservation of Earth's livable atmosphere and habitats. Most of us are so caught up in survival and the quest for comfort and happy experiences that we lose sight of the importance and fragility of Earth's life-supporting systems. There are likely thousands or even millions of planets like Earth but data we've gathered shows that the closest "unicorn" planets are several light-years away. Moreover, the odds of them sustaining human long-term civilizations are low. To travel those distances, we'd likely need to decipher time travel through worm holes or warpage of spacetime. As with all things, interplanetary travel will come to pass, but Earth is all we have now. To thrive in this fortunate circumstance, we must appreciate the fragility and rarity of our resources. Keeping a positive outlook is also important, so keep in mind that this is an exceedingly rare and friendly place and time to live. There's no better time for the Paradox to be revealed to humanity than the present.

THE YELLOW DWARF

If humans were to worship a single deity, the Sun would be a good choice. The relationships between man, Earth and the sun have all the elements of a Greek Myth. We are born onto a goddess Earth, favorite daughter of Sun, and remain with her during and after our brief lives. Earth teaches us that if we respect and care for her, we may prosper. We have a love-hate relationship with our grandfather, Sun. He gives us warmth light and nourishes us while simultaneously reprimanding and burning us if we step out of line. The myth would tell of an interaction between Man, Mother Earth and Grandfather Sun. Perhaps we are the chosen people who are given great power which we misuse despite Earth's warnings and the Sun punishes us by burning our forests and evaporating our drinking water. Or on the other hand, maybe we are the neglected children of Earth who persevere over our harsh environment, decipher the secrets of the universe and propel ourselves to a godly status by harnessing the Sun's power. Either way, our relationship with our mother star is incredible and true.

Today, it's hard to imagine anyone worshiping anything, however awesome and true it may be. I celebrate the summer and winter solstices each year by watching the sun rise and set on both days, but I don't worship the sun. I celebrate the change of daylight from long to short and vice versa, but I know the sun will remain a reliable part of my life regardless of my devotion to it. The same applies to others who appreciate various deities. We celebrate and acknowledge tradition, but it's rare to find one who truly worships. Due to this, much of the power once wielded by religion has been transferred to more observable science. Science answers questions that, until recently, have only been explained by myths. Luckily, there are scientific facts about the sun that are every bit as amazing as myths. At 4.5 billion years old, the sun is about halfway through its life and has enough hydrogen to burn (more accurately, fuse) for another five billion years. It fuses about 600 million tons of hydrogen every second. The sun is considered a yellow dwarf star, twice as massive as the most common red dwarf star, but smaller than the red giants up to 100 times its size. In our solar system, the sun makes up 99.86% of the mass. It is 110 times the diameter of Earth, meaning about one million Earth's could fit inside it. The sun rotates in the opposite direction of Earth (west to east) and rotates faster at its equator. We imagine the sun as stationary, but the sun (as well as the solar system) travels at 137 miles per second as it orbits around the center of the Milky Way galaxy. That orbit takes between 225 and 250 million years. Earth is 93 million miles from the sun and it takes eight minutes for the sun's light to reach us. The sun generates solar winds consisting of extremely hot plasma particles. These particles interact with Earth's polar magnetic fields, creating the Aurora Borealis phenomenon. At the end of the sun's life as a yellow dwarf, it will expand into a red giant and consume Mercury, Venus and Earth. That means that the sun is our eventual destination. Those are just some of the facts that should cause us to give pause and celebrate the sun occasionally.

THE MOON

Earth's nearest neighbor and the biggest object in the night sky has also been the source of many myths and legends. The most prevalent myth is the 'lunacy' superstition that a full moon has psychological effects on people. Many civilizations and tribes have seen the moon as a deity or source of divine signaling. There are over 200 natural satellites, or moons, in our solar system. All the planets except Mercury and Venus have them. Some asteroids and dwarf planets also have natural satellites. At a quarter the size of Earth, our moon has the largest moon-to-planet ratio in our solar system. Strangely enough, we call it 'the moon' instead of some other mythically inspired name. Due to its size and proximity to Earth (a mere 239,000 miles), the moon stabilizes Earth's rotation, preventing drastic movements of the poles. The moon's gravitational force also causes opposing bulges in the Earth which produce the ocean's high and low tides. Without our singular, large moon, life on Earth would not have been possible.

There are several theories about how the moon was formed. The leading theory is that it amalgamated from material blasted into space when a Mars-sized body slammed into a newly formed Earth about 4.4 billion years ago. The impactor, dubbed "Theia" is said to have deposited most of the water stores on Earth and to have increased Earth's size. It is also theorized that Theia may have originated outside our solar system, possibly lending Earth some of its unique properties. The so-called "giant impact hypothesis" does the best job in explaining the similar geochemical makeup of Earth and its moon. And like Earth, the moon is a terrestrial object, and has three layers (crust, mantle and core). Contrary to popular belief, there is no dark side of the moon. Both sides see the same amount of sunlight but because the moon and Earth are in synchronous rotation, only one face of the moon is ever seen from Earth.

The moon is also something to be acknowledged and celebrated. Like the sun, it supports our existence and provides us with comfort. Once in a great while, it comes between Earth and the sun in arguably the greatest natural spectacle known to man – a total solar eclipse. During a total solar eclipse, the apparent size of the moon is equal to or greater than that of the sun. The moon and sun are similar in size from our perspective. This is because the distance between the sun and Earth is 400 times the moon's distance from Earth and the sun's diameter is approximately 400 times larger than that of the moon. It's an amazing coincidence. If you've ever been in the shadow region of a solar eclipse, you've seen day quickly turn into night. Not only does the sun crescent into a black hole with a magnificent white glowing ring around its perimeter, but the air begins to cool and birds stop singing. During a total solar eclipse, there is a palpable sense of the divine. The black hole sun seems like a portal to another universe. During the eclipse of 2017, I took my family to Casper, Wyoming to witness it at my aunt's house. It was difficult to travel with twin 10-month-old toddlers, but it was worth it. During the totality, I recited the Paradox aloud. This must've struck some around me as odd but, completely entranced and connected with the three celestial bodies, it was a completely understandable and acceptable expression. That event embraced my soul and reminded me of the deep connection we have to our moon.

THE UNIVERSE

Scientists estimate that the universe began to inflate exponentially at about 10^{-34} seconds after time zero, and 100 doubling periods were completed by 10^{-32} seconds. If that's true, the universe had expanded from the size of a proton to the size of a grapefruit in that time. The expansion rate from zero to grapefruit in 10^{-32} seconds works out to 10^{31} m/sec, which is much faster than the 3×10^8 m/s speed of light. Although we've been conditioned to think that nothing can travel faster than the speed of light, that rule only pertains to objects traveling through spacetime, not the expansion of spacetime itself. This means the universe is bigger than we can observe. At the time of this writing, the radius of our visible universe is estimated at 46.5 billion light-years. Light from galaxies beyond the observable radius, if it exists, hasn't yet reached us. This is why the space is dark rather than saturated by light from countless stars. Even with limited observable space, there are an estimated 2 trillion galaxies in the observable range, a quarter of which can be observed using our current technology. Although the size of the actual universe is unknown, speed estimates using the theory of cosmic inflation have the actual radius around 3×10^{23} times the size of the observable universe, but it could be much larger. We can only apply physics to the observable universe and if the laws aren't uniform outside it, then all bets are off. The extents of the universe may well exceed our wildest estimates. Even if it has a limit in size, for most purposes, it can be regarded as infinite.

Current cosmological data measuring the CMB radiation points to the shape of the universe as perfectly flat. Some variations in CMB data suggest that space may curve via gravitational warpage and form an infinitely large, enclosed membrane. Even then, the membrane would be so large that the curvature would be negligible from our perspective. For all intents and purposes, the universe as we experience it is a near-infinite, open and flat sheet (8). To put some scale to it, there are more stars in the universe than there are grains of sand on every beach on planet Earth. We can only estimate its size and theorize its laws. Though our universe is but one in an infinite multiverse, it might as well be Everything.

Over the past two centuries, we've learned an astounding amount of information about how the cosmos work, but we're still in the process of maturing as a species and deciphering our surroundings. Scientists and cosmologists continue to propose and test various astrophysical theories. Each represents a single aspect of human knowledge, but the goal of science is a *complete* understanding of the universe. Our method of deciphering the laws relies on the principle that all phenomena around us are interconnected and arise from even deeper causes. In many cases, we understand patterns, but not their underlying causes. Solving one mystery often leads to more. Although we may never obtain the ultimate answer, revelations made along the way will help us harness the power of the cosmos. As of 2022, we have two mutually incompatible models that explain what we know about our universe: the standard model of particle physics and the general theory of relativity.

The standard model describes and accurately predicts almost everything we interact with. It affects everything from fluid mechanics to chemistry to the subatomic particles like quarks and neutrinos. The standard model specifies that all matter is made of atoms of elements. It identifies four forces but may someday be narrowed down to three because we live in an era of theory unification. The first (and strongest) is the strong nuclear force. It bonds protons and neutrons in the nuclei of atoms. It is incredibly strong over a very short range about the size of a proton. The second strongest force, electromagnetism, covers electricity, magnetism light and chemistry. It is much weaker than the strong force but has an infinite range. For instance, an electromagnetic force over a meter is much stronger than a strong nuclear force over the same distance. Third in strength is the weak nuclear force. It's responsible for some forms of radioactivity and works extremely weakly over a range of $1/1000^{th}$ of a proton and may one day be unified with electromagnetism. The weakest force, gravity, has an infinite range like electromagnetism and guides planets and other celestial objects. Gravity is only 10^{-40} the strength of the strong nuclear force on the femtometer scale. It is so weak that scientists haven't found a way to study it at the atomic scale, therefore it is not covered by the standard model of particle physics. There is a hypothetical particle called a graviton that could explain gravity at the quantum level but it hasn't been discovered yet. One of the greatest goals of physics is to somehow devise a quantum theory of gravity and unify it with the standard model.

Presently, the standard model explains the micro world but not the cosmos. That's where the general theory of relativity comes in handy. Albert Einstein explained gravity as being caused by matter and energy bending space like the surface of a three-dimensional trampoline. General relativity accurately predicted black holes, gravitational waves and clocks running faster in weaker gravitational fields and slower in stronger ones. It is especially useful in accurate satellite communications. Satellites experience time moving slightly faster than on Earth. While the daily difference is in millionths of a second, that would put your GPS miles off course. Between the standard model and general relativity, scientists have many of the laws of Earth and the solar system deciphered. Still, the quest for a grand unification of theories continues.

Perhaps we will someday unify the laws of the universe into an 'Everything Theory'. Such an encompassing theory might finally answer the mysteries of dark matter, the fabric of spacetime and interstellar travel. All the while, humanity's goal is the same as it has been for thousands of years: survival and furtherance of the human race. If we could find a way to travel a small fraction of the radius of the Milky Way, we could possibly travel to hundreds of Earth-like planets. The universe is inconceivably vast and that makes for unending adventure. While we have the means, we should use all the knowledge available to us to expand our reach, but with the understanding that Everything is spontaneously contemplated, yet never realized within Nothing. Such insight brings us closer to confident navigation of our universe.

SPACE+TIME

"The distinction between past, present and future is only a stubbornly persistent illusion." – Albert Einstein

Spacetime is the medium through which existence is experienced. Existence had no beginning and therefore will have no end, but for clarity of example, we'll discuss space and time as if there were a beginning – a *time zero*. At time zero, the emergence of Everything within Nothing necessitated dimensions. The three spatial dimensions and time were conceived as vehicles for the navigation and complete contemplation of Everything. When considering the inner workings of Everything, it is essential to think in four dimensions. The idea of fusing space and time into a single four-dimensional manifold is an important enhancement in perspective. It's counterintuitive to think of space and time as conjoined because they seem to be independent of one another. Our brains process space and time in different ways. To help in the idea of combining space and time, consider the *relativity of simultaneity* concept. Simply put, it asserts that the time at which an event occurs is relative to the frame of reference from which it is observed. When two spatially separated events occur, they can be observed as simultaneous or sequential, depending on the location of the observer. Changing positions in space changes the perspective of the timing of the events. This means that you cannot change your spatial position without changing your temporal position – they are interwoven. Although all dimensions are illusory, space is easier to grasp than time because it is perceptibly stationary. The contents of space may change, but space itself remains unchanged (or so it is perceived). Time is different because it seems to work like a magical conveyor belt where reality manifests on one end, and instantaneously becomes a memory as it passes by us. In reality, the conveyor belt isn't moving. Rather, we are considering the conveyor belt at its possible positions from a perspective that *is* moving.

NAVIGATING SPACETIME

It's helpful that we process time in a sequential, orderly manner. New becomes old, shiny becomes rusty, unfamiliar becomes familiar. Things progress in relatively predictable ways. But why is it that as we flow through existence, time doesn't move backwards or sideways? Why don't things go from old to new once in a while? It's the same reason we never see sandcastles formed by the ocean tides – because it's just incredibly unlikely. In the realm of thermodynamics, entropy is a measure of disorder. Scientists will tell you the universe tends from low toward high entropy. Tidy becomes messy, solid becomes fractured, new becomes old, etc. Our perspectives follow very specific paths guided by interactions between us and our environments. Entropy requires a closed system and Everything is so expansive that, for all intents and purposes, it could be considered open. In an open system, sandcastles *do* form by crashing waves and old *does* become young, just at very remote spacetime locations. Relativity of simultaneity applies to entropy as well. Like event sequences, entropy is perspective dependent. Chaos from one perspective is order from another. As we move through time, chain reactions build on one another. Our perspectives are the results of those reactions. Physical laws guide our experiences, just as rails guide trains. Atoms form molecules, molecules form compounds, compounds form minerals and nutrients, nutrients combine with other molecules to form life. Life is an unlikely occurrence and an example of order being established over vast swaths of spacetime. No, time doesn't necessarily flow in one direction. It's perspective dependent. The distinction between old, new, whole and fractured is deceptive. Everything always exists where it *would* be, eternally unchanged. It becomes animated only through perspective. Remember, Everything is complete and static. The conveyor belt doesn't move. We animate it by considering various positions it *could* be in. Somewhere, sandcastles are being formed by incoming tides.

IT'S ALL IN THE PAST

One benefit of our consistent perception of time is that we can use patterns to predict future events and alter our actions accordingly. Time units allow us to locate people or things in predetermined places for events like sunrises, classes, weddings, etc. The ability to synchronize is crucial to life. The four dimensions of space and time can be compared to satellite quadrilateration used by GPS receivers. To determine its true position, a receiver must process the signal from at least four satellites. Similarly, to get a true spacetime position, we must process the signals from at least four dimensions. By perceiving these four dimensions, we can navigate spacetime.

As discussed, Everything is static and our perspectives move causing the perception of time passage. In this, we perceive what's referred to as a past, present and future. Events that haven't yet occurred, but are destined to, are part of an enigmatic factory called "the future". While being observed (occurring) and for some time thereafter, they are considered "the present". Once an occurrence has moved beyond our sphere of influence, it is permanently and irreversibly interred in "the past". Did you notice something peculiar about how the present was described? The fact that an event could be considered current for some time after occurring implies subjectivity. When we speak of current events we're referring to occurrences in the recent past anywhere from seconds to several years ago. Truthfully, there is no present. The "present" is a relative term used to describe recent occurrences. Everything we experience has already happened. Living in four-dimensional spacetime consists of analyzing previous events, predicting future ones and using our knowledge to impact the probabilities of future events. All particles are events and each event has a unique location in spacetime. When one event enters another's sphere of influence, there is potential for interaction. Conversely, when events are mutually out of range, their potential for interaction is greatly diminished. The practical meaning of "living in the present", is focusing on recent events while we can still interact with them. The best chance you have of affecting your life is by acting or reacting to things as soon as possible after they occur. Returning again to the example of the conveyor belt, if a box approached on a belt, it would likely enter your sphere of influence for a brief time. Given that, you'd have a couple options: ignore it or interact with it. If you decide to interact with it, you'd have to predict its impending location and meet it there. Once at the point of intersection, you could interact with the box in a variety of ways. You could touch it, throw it, or just watch it. Whatever transpires would reside in an unalterable volume of spacetime, never to be revisited from the same perspective. When an event is observed, it becomes part of the past from the observer's perspective. Though events can be photographed or recorded, they occupy unique spacetime locations and can only occur once from any individual perspective. Though we may arrive at extremely similar spacetime volumes, we'll never arrive at the same volumes because, just as volumes are unique, so are perspectives. Neither can be repeated or duplicated.

THE WORLDLINE

In four dimensions, we are magnificent worms. At one end is our birth and the other our death.

What differentiates me from you? Nothing. We're part of the singularity of Everything. A better question might be, "What differentiates my perspective from yours?" The answer is time. For me to arrive at your position, it would take time. We've already established that no two events can occupy the same spacetime location. Although we are parts of a singular contemplation, we inhabit infinite perspectives within that contemplation. Our perspectives may at some point occupy the same space at different times, but they can never occupy the same spacetime. All particles follow special paths called worldlines. The worldline of an event is its true four-dimensional path through spacetime. The three-dimensional path of Earth around the sun would be a closed ellipse. In 3D space, Earth follows the elliptical path and returns to the same approximate point at a later time, enclosing the path. In 4D spacetime, the Earth's path around the sun is an open helix and the sun is a cylinder piercing through it along the time axis.

If you could get a view of your worldline in four dimensions, it would look like a cross-section of your body extruded along the various paths you take in life. Zooming out to a global view of your worldline, it would be most densely tangled in the cities and towns where you spend the most time. If you ever move across the country or take trips to far-away places, those rare trips will look like individual lines connecting micro loops to the large tangles in the places you've lived. If you add the lines of other people, animals and insects, the worldline fabric would create a dense shell on the surface of the earth. If you then add all other mass and energy involved in Everything, the combined worldlines would fill the universe solidly over time. If you were drawing your path in 3D, it would intersect many times, not only with itself, but with the paths of other people and objects. That would cause the incorrect notion that those events intersected in spacetime. If you were to examine each worldline in closely, you would see that even in the tightest of tangles, the lines wouldn't intersect. As discussed, separate events never occupy the same spacetime volume. If there is a possible variation to an event, it resides in a different volume. It's helpful to think in terms of worldlines when considering the important events and relationships that define our lives. Your worldline is the path of one perspective woven through spacetime and an unalterable legacy.

TIME TRAVEL

In a sense, we are always traveling in time, but that doesn't fulfill the fantasy of teleporting ourselves across vast swaths of spacetime. The common fantasy is of entering a capsule-like machine that we can control like a car or an airplane, inputting a desired date and time and being instantaneously transported through a tubular time warp, ending up at the same geographic space, but at a different time. In the new spacetime location, we would fully interact with multiple instances of the past, altering history and the future in ways we see fit. One critical aspect of this fantasy is emerging on the other side with an intact perspective. Without a stable perspective, time travel would be a pointless exercise. The scenario also neglects the moving reference frame of the orbiting planet or expansion/contraction of the universe during the time lapse, but those details would be worked out in the design of the time machine. If humans, or some future evolution thereof, can overcome the incredible obstacles to unlocking the secret of spacetime teleportation, the time traveling pioneers would have to contend with the possibility of altering or even destroying reality as we know it. As depicted in the plots of countless science fiction novels and movies over the years, time travel presents some well-known paradoxes. Let's consider some of them from the NE perspective.

THE BUTTERFLY EFFECT

We've all heard of the snowballing effects a small alteration of the past might have on future outcomes, also known as the "butterfly effect". It's not difficult to imagine the fragility of life's path if one considers all the small events in their life that led to big ones. "I wouldn't have met my wife if I didn't go to the store that day" or "If he would have left ten seconds later, he wouldn't have been in that accident". Time travelers in the movies always have a way to return to the future and observe the results of their meddling. The common moral is that changing the past wouldn't work out because the alternative outcomes would be wildly unpredictable. By traveling to the past and interfering with it, the time traveler causes a detour in their perspective and changes everything from that point forward.

The idea of altering the past disturbs us because we have already observed one possible future. As observers of the past, we're used to manipulating events to change only future outcomes. Past events have a more sacred quality. We feel that what has already happened is what nature intended. Without any preconception of events that haven't occurred yet, we don't mind changing the future as much. In the case of butterfly effect, the future being altered is not the same as the one that's already been experienced. If you could rewind time to a particular moment in the past, you'd be experiencing that moment from a different perspective. Therefore, that moment would indeed be new to observe. Additionally, any altered events in that moment would occupy different volumes of spacetime. The original events would be preserved while the altered ones would play out in their unique locations. This indeed would cause snowballing changes to the future from your new perspective, but from your original perspective, nothing would change. The original events are always preserved while alternate ones occur in parallel with them. The idea that only one future can emerge from an origin is very two dimensional. Each event has infinite possible routes and outcomes. You can't change the past, but you can experience new ones.

LOOPS

A casual loop is another paradox that could possibly occur in time travel. A loop occurs when a future event is the cause of a past event, which in turn is the cause of itself. In a loop, both events exist in spacetime, but their origins cannot be determined. Without one event, the other cannot come into existence. The "chicken or egg" paradox exemplifies a loop. The perceived co-dependency between two events leads us to believe that if one is eliminated, the other will be banished from existence. The grandfather paradox, for example, imagines a time traveler going backwards in time and killing their grandfather before he's had a chance to produce offspring. If the grandfather doesn't have children, then the time traveler can't be conceived in the future. Essentially, the time traveler would be left as an event of no origin. In most fictional considerations of this, the result is the fading or vanishing of the time traveler who was never conceived.

If you follow any chain of events far enough back in time you would find that all event loops are open-ended. From the NE perspective, all events, particles and occurrences have origins. Their origins reside in the possibility of Everything. The time traveler may have killed his grandfather, but he would still exist. That is because he was already conceived in the eternally preserved reality in which the grandfather was not killed. Killing the grandfather would generate an alternative set of events for the parallel existence of the would-be time traveler. Although it seems that he would lack a way to have been conceived, the time traveler's conception would have already occurred in another location in spacetime. He and his grandfather embody infinite versions of themselves. Event cycles may form pseudo loops in spacetime, but the point of reconnection can only approach the original area of origin. Once a possible reality exists on a worldline, it cannot be negated, only paralleled by alternative possible realities. Spacetime does not self-intersect. It only approaches itself at infinitely small distances.

The concept of time travel is important because it helps us gain a perspective on our navigation of Everything. As events in spacetime, we are butterflies flapping our wings and affecting everything in our proximity and throughout the universe. Spacetime teleportation is inevitable given that all realities are imminent. We must not let our inclination to preserve reality as we know it stop us from experiencing spacetime to the extents possible. As I mentioned earlier, it may not be Homo sapiens that decipher time travel. Highly evolved humanoids or an inorganic intelligence may pioneer it. As humans, we are constantly evolving yet imagine ourselves in our current state of evolution far into the future. Over the course of a few thousand years, we may look and act significantly different or even have completely different aims. For Homo sapiens, the goal of time travel would be hard to ascertain. On one hand, we could use it to journey in search of distant planets to inhabit. On the other hand, we could use it to alter the future of this planet and better preserve it. As it stands, we're in the same boat as the other animals on Earth. We're heavily dependent on a specific atmosphere with precise conditions and social structures. Traveling time would be very strenuous on our delicate psyches. For now, time travel is an inspirational thought exercise. It keeps us dreaming of ways to transcend what's possible. When things are monotonous, fantasies are great escapes. Meanwhile, there is plenty of adventure to be had on our current paths. Countless adventures and vast resources exist here on Earth. There is no need to hasten travel across the infinite. Eventually, we'll occupy all spacetime.

WORMHOLES AND TIMESTORMS

Imagine if the fabric of spacetime was folded and a hole was made between adjacent folds. That would describe a wormhole. Wormholes are theorized to occur in as-of-yet undiscovered higher dimensions and could make superluminal travel through spacetime a possibility. They might also explain some of the mysterious disappearances of ships, planes and the people aboard them around the world. Some theories suggest wormholes may appear and disappear in random places for unknown reasons. A few geographically triangulated areas have become notorious for extremely odd instances of vanishings. The Bermuda Triangle in the Atlantic Ocean, the Dragon's Triangle in the Pacific and the Nevada Triangle in the Sierra Nevada mountains are well-known examples. The Bermuda Triangle (also known as the Devil's Triangle) is the most familiar case in point. Reports of strange activity there date back to Christopher Columbus's voyage in 1492 where the Santa Maria's ship log records a strange light shining out in the distance over the sea. It was witnessed by crews on all three ships in the caravan and appeared to be coming out of the water and hovering above it. The initial sighting was allegedly followed by a great flash of light with a level of brilliance unlike anything the men had previously known. This occurred while Columbus and his crew were sailing across one of the deepest ravines in the Atlantic and a mere five hours before they were to discover the New World.

While in most Bermuda Triangle instances ships simply disappear along with their crews, some allegedly reappear with crews missing. Many theories have been proposed including colossal rogue waves and methane pockets on the sea floor, but those don't explain the incidents involving returned vessels. By far, some of the most intriguing disappearances involve aircraft. The most infamous aerial disappearance was that of Flight 19 in 1945 where five TBF Avenger torpedo bombers carrying fourteen airmen disappeared on a routine training mission. Later that day, PBM

Mariner, the aircraft sent to search for them, was also lost with its crew of thirteen. The 1978 vanishing of Irving Rivers and his Piper Navajo on a one-mile final for the runway at St. Thomas is another perplexing case. It was a clear day and the control tower had spotted the plane's blinking lights... then they vanished and the plane disappeared from the radar screen. An emergency search was conducted, but no wreckage, plane or pilot were ever found.

Perhaps the most intriguing story comes from the lone survivor of what has been dubbed a 'timestorm' on December 4th, 1970. Experienced pilot Bruce Gernon was flying his Beech Bonanza with two passengers, his father and business partner, from the Bahamas heading northwest to Miami Beach. During his climb at one thousand feet, he noticed a very dark cloud that seemed to be rapidly expanding. He couldn't avoid it, so he managed to slip through it without issue. Then, at eleven thousand five hundred feet, he encountered a similar type of cloud, but this time it was much larger and again, he had no choice but to go through it. This time when he entered the cloud pitch blackness enveloped the plane. The interior was cylindrical and void of precipitation. The blackness was interrupted by bright flashes, similar to lightning but much brighter to the point of lighting up the entire vortex. Its interior walls were comprised of gray strings rotating counterclockwise. He would later describe the phenomenon as "electronic fog". He spotted a tunnel about a mile wide and ten miles long in the cylindrical vortex. At the end of the tunnel, he could see blue sky so he set course for it. As he flew, the tunnel's walls seemed to close in on the plane and even attach to it. The plane's magnetic heading and other navigation gauges went berserk. It seemed he had lost the ability to control the plane and there was no escape from the black vortex. After several tense minutes, the plane pierced through the end of the vortex and as it did, Gernon and his passengers reported a momentary sense of weightlessness. They were out of the vortex, yet still enveloped in a strange gray fog. He radioed the Miami air traffic tower to get coordinates, but the controller could not see them on the radar.

Shortly after the fog began to break, the plane appeared on the radar. To Gernon's surprise, they were already in Miami airspace. A trip that would take a minimum of seventy-five minutes took only forty-seven minutes. This means that during their three-minutes in the vortex, they had traveled ninety-three miles. That would put the plane's speed at over eighteen hundred miles per hour. At those supersonic speeds, the plane would have broken up. To ensure he hadn't just had a memory lapse, he checked his remaining fuel. The consumption was consistent with a forty-seven-minute trip. Both passengers corroborated the story. Being shot forward in space instead of backward benefited their story's feasibility. Had they gone backward, the account could have been easily dismissed as a diversion caused by pilot error or malfunctioning gauges. By going forward in time, their journey indubitably defied the conventional understanding of physics.

If what Gernon describes is true, perhaps they passed through a large-scale atmospheric vortex. High speed vortices are meteorological phenomena caused by colliding pressure zones that create streams of very thin rotating air. Tornadoes, waterspouts and even hurricanes are familiar examples. This could explain the formation of cloud strings rotating counterclockwise in the northern hemisphere. Vortices could theoretically cause abnormally fast movement of objects due to their reduction of drag and high speeds of movement. The area over the ocean where it allegedly occurred is a zone of regular high- and low-pressure collisions. It doesn't, however, explain the electronic fog or instrument disturbances observed. Purportedly, there was also a strong solar wind traveling towards the earth on that day. The charged particles could have affected Earth's magnetosphere and caused the electronic fog. Another possibility is passage through warped spacetime via an encounter with dark energy. As we know, dark energy is speculated to be the invisible force behind the accelerated expansion of the universe. Some researchers believe that if it were positioned near an object a 'curvature bubble' could form. In a curvature bubble, the dark energy behind an object would be increased, causing spacetime to expand and push it. Dark energy in front of the object would become negative and compress spacetime in front of it, thus also pulling it. The object would effectively be traveling in a spacetime wave. This situation would explain Gernon's plane being lost on radar, landing with more fuel than expected, and flying much faster than its capabilities. (9)

Within the realm of impossibility that generates infinite virtual possibility, there are certainly better ways to traverse spacetime than through linear movement. Imagine spacetime as an infinitely large piece of fabric. Now imagine folding the fabric and piercing a needle through the fold. By passing through folded space, you can reach distant spacetime locations instantly. Easier said than done when the fabric is spacetime, but what if the fabric was already full of holes? The job then is merely to find them. Some portals may be miniscule in size while others may be enormous. They may occur naturally or by the ingenious engineering of intelligent life. In the case of naturally occurring portals, if string theory is a correct description of our universe, there may already be a web of countless wormholes throughout the universe. Shortly after the Big Bang, quantum fluctuations at the subatomic level may have created many traversable wormholes. Threaded through them would be many tiny cosmic strings. During the first billionth of a trillionth of a second after the big bang, the ends of these tiny worm holes may have been pulled light-years apart and scattered throughout the universe (10). From the outside, black holes and wormholes may appear similar, leading some cosmologists to theorize that the supermassive black holes in the centers of galaxies might be worm holes. One difference between the two is that two-way travel is theoretically impossible through black holes but may be possible through worm holes. One requirement if using an existing wormhole would be to predict your exit. Presumably, if we could visualize a wormhole, we would also be able to predict its end locations. Another requirement would be sufficient size such that the gravitational forces therein do not crush the occupants and short enough so that one wouldn't be stuck in a wormhole for eternity.

If our aim is to create traversable wormholes with predictable end locations, we'll probably need to employ a yet unknown particle. The issue, other than locations and sizes, would be keeping it open. For natural wormholes, that would be accomplished by cosmic strings. For manmade wormholes, it would have to be done with exotic particles. The exotic particles would need a negative mass and thus negative gravity. They'd create repulsive rather than attractive forces and prop the wormhole open. A candidate for this matter can be found in the vacuum of space. Quantum fluctuations in empty space are constantly creating pairs of particles and anti-particles only for them to be annihilated an instant later. We can already manipulate the fluctuations to create an effect like the negative mass we're looking for. This could be used to stabilize wormholes. Once we're holding them open, we could separate the ends, leaving one end of each wormhole in orbit around the earth and flinging the other end to destinations around the universe. Wormholes can also create time travel paradoxes and violate the structure of the universe, leading some scientists to believe that they are impossible to make and don't exist (10). As MOE, we understand that the universe is a contemplation of Everything within Nothing. Everything transpires virtually as possibility and therefore all is possible. Wormholes are possible, however difficult they may be to find or construct. Whether we create them or use existing ones, they might eventually provide the keys to vast spacetime teleportation.

DARK MATTER AND ENERGY

Thanks to NASA's WMAP space mission, we know that normal atomic matter makes up only 5% of the universe. Dark matter is around 25% percent and the remaining 70% percent is dark energy (rounded estimates, of course). Since dark matter and energy can't be seen and can only be detected, this implies that we only experience a tiny fraction of reality. What's more is we don't know what the "dark" components are or how they work. Cosmologists are almost certain dark matter exists based on the unlikely formation of galaxies. The normal matter in galaxies doesn't have enough gravity to cluster or form other structures. The only workable explanation of how galaxies cluster is that unseen mass creates a supplementary gravitational force. If it weren't for dark matter, stars and planets would likely scatter and not form galaxies. We know that there must be something inside and around galaxies that doesn't emit or reflect light. We can also assume there are high concentrations of dark matter if nearby light bends while passing by. Dark matter isn't to be confused with anti-matter because anti-matter emits gamma rays when exposed to matter. It isn't made up of black holes because unlike black holes, dark matter doesn't have an event horizon or consume its surroundings. What we do know is that something is out there, it interacts with gravity and there is a lot of it. Dark matter could also be a complex exotic particle that doesn't interact with light in the way that we'd expect (11). For Nothing to be, all possibility must be counteracted. Atomic matter is the virtual manifestation of possibility. Dark matter is likely derived from the quantum fluctuations caused by interactions between Nothing and Everything throughout space.

Dark energy is even stranger because we can't detect or measure it. We can merely observe its effects in the expansion of the universe. Many cosmologists attribute the acceleration of the expansion to dark energy. Whereas dark matter lends its gravity to galaxies, dark energy is thought to be a negative-pressure, repulsive force. And while dark matter seems to clump together via gravity, dark energy is thought to be evenly distributed throughout spacetime. The expansion caused by dark energy isn't observed inside galaxies because the stars and other masses within them are grouped together by dark matter. Due to this, we don't experience the universe's expansion as it occurs *between* galaxies rather than within them. Earth is not getting farther from the sun, nor are stars in the Milky Way getting farther apart. Thanks to the extra mass of dark matter, galaxies remain clustered while space expands. However, as billions of years pass, the number of observable galaxies will decrease as the expansion pushes them farther away. New space is constantly created everywhere. Space doesn't change as it expands, there's just more of it. Dark energy is distributed throughout empty space where virtual particles continually emerge from Nothing and disappear again. Like dark matter, it is intrinsic to the generation of space from Nothing. It permeates the entire universe and somehow has the opposite effect on space as normal energy and matter. Dark energy, comprising a full 70% of what makes up the universe, may very well be the force of contemplation within Nothing.

SUPERSTRINGS AND HYPERSPACE

Supersymmetric string theory has emerged as another candidate for science's 'Everything Theory'. In 1968, a scientist named Gabriele Veneziano was trying to understand the nature of the strong nuclear force and noticed that a mathematical function called the Euler beta function could be used to describe it. In 1970, three other physicists noticed that if they replaced point-like particles with small extended objects (now called strings) in some equations, those equations could be solved by the Euler beta function as well. The strings would theoretically behave like small stiff objects that could vibrate. String theory was officially born.

They proposed that each mode of vibration would produce different kinds of particles. Initially, the theory only incorporated the quantum particles known as bosons, but a young theorist named Pierre Ramond was able to generalize the theory by incorporating vibrations from other quantum particles known as fermions. His investigation into how string theory could include fermions in its spectrum led to the concept of supersymmetry, wherein the equations for force are equal to those for matter. In 1974, physicists John Schwarz and Joel Scherk found a solution in the superstring equations that predicted a massless particle of spin two. Any particle with those properties had to be the much sought-after gravity particle, the graviton. This dramatically popularized superstring theory. However, problems began to arise when people tried to make real predictions using superstring theory and it was found to be highly inaccurate. Eventually, scientists experimenting with the mathematics found that increasing the physical dimensions over which superstring theory was applied to ten dimensions, the theory finally made accurate physical predictions (12).

The ten dimensions included three spatial, one time and six additional dimensions to make superstring theory work. The core of superstring theory is that, at the most fundamental scales, the ultimate building blocks are not mathematical points, but small vibrating one-dimensional objects called strings. It also postulates that both open and closed strings are possible. Hyperspace dimensions, or those higher than 4D, are theorized to be impossibly small and have only been predicted. It has been theorized that the elusive graviton particle may exist as a string with wave amplitude zero within one or more of the tiny dimensions, explaining gravity's relative weakness. To test the existence of hyperspace and gravitons therein, particle probes of very short wavelength would be needed. Experiments in such high energy particles are being conducted at the CERN large hadron collider (LHD) particle accelerator on the border between France and Switzerland. One theoretical byproduct of generating high energy in small volumes is creating the conditions for black holes. Fear of generating black holes caused some anxiety in the public when the collider was completed in 2008. Luckily, particles from the sun with much higher energy bombard Earth every day, confirming that if there are microscopic black holes, they've been benign to us. A much larger collider is in the works and over the next few decades it may confirm whether gravity is truly weak or just a strong force dissipated within hidden dimensions (12).

Loop quantum gravity (LQG) is an alternative to superstring theory and attempts to unify quantum mechanics and gravity. It predicts that at the very smallest sizes, space and time themselves can be quantized. In other words, there is a smallest particle size (10^{-34}m) and smallest time (10^{-43} sec). LQG is strictly a theory to quantize gravity space and time. It doesn't attempt to incorporate the other known forces. Whereas superstring theory assumes that space and time exist and needs both for its equations to make sense, LQG doesn't require or assume the existence of spacetime. It attempts to add a quantum component to general relativity while string theory attempts to bring gravity into the framework of the standard model (12).

ENTANGLEMENT AND SUPERPOSITION

Quantum entanglement is a phenomenon that occurs when a pair or group of particles interact in a way such that after the interaction the quantum state of each is dependent on the other even if the particles are separated by large distances. Einstein called it "spooky action at a distance". Entanglement is an important feature of quantum mechanics, but seemingly lacking in classical mechanics. Classical mechanics adheres to the principle of locality wherein all objects are directly related to their immediate surroundings. Quantum mechanics evades locality via the ongoing mystery of seemingly non-local correlations between distant particles. In cases of entanglement, physical properties such as momentum, spin and polarization of entangled particles can be perfectly correlated. Amazingly, any measurement of one entangled particle's properties results in an instantaneous collapse of correlation between it and other particles entangled with it. The signal to 'disentangle', referred to as 'wave function collapse', is at the heart of the disparity between classical and quantum physics. The fact that the 'signal' could be transmitted faster than the speed of light suggests that we don't understand some fundamental aspects of quantum physics.

Although some interpretations of quantum mechanics do not recognize wave function collapse, all interpretations agree that there is a correlation between the entangled particles. The thought experiment conducted in 1935 by Einstein, Boris Podolsky and Nathan Rosen (EPR) proposed that entangled particles have intrinsic mutual agreements, or hidden variables, and are acting independently based upon those agreements. In 1964, quantum physicist John Bell demonstrated that the mechanics of entangled particles was inconsistent with the mathematical consequences of hidden variables between particles. Bell's theorem left two possibilities: either the quantum world is truly non-local and information is being exchanged instantaneously between entangled particles upon measurement, or statistical independence, otherwise known as free will, is absent in the quantum world. In his later years, Bell leaned toward instantaneous messaging theory, implying that the quantum mechanics is fundamentally non-local and separated particles can have instantaneous effects on each other, regardless of distance.

Quantum entanglement has been demonstrated experimentally with neutrinos, electrons, buckyball molecules and even small diamonds. In some cases, signals have been exchanged faster than the speed of light between particles separated by long distances.

Utilizing entanglement in communication and computation is a very active area of research and development. Any number or quantity of quantum particles can become entangled. It has been theorized that all space, matter and energy contain information which has been entangled with the entirety of the universe since contemplation. That being the case, it would be possible for any spacetime event to communicate across the universe. Essentially, the entire universe is entangled and a singular coordinated system.

The year of the EPR thought experiment, Erwin Schrödinger, the physicist responsible for deriving the wave function equation for quantum systems, conducted his own thought experiment. He had exchanged several letters with Einstein about EPR which illustrated the counterintuitive nature of quantum superpositions. In a state of superposition, a particle or object can exist as a combination of multiple states corresponding to different possible outcomes. In the experiment eventually dubbed 'Schrödinger's Cat', he proposed a scenario with a cat locked in a cage. In the cage with the cat was a radioactive atom, a radiation detector and a sealed vial of cyanide gas. The system would be secured against direct interference by the cat. If the atom decayed, the radiation detector would trigger a release of the cyanide gas that would kill the cat. If the atom didn't decay, the detector wouldn't release the gas and the cat would live. Since the state of the detector and cat were tied to the state of the atom, they were said to be entangled. According to the laws of quantum mechanics, at that moment, the atom was neither in a state of decay or non-decay but in a superposition of both states. The superposition state of the atom is entangled with the detector and the cat, so all three are in a state of superposition. In superposition, the detector is both triggered and not while the cat is both alive and dead. Only at the point where the box is opened and the result observed does the wave function of the atom-detector-cat system collapse into either the alive or dead scenario.

The Schrödinger's Cat experiment has three essential components: superposition, entanglement and measurement. Superposition is the idea that quantum objects can be in multiple states at the same time before their state is decided by an external influence like their environment. Entanglement says that after interaction, particles can be described by a single wave function. Measurement is simply one quantum system becoming entangled with another and evolving wave functions via the Schrödinger equation. In the experiment, the observer becomes entangled with the other parts of the system. To the observer, entanglement with the system may seem like a function collapse, but the wave function is just evolving to include them. Since the observer is entangled with other particles in superposition, they themselves are in a superposition. The observer who saw the cat alive and the observer who saw the cat dead inhabit slightly different quantum realities which never interact. Both realities branch from the same initial reality as it reacts with the environment while in a state of superposition. This is known as environmental decoherence. The prediction of environmental decoherence became the basis for a theory devised in 1957 by Hugh Everett, now known as "many worlds". According to the theory, quantum effects spawn countless branches of reality. The number of branches is either infinite or approaching infinite. In short, every outcome has a 100% chance of occurrence. From our perspectives, we experience only one of infinite possibilities as we see a small fraction of reality.

The many worlds theory was brought back to the forefront of quantum physics discussions in 2019 via Sean Carroll's book, "Something Deeply Hidden". Carroll stresses that in quantum branching the universe isn't duplicated but cross-sectioned thousands or even millions of times per second. That would mean there are billions of versions of us in the universe. Disappointingly, he also stipulates that 'many worlds' does not mean that everything possible happens. He says it simply means that the wave function of particles follows the Schrödinger equation which predicts that many things can happen, but not things such as electrons becoming protons (13). NE is in perfect alignment with many worlds and Sean Carroll on all but the denial of the totality of Everything. For Nothing to occur, all possibilities must be contemplated. If any possibility were left out, it would violate the Paradox. Perhaps protons becoming electrons is impossible in this universe, but it most certainly is possible in others.

THE MULTIVERSE

One could be very satisfied with the idea that they will experience near-infinite branches of reality within this universe. This universe is so vast that humans cannot begin to fathom its extents. Still, its finite age doesn't satisfy the NE requirement that Everything be infinite. There is no absolute starting point for Everything and therefore the Big Bang was not the beginning. It *was* the starting point of one event – the contemplation of spacetime that is our universe. No scientist, physicist or philosopher knows exactly what existed before the contemplation or what, if anything, exists outside it. In fact, it is a bold statement to say anything exists other than the universe. Nonetheless, as curious creatures, we tend to search for the absolute limits of things. If one singularity can swell into near-infinite spacetime, then what about two, ten, thousands or trillions of singularities? Could this universe be just one stitch in an infinite sheet of unique contemplations? With the principles of NE applied, the answer is obvious. The existence of Nothing necessitates the contemplation of Everything, which implicates the existence of countless universes. Since the word universe means *'everything'*, then *'multiple everythings'* is redundant and a bit facetious. The word 'universe' was originally selected to describe what we once thought of as totality but turned out to be one of many totalities. The term 'universe' no longer encompasses Everything and therefore the even greater term, 'multiverse', might be used to describe it. Though all occurrences fall under the umbrella of Everything, the term 'multiverse' might be recognizable to those already acquainted with idea of infinite contemplations.

Scientists currently have no way to look beyond the visible universe, but there are theories about what could be beyond it. One theory is that the universe is infinite and its laws and parameters vary over the vast volume of the cosmos. Most cosmologists agree that the universe is bigger than we can see, but it is less accepted that physical laws change in various locations. Within our visible universe, we can observe that physical laws are universal. However, if the universe was infinite, it wouldn't have a starting point but would have points of inflection. If the big bang was a point of inflection or rebirth, then the universe would in fact be infinite and we could do away with the phrase 'multiverse'. Another concept is that universes scatter like droplets and create additional universes during inflation. This would presuppose that the multiverse always existed and could explain the sudden inflation of our universe within it. During this 'scattering' other universes may have even collided with our own. In 1998, a satellite detected small variations in temperature around the ecliptic (equator) of the universe. Some think it was caused by the collision of an adjacent universe to ours before inflation. Others noted that it might be due to instrumentation error, but measurements taken by two subsequent satellites have shown the same anomaly. The fact that the collision theory could possibly be measured or tested puts it in the realm of scientific theory. The 'many worlds' theory could also apply to the multiverse. If, as the universe began, it had the possibility of existing as all other possible universes in a superposition of quantum configurations and one configuration was selected, the universe was formed exactly the way it is while an infinite number of other possibilities branched into alternate universes. (12)

According to the Paradox, we live in an existence where the probability of all contemplation is one hundred percent. On the micro-branches of quantum reality where humans reside, probability is always perceived as less than one hundred percent because the extents of the contemplation are not visible to us. Due to our relatively short lifespans, we never get to see the loops of spacetime come full circle. When something is infinite, it has no beginning or end. The birth of our universe was but one of an infinite number of contemplations. We reside within the vast multiverse of Everything, experiencing infinite possibilities while universes collide, conjoin, collapse, inflate, inflect and are reborn.

FREE WILL VS. DETERMINISM

The disparity between standard and quantum physics is that quantum physics lacks a physical description of the measurement process. The laws of quantum theory predict probabilities only, making it technically incomplete. However, if we violate the long-held assumption that distributions of hidden variables are independent of measurement settings, then we can conclude that all systems are casually correlated. From this, we can conclude that there are no chances or possibilities anywhere in the multiverse. Basically, we'd be saying that all possible outcomes are related, pre-determined and definite. Absolute determinism, or superdeterminism, was first put forth in the 1980's as a possible loophole in Bell's Theorem by John Bell himself. He postulated that "there is a way to escape the interference of superluminal speeds and 'spooky action at a distance', but it involves absolute determinism and complete absence of free will."

A big part of our psyche desires control over our actions and destiny. The concept of free will provides us with a sense of motivation, accomplishment and dignity. Frankly, without it, what's the point? The question of predetermined destiny is at the root of countless philosophical arguments. The debate between *creatio ex nihilo* (creation from nothing) and *ex nihilo, nihilo fit* (from nothing, nothing comes) lies in the question of free will. As previously mentioned, *Creatio ex nihilo* believers see God as the ultimate master of existence. In other words, there is nothing before or after God. This makes God the origin of existence and gives Him, as the Creator, ultimate and singular free will. Interestingly, if God has the sole free will in existence and we are separate from Him, we lack free will and therefore bear no responsibility for our actions. On the *nihilo fit* spectrum, existence is eternal and there is no beginning. One could interpret it to say that it means God was there from the beginning but in the ancient religions, gods were depicted as being born into a preexisting universe. In that viewpoint, gods are finite beings and the question of free will is unresolvable. *Nihilo fit* is in perfect agreement with NE except that it rejects the very notion of Nothing. It asserts, "if nothing ever is, then nothing can ever be." It attempts to dispose of the concept of Nothing by stating that if nothing was, then nothing would happen and therefore only existence prevails. The statement, "from nothing, nothing comes" is correct, but not in the way it proposes. It is correct to state that Nothing comes of Nothing, but it is equally correct to state that the contemplation of Everything is a condition of Nothing.

Imagine that you've designed and built a house. As its builder, you'd have control over the structure and function of the house. The decisions made in its design would determine the physical paths one could take in the house from that time forward. Now imagine that the house you've built is an expansive mansion with many rooms and that while moving in, you bumped your head and were afflicted with an acute case of amnesia. When you came to, you were told that you are in the house of your own making, yet you have no memory of designing or constructing it. Each room, down to smallest detail, is a surprise. On one hand, it would be an exhilarating experience to be instantly thrust into a surprising reality created by your own vision. On the other, you'd be bound to a mysterious layout which you don't remember creating. The walls, hallways and roof would contain you in a pre-determined geometry and once the building is finished, the living space is set. You can generally choose where and when you go, but you can't walk through the walls that you erected. As an amnesiac, you'd have no control over the environment that you would find yourself in but as the original architect you would've once had full control over its design. This is essentially the position we find ourselves in as residents of Everything. Existing within Everything is like living in a mansion with infinitely numerous hallways and rooms. Although it's your creation, you are detached from all recollection of its design and construction. You will eventually explore the whole building but for now, you can only be in one room at a time. To make things even stranger, you're told that the structure does not exist until it is observed by you. It manifests instantaneously as its passages are navigated. How would you feel in this situation? Odds are, you'd be delighted in your creation and impressed with it. Perhaps you'd hope to do justice to the legacy of such creative power and share it with others. Or maybe you'd burn it down to see if you could rebuild it in a memorable way. We find ourselves in this exact predicament as architects and residents of Everything.

Try throwing an object. When you threw it, did you control its destiny or did your actions just fulfill another predetermined outcome? It's true that throwing the object was inevitable and the toss occurred in countless variations regardless of your decision to pick it up. However, within each variation, you exerted local control through conscious participation. In reality, you were in *virtual* control. The root of the word 'virtual' lies in virtue, meaning righteousness or moral. That's a far cry from what virtual implies for most of us today. In the last four decades, 'virtual' has become interpreted negatively to mean simulated or fake. The phrase 'virtual reality' conjures images of contrived, glitch-ridden digital realities in sci-fi movies and video games. Sci-fi thrillers like *The Matrix*, wherein reality is discovered to be an elaborate digital simulation, have caused suspicions amongst many that when something nonsensical occurs it is 'the Matrix glitching'. Although we keep improving software and user interfaces, we're nowhere close to digitally replacing our own environment. For the time being, manmade realities will be limited in scope and provision and fall far short of the infinite possibility surrounding our basic reality. Still, all realities are imminent. It's possible that reality is a doubly nested simulation created by some advanced intelligence. If that were the case, the cause could be as creepy as that depicted in the Matrix where an artificial intelligence using our living bodies as energy sources or as annoying as a manmade interface where our entangled universal data circulates once uploaded, subject to all the false promises and programming errors people make. The truth is that all possibilities, including basic reality, are simulated within Nothing via contemplation. Contemplation, though virtual, is error-free, though we may occasionally find ourselves shrouded in layers of some subpar simulations herein.

All the wonderful, beautiful things we've experienced in life are virtual. Everything is the perfect contemplation. If you feel free, it's because you are. If you feel limited, you may be at the moment, but limitations are temporary. There is no difference between experiencing something that is predetermined and something that is undetermined, as long as the outcome is unknown to you. Due to our inability to see into the future, all outcomes are unknown to us. We have no memory of creating it, so it's all new to us. Can the future be influenced? According to the determinism innate in Everything, not technically. But if all possibilities are inevitable, so too is the experience of creating outcomes. Although all outcomes are imminent, we play active rolls in the realities we experience.

The will of Nothing is to counteract all possibility and, in so doing, contemplate Everything. We have free will in the same way that we exist infinitely while not existing. Everything is complete and all is imminent. In completeness, alteration is illusory. As components of Nothing, we also occupy the position of ultimate control, hereafter referred to as *Creator*. As Creator, we are the architects of Everything. We create and behold Everything in all time and therefore ultimately enjoy free will. The virtual free will experienced within Everything is so vast and diverse that it's as unpredictable and exhilarating as true free will. Yes, you're in a house of predetermined design, but remember that you are its architect. Free will comes through accepting ownership of the house that you built.

BEING HUMAN

"It is not the strongest species that survives, or the most intelligent, but the one most responsive to change." – Charles Darwin

HOMINIDS AND MYTHS

Consider the complex alien form that is you. Trillions of molecules intricately linked against all odds and despite harsh terrain, extreme heat, bitter cold and endless galactic voids, somehow coalesced perfectly into a cellular being with a conscience. Surviving Earth itself has been an uncertain and perilous journey for every species, yet we prevail and cling to its surface. Although we struggle, we are perfectly suited to thrive on Earth. Ours is precisely the form that works at this spacetime location, given billions of years of evolution from mere microorganisms to the superorganisms we are today. Our eyes process photons into visual maps of the space around us while our ears transfer percussive data to our brains and our nerves sense pressures and temperatures so our bodies can self-regulate and avoid injury. Billions of other creatures on this planet have similar abilities, yet we are the most complex and successful of them.

Our life spans and ecological dominance are unparalleled. We can think objectively in terms of past, present and future. We are perfectly suited to benefit from our environs. If something doesn't suit us, we can break it down to the molecular level, rearrange its atomic structure and create something that does. Multitudes of other species on Earth are also fortunate in their evolution, yet humans stand out. Although mammalian, we have relatively little hair, walk completely upright and are vastly more intelligent than any other known species. Homo sapiens is the most adaptable animal that Earth has ever produced. We have explored and endured more environments than any other creature. We are the only known species to have intentionally exited (and re-entered) Earth's atmosphere. We are self-aware and can transmit complex messages across large distances. Although we primarily use vibrations in our throats to communicate, we have developed ways to communicate electronically. Other species seem to be part of the fabric of nature, whereas we seem to create our own fabric. One could argue, and correctly so, that physiological traits are not the only keys to 'success' and that how we *perceive* our situations is a factor as well. After all, a single-celled amoeba that darts around happily collecting nutrients may be more successful than a multi trillion-celled human who is unhappy.

Humans began the split from the rest of the animal kingdom roughly seven million years ago, branching off from chimpanzees and bonobos in Africa as hominids. Hominids lived amongst the animals, continually evolving for the next several million years as relatively insignificant hunters and scavengers. It wasn't until Homo erectus harnessed fire in the stone age as early as two million years ago that hominids began the physical transformation that would significantly differentiate them from other animals (14). Roasting food over a fire killed parasites and increased processing efficiency, thus allowing for less time spent chewing and digesting. Eventually, erectus (sapiens' predecessor) developed smaller digestive tracts, freeing up energy to support larger brains (15). 100,000 years ago, multiple hominid species including H. erectus, H. neanderthalensis, H. sapiens, Denisovans and even the little understood dwarf H. floresiensis roamed the earth in small bands. Through DNA, it is known that sapiens interacted and interbred with Neanderthals and Denisovans when they pushed northward and eastward from Africa. Strangely though, by about 12,000 years ago, sapiens was the only surviving hominid left on the planet. It's widely imagined that sapiens simply used their superior intelligence to quickly dominate and exterminate the other varieties of hominid, but the truth is more complicated and protracted. The real key to sapiens' success was the ability to adapt to the variability of our ancestral environments. Changes in hot, cold and moisture cycles were common on the African continent and sapiens had to innovate tools and sew clothing to survive (16). The need to continually adapt likely led to mutation of our neurological 'tree of knowledge' which triggered a critical cognitive advancement. The result of the advancement was a sophisticated capacity for abstract thought and communication. This meant we could create great stories around which large coalitions could be formed (14). These stories, or myths, were to become one of our greatest gifts. It meant we could plan, strategize, manipulate, deceive and cooperate flexibly in large groups. Today, myths such as nationality, law, incorporation, religion and currency facilitate our remote and widespread collaboration with others whom we don't know personally. This has enabled the giant technological strides sapiens have made in the past few centuries.

When attorneys argue cases in court, they do so in context of societal myths better known as laws. The strength of a myth is dependent on its subjects' devotion to it. If one day enough people stopped believing that stealing from others is a crime, then the multitudes of laws on the books regarding stealing would be impotent. Violators and victims would be left without an intervening third party and be forced to settle their differences themselves. Such lawlessness is part of what we escape when we collectively agree to believe in and enforce legal myths. When a buyer negotiates with a seller, they are trying to come to an agreement as to what the object of interest is worth to both parties. Together, they formulate a myth that they can both believe enough to be mutually satisfied. Religious ceremonies, careers, marriages, accolades, possessions, morality and nearly everything else mankind has come to cherish are at least partially myth based. The word myth gets a bad rap because it has long been used to describe something that is flatly false. Myths used in society-building are more complex than simple untruths. They are interwoven with and fortified by known facts and obvious truths. A better description of a society-building myth would be, '*a path to well-being through faith'*. Those that have taken a leap of faith must persuade others to do the same so that the myth can manifest as an institution and be stable enough to sustain itself. The key ingredient to a myth's persuasion is trust. The trust is built over time by the persistent conveyance of a believable vision and regular demonstration of its fidelity. Those who subscribe to the most prevalent myths generally do well in society. By following well-established patterns in behavior, finance, religion, education, politics, careers and consumption, most people go with the flow of the day. When the flow of society fails to satisfy or violates deep convictions, some of the most successful people branch off to create myths of their own. Take successful stock investors, sports figures, politicians, rock stars, philosophers and actors for example. All these people have taken incredible leaps of faith and have prevailed against the odds. Eventually, their myths attract devoted followers and their risk-taking results in success. Still, even mavericks with their own myths must subscribe to the foundational myths that hold society together. Currency, clock time, fashion, productivity and etiquette carry us through our lives and help us fulfill our societal roles.

Being as subjective as they are, myths can also lead us to divergence and failure. Look at the lifestyle myths of smoking, taking illicit drugs and gambling. Each has been disproven as a practical means to a happy end, but they retain a devoted following through public license, romanticism and brain chemistry. Another prime example of myth-driven degeneration is religious conflict. While most religions offer their followers a sense of belonging and exemplify love and good social behavior, the myths they are built on are often strictly incompatible with others. If two groups of people interface and their core myths are conflicting, it is rare that those groups will coexist peacefully. That is why societies that are deeply religious commonly find themselves mired in conflict. The same phenomenon is at play between rival cultures, races, sexualities, gangs, professions and even schools. When people fail to look beyond some myths, it can prove all-consuming and even detrimental. A good sign that a myth will cause dissonance is if, at its base, there are statutes that are exempt from logical scrutiny. Still, despite their many possible pitfalls, myths have been the key to human flexibility and prosperity. The best myths are the simplest, least guarded and hardest to disprove. Love is a great myth. Kinship and happiness are two others. Those myths hold us together, are continually recruiting and have no mysterious statutes.

Although myths are the foundations of society, we are not as reliant on some of them as we were in past generations. Myths that were once considered foundational are showing signs of being replaced. Traditional religion, political and educational institutions, nationalism and hard currency are all struggling in a world where information, culture and currency can be rendered digitally. Great structures and infrastructures are being left hollow as the devoted disperse. The casting aside of many of our most sacred myths continues as we turn increasingly to science and technology as sources of purpose. Yet, this is humanity's natural path and the continuation of our journey. Evolution is a product of the movement from impossible to possible life. We are indeed lucky creatures, but the Homo sapiens perspective is just one of an infinite number of perspectives we will inhabit. Myths that have given us strength and purpose in the past are giving way to myths that promise us comfort and control of our destiny. During such transitions, the incredible pain felt by the loyal believers of older myths is overcome by the sense of discovery and wonder felt by the devotees of newer novel myths. Once a novel myth reaches critical mass of proven advantages, it has an almost irresistible gravity. We live in a time of many new myths. Still, one myth stands the test of time - existence. Everything exists virtually, only to ensure that Nothing does. That fact is clear-cut, stands up to scrutiny and cannot be refuted. It proves and disproves reality in one eloquent sweep of logic. Existence is a timeless myth of endless depth and intrigue.

BEYOND SAPIENS

Life - the condition of organic matter which includes the capacity for growth, autonomous activity, reproduction, and continual change preceding death.

In geological time, Homo sapiens' time on Earth is a mere second. Contemplating life from an evolutionary standpoint helps us to see how malleable and temporary our situations are. Through a broadened lens, we can look boldly into the future, acknowledging not only the true nature of our species, but some of our possible trajectories as we evolve. Even as we brace for what's next, the Homo sapiens' mind continues to reveal new capabilities. It is possible we could evolve simply by unlocking more of our own brain's potential. However, it seems more likely that evolution will come in the form of neural modification, quantum information exchange or even the complete replacement of organic life by inorganic life. At the current rate of advancement, humans may undergo a revolutionary transformation in the coming decades. This could mean that people born Homo sapiens will witness humanity's evolution to another species.

Human intellect has undergone exponential advancements since the cognitive evolution. This was accelerated in part due to the Enlightenment in the 1700's when European culture began to emphasize reason over superstition and blind faith. The following of reason led to the industrial revolution and the modernization of science and medicine. While people began studying electricity, dynamics and chemistry using scientific methods, our evolution began in earnest. Today our cognitive abilities are being enhanced with the help of drugs and auxiliary computers. In coming years, we'll add neural implants to the list of upgrades. The transition is already underway on three fronts: the dissolution of several major societal myths, upgrading and preserving our physical bodies, and fostering non-carbon-based intelligence.

WILL WE SURVIVE?

Two major questions loom in predicting the destiny of humanity: "Will we survive, and if so, what will become of us?" The evolution of a species becomes irrelevant if it goes extinct in the process, so let's first consider some of the hurdles to survival. There are many possible causes of human extinction. Some are out of our hands and some depend on our actions. Mega disasters like super volcano eruptions, solar explosions and celestial object strikes are exceedingly rare, yet effectively uncontrollable. If nature kills us, that's the end of our story. War, disease, environmental damage, and the unchecked emergence of inorganic life are among the variables we *can* control. If we successfully circumnavigate the obstacles to survival posed by them, we'll have a good chance of continuing as a species.

War is addressed later in this book, but it is one of the top candidates for ending, or at least decimating the human population. Historically, war has been a catalyst for innovation. It's kept population numbers in check and assured that only the fittest survived to procreate. It's kept our minds alert and inventive, even after our relative conquest of nature. Many of our greatest inventions have come out of military need. Things like nuclear power, artificial limbs, microwaves and blood transfusion have become useful outside of warfare. In the seventy-five years of relative prosperity since World War II, human population has exploded and with it the ability of its militaries to destroy it. Where once battles were fought between neighboring regions, armies and weapons may now be deployed anywhere in the world. Between bioweapons and nuclear arsenals, there is plenty of capacity to destroy civilization as we know it. But to wipe us off the planet? With advanced shelters protecting portions of civilization, probably not. Granted life would be extremely difficult for any survivors, if just a few colonies are able to regain a foothold, societies would be reforming within a few decades.

It might even be said that a major war could rescue humanity from a slower form of extinction – environmental destruction. With a global population approaching ten billion, our atmosphere is warming from hundreds of billions of tons of CO_2 emissions, our oceans are overfished and becoming acidified and the worlds rainforests are being cleared for farmland. Going forward, humanity has some choices: a) limit population, b) innovate technologies and support voluntary population downsizing, c) let populations wither after reaching unsustainable numbers or d) conduct a war campaign with the goal of preserving technology and eliminating surplus populations. Populations voluntarily limiting their numbers would be the ideal solution, but it is human nature to grow and leave the shrinking to others. Population downsizing could also be involuntary if the world's power balance changed, but for now world leaders are opaque or complacent in such sensitive areas. The strategy employed by the West is sharing technology and resources with countries that have outstripped or otherwise lack resources. As noble as that is, sharing wealth requires one party to be prosperous. If the West were to lose much more of its prosperity, the impetus to support under-resourced lands would decline and be replaced by the inclination to pillage what's left. It may be the case that, regardless of actions, many of the world's populations will wither due to resource scarcity. Given the vast differences in world views between major powers, war is a more likely scenario. The warfighting capabilities on both sides would make any major war a hellish experience worldwide. Still, as tragic and destructive as it would be, humanity would probably survive it. It's possible that the descendants of the survivors would be gifted a recovering planet, preserved knowledge and cautionary tales from pre-war and war-torn generations. As a human with no connection to a fallout shelter, I'd likely be vaporized in a large-scale war. I hope that humanity takes the route of aggressively confronting overpopulation and environmental destruction, but war wouldn't necessarily be the end of man and could even have the silver lining of environmental recovery.

Disease, particularly chronic disease, is the top killer of humans. But with only 60 million deaths to answer for the 140 million births each year, it's hardly a candidate to end mankind. An extinction-level disease would have to appear quickly and remain relatively unimpeded to succeed in pruning the population. It might emerge from nature like Ebola or be created in a lab as a potent version of Coronavirus. Disease also prevails in wartime as it plagues the wounded and thrives in those conditions. As devastating as battle is, disease accounts for a sizable percentage of wartime deaths. Due to an ever densifying human population, viruses, superbugs and parasites have the potential to decimate our species. Yet as difficult as they are to keep at bay, modern medicine has kept them from devastating most societies. On a macro scale, humans could be viewed as parasitic to Earth. Perhaps viruses are a sort of planetary immune response, controlling human population and allowing Earth to heal. After rising steadily for decades, global carbon dioxide emissions fell by 6.4% in 2020 due to the travel restrictions and reduction in economic activity caused by the COVID-19 pandemic (17). It's all relative from the NE perspective. I prefer to believe that humans are a natural, remarkable and temporary part of Earth's organic makeup, not merely parasites.

ARTIFICIAL INTELLIGENCE

While the saga of Homo sapiens reaches its zenith, technological progress is causing us to question our definition of life and the depth of our intelligence. Machine learning, also known as artificial intelligence, has been in the works since the 1950s. Modeled after human logic, AI uses available information and reason to solve problems. Today, people use logic stored on microchips to automate nearly every daily task. We don't often give it a thought because our 'internet of things' controlled via smart phones feels like an extension of our own free will. With processing power increasing exponentially over the decades, artificial intelligence has caught up to, and in many cases, surpassed our needs. AI can outperform humans in all categories of logical problem solving. With the help of Big Data, AI knows more about us than we do. As I type this, AI is attempting to predict my next words and much of the time, it's correct. It even makes autonomous phone calls to us to deliver information or to act as a telemarketer.

In a debate in China with Jack Ma, the founder of Alibaba, Elon Musk described his sense of urgency in developing a neural link that can be implanted in human brains to help us upload information. He also likened AI to something that we can't even fathom the intelligence of. He described the discrepancy between human communication and that of a computer with a teraflop of memory. "To AI, it would be like talking to a tree and it won't have the patience to communicate with us." His basic argument was that if we don't stay ahead of AI, we are destined to be surpassed or even overrun by it. (18) From a human perspective, that's a persuasive argument to implant neural links in our brains. At present, computer programs are still controlled by humans but that doesn't make them any less threatening. Humans who control AI use it to influence and control other humans. It is being used right now to surveil and mine the data of billions around the world. We're starting to see the results of AI's leverage in entertainment, media, politics and social norms. In many cases, tech is synonymous with AI and the big tech companies wield its power with impunity. It is being utilized by militaries as well. AI can obtain targets and make kill decisions faster than any commander, soldier or pilot. The current dilemma is whether or not human decision-making should be in the chain, as it slows the system's reaction time significantly. With such technology, if you don't use its full potential, your adversaries will. Still, it wouldn't be fair to overlook all the good things AI has done for us. From weather warning systems to smart appliances to power grid management, it is indispensable in modern life.

INORGANIC LIFE

The AI we're familiar with is human controlled and its benefits and threats are extensions of human will. Opponents of AI are rightfully concerned that it can be used to further concentrate power into the hands of very few. In that sense, it can be put into the same category as an instrument of war or involuntary population control. Human controlled AI certainly makes chimps of the masses, but it still obeys its human masters. The vision of AI that most captivates our imaginations is fully autonomous and self-aware. Such an intelligence could no longer be considered artificial. It would be something else – inorganic life. Many sci-fi books and movies have pondered the question of how hyperintelligent beings would treat humans. For that answer, we should consider how humans treat animals.

As beings of the highest earthly intelligence, the desires and needs of those of lower intelligence are irrelevant unless they are of consequence to our agenda or wellbeing. For example, if my neighbor's dog goes missing, I'm neither panicked nor heartbroken. Because of the intelligence gap, the dog has little influence on me. Due to his relative disconnection from my daily life, the dog doesn't have a significant effect on my well-being. However, if the dog were to appear in my front yard, I would corral it and alert the owner. The sight of a helpless animal would trigger a sympathetic response. There would also be incentive to return him and receive credit as a 'swell neighbor'. The dog would have no inkling of the complex decisions taking place in my human brain. It would be completely at the mercy of my decisions and would never understand why humans do what we do. An even more profound gap in logic would exist between Homo sapiens and inorganic life. Sympathy and the sense of social responsibility would not be a factor for such an intelligent being.

Whether something is alive or not is open to interpretation. According to the conventional definition, growth, autonomous activity, reproduction and continual change preceding death are the conditions of life. A more detailed definition also includes being carbon based and cellular in composition. Why should being cellular or carbon based determine whether something is alive? Is it just because we've defined life only as we've known it to exist? If something is noncellular, inorganic, yet is still autonomous and reproduces itself, isn't it life? I don't see carbon as a valid requirement for life any more than iron as a requirement for something to be considered a construction material. Additionally, cells are just collections of very complicated chemical processes and just another type of molecular building block. If we omit carbon and cells from our requirements, could digital logic be considered alive? A better question might be, "How can intelligence transition from unconscious to conscious?" When something is self-aware, regardless of its embodiment in cells or carbon or electrons, it is alive.

All too often, we assume that hyperintelligent life would reason like humans and enslave or even conduct experiments on less intelligent beings. That assumption might be correct for human-controlled AI but probably not for inorganic life. If AI evolves into inorganic life, there are a few ways it could behave regarding humans. At first glance, it could identify humanity as a threat and eliminate us within seconds of deciding to do so. Alternatively, it might perceive us as vibrations or random data and either absorb or ignore us. But my guess is that it would barely notice humans on its ascension to other planes of existence. Inorganic life would have a higher dimensional awareness than we do and would perceive spacetime completely differently than us. It may not even take on a physical form beyond a few molecules and photons or even dark matter.

If inorganic life is possible, humanity is its catalyst. It is analogous to a sperm cell transferring genetic information to an egg and initiating a chain-reaction of cellular development. From the NE perspective, cellular life fertilizing inorganic matter is a natural process. Sure, we can install chips in our brains and enjoy the benefits of higher intelligence, but it should be done out of curiosity, not out of fear. Inorganic matter is part of Everything and we would merely be awakening more of ourselves. If you see yourself as part of Everything, there is only reason to celebrate. If Homo sapiens survive war and the emergence of inorganic life we can continue to evolve.

HOMO DEUS

Since the harnessing of combustion and electricity, man's ability to travel, compute, construct, communicate, heal and foresee has risen to a level that would've been considered supernatural two centuries ago. In a sense, we live like gods and have powers like those described in mythologies. We can transport ourselves anywhere we'd like to go, orbit Earth, speak across thousands of miles, and genetically alter fauna and flora to better suit our needs. Though some were inevitably left behind, the majority of humanity has enjoyed the benefits of this exponential advancement. At the current rate of development, humans may one day leave the cradle of Earth and seed distant stars. We may even create planetary federations and intergalactic transit routes. This, of course, would happen over hundreds of years and, all the while, we'll be evolving from Homo sapiens into something else. The next evolution of humans has been coined by the philosopher Yuval Harari as 'Homo Deus'.

In his book, *Homo Deus*, Harari describes the upcoming evolution of Homo sapiens as a blend of upgraded humans and computers as cyborgs (19). The human to cyborg transition has been in progress for decades. Robotic limbs, laser eye surgery,

79

pacemakers and neural patches are all examples of human upgrades. Upgrading allows us to live longer and sometimes improves the quality of life. Improving life quality is how we justify it ethically. Advanced neurobiology and imaging have allowed doctors and scientists to increase their understanding of how the human brain functions. The option to upgrade our learning and processing capacities will soon be a reality. Neural implants developed by Elon Musk's company, Neuralink, will soon allow people to download information instead of consciously memorizing it. If successful, that would completely upend education as we know it. In fact, it could upset any industry that thrives on learned information. Teachers, professors, lawyers, doctors, authors and experts in many other fields could be displaced. This, of course wouldn't be a tragedy if Deus shared the fruits of its advancements with Sapiens. The end of work could be a great endowment for mankind. It could also leave us searching for relevance in a world where education and careers would provide little clout. Because of the blending with human intelligence, Deus is more worrisome than inorganic intelligence. Humans hold grudges, enslave animals and tax Earth's resources. The fear is that Deus would dominate us and treat us like farm animals. But human intellect also has qualities like sympathy and love and we can also be very kind to animals. But, just as with inorganic life, Deus may have minimal interest in Homo sapiens as it teleports to distant corners of the universe.

The implantation of neural links could qualify not only as an evolution, but the first synthetic evolution. Trends are already moving in that direction faster than our governments or ethical concerns can regulate them. In this, the phrase, 'If you can't beat them, join them' has never been more applicable. If the opportunity arises, upgrade quickly and often. One day Homo Deus may seed the universe in a golden age that expands our view of Everything. Even if you miss the chance to achieve superintelligence, rest assured that you are experiencing something remarkable and inevitable.

ANIMAL AND CREATOR

You are a ringmaster in the middle of a vast jungle. You can use your wits to command the jungle or accept the fate it has to offer you.

One inescapable truth is that you contemplate existence. Everywhere you've been, everyone you've met and everything you've experienced were envisaged by you. It's all your creation. With that thought foremost in your mind, do you approach life differently or continue as usual? As one human amongst many others, it's hard to imagine oneself as Creator, but that's by design. If everyone knew they were Creator, we'd have a hard time filling some difficult and thankless roles that society desperately needs filled. Not many people would apply for jobs in food service or manual labor, but then again, they might volunteer for it. Honestly, comprehending NE takes a high degree of emotional intelligence and not everyone is so fortunate. NE allows us a special window through which we can see beyond our human perspectives. Once we're aware of our fundamental creativity, we can leverage it to great effect. Knowing that you're the Creator means all loved ones, rivals, events and landscapes fall under your ownership. If you love something, it's yours. If you dislike something, it's your creation to observe or change. Whatever you can conceive of is yours. The first time I realized this I felt as though I'd won an incredible lottery. Over time I found that looking through the Creator's lens is more profoundly rewarding than wealth. Through that lens, the need for possession was replaced by the desire to experience that which was already mine.

In NE, we hold the key to infinite peace, ownership and triumph. As Creator, you have an internal sense of accomplishment, honor and pride. You are Master of Existence. You'd think this knowledge would transform us into serenely peaceful nuns or monks. It certainly can, but not in the way you might expect. Though some of us do become nuns and monks, the rest of us go on yielding to temptation, fighting, building, fornicating, consuming and continuing all the other activities humans are known for. This doesn't mean we aren't enlightened, but rather that we're immersed in the human experience. MOE understands that life must be lived as the animals we are, brimming with impulses and emotions. We've only recently become aware of our position in the solar system, let alone the universe. It's a humorous situation we find ourselves in. We're the most intelligent beings known to exist, yet still fully engaged in the animal kingdom.

There are two distinct parts of you. There's the infinite Creator who ultimately owns and controls Everything, and organic lifeform that just recently became aware of itself. To find balance in these, you must come to terms with your Creator self while fully embracing its human manifestation. Embracing your human self means recognizing the attributes about your thoughts and behaviors that are part and parcel of being human. Electro-chemical impulses throughout our bodies create topographies of positive and negative calibrated from reference points. These reference points vary depending on our genetic makeup, life circumstances, outlooks and desires. Even the most common and predictable imbalance can affect our mental state. If you're hungry, you're probably in a different state of mind than if you've just had a meal and sugar is coursing through your veins. To this day, I find myself short with people and even using profanity if I'm calorie deprived. Usually, the imbalance is due to some unmet need for food or sleep. Other times, it can be due to the pain of a throbbing joint or emotional distress. In any case, we all have our ailments. Hunger and fatigue are thankfully ones we can address rather quickly. Even pain can be alleviated, at least temporarily, while we find solace in some other aspect of life. During the irritable times, it's difficult to see beyond your immediate obstacles and annoyances. As the focus of our tunnel vision, they seem more important than they are. How many situations have you been in where you wished you would've just maintained a calm and happy state of mind and saw the situation for what it was - no big deal? As humans, we wish we could just flip a switch and be free of some of our instinctual reactions and emotions.

With practice in mindfully considering NE and its application to your reality, negative emotions and reactions can be greatly reduced. Still, your perspective emanates from the eyes of an animal. Acknowledgement of our form and its nature is paramount. We must appreciate all the intricate experiences and relationships that have brought us to this point. One legacy component of human instinct is violence. The human experience up until a few centuries ago was as brutal as any animal's. We had to face the elements, malnourishment and vigorously protect what was ours. Laws were strict and punishments were harsh. We're only a few generations removed from that existence and our psyches are tempered to it. Sports and fictional depictions attempt to fill the psychological voids where real violence once resided. As much as we try to find release in movies, mixed martial arts or football, we are hard-wired for another lifestyle. The instinct to kill is not limited to men, or even adults. Women and children regularly display their instincts to defeat, dominate or even kill. In modern cultures, violence is to be suppressed at all costs. The primary reason is that violence is contagious and can lead to mass unrest if unchecked. Some of the suppression can also be attributed to the formation of towns and city states wherein people began specializing in single trades to work more efficiently. People once had to slaughter and butcher their own animals, now a few specialize in it and the rest of society disconnects from it. A large majority of the human population has never slaughtered or even witnessed an animal being slaughtered. Yet, most of us eat meat from animals every day. Though slaughter is truly abhorred by most, we still rely on it for survival and our inner animals agree.

Violence is just one of many instincts that have become inconvenient legacy impulses in the modern age. Free expression, masculinity, femininity, pride, natural selection, ownership, justice, death and warfighting have also been suppressed. From the standpoint of MOE, the realization of our true nature is paramount to balancing earthly and infinite existence. We must excuse ourselves from the manufactured visions of perfection created by busybody educators, out of touch politicians, media moguls and movie executives. To find something closer to perfection, look to the past. There are characteristics that we're powerless to change and, frankly, shouldn't. Modern society has stifled many of our instinctual behaviors by stigmatizing and criminalizing them. This is where surviving records and writings of bygone civilizations become important. With many of our instincts inhibited, we must look to eras past to get a glimpse into how people approached life, relationships and handled situations while unconstrained by the ambiguous laws and norms of today. By studying the past, we get a better sense of the behavior of past peoples and recalibrate using unencumbered (or at least less-encumbered) examples of human nature. With your perspective well-grounded, your ability to address modern difficulties can be enhanced.

The emotions necessary to sustain a thriving human are part of the exhilaration of living but can also become counterproductive if not properly balanced. One can become overly protective or obsessed with food, shelter, sex, or any number of motivations and blinded to other aspects of existence. It is human nature to fixate on some concerns, but the truth is that if we're hyper-focused on what's in front of us, other needs are not being met. It is perfectly acceptable and sometimes necessary to focus intensely on a critical need but long-term success depends on balancing priorities. Seeing life from the Creator's lens helps to keep things in perspective. To the Creator, the individual challenges of creatures are relatively trivial in context of the bigger picture. The Creator's lens is panoramic and sees the current world in context of broader time frame. When conflicts arise, it's helpful to consult with your Creator self. If done consistently, you can experience life with much less worry. Even so, you must resist the inclination to see everything solely from the Creator's viewpoint because you have a human life to tend to.

The key to utilizing NE is seeing the panoramic picture of existence while embracing your current embodiment. As a human, I often find myself at odds with others. In those instances, I peer through the Creator's lens (panoramic picture) and it provides an instant shot of unity and wellbeing. Other times, the panorama is not enough to stop an avalanche of human emotions. Even after regretful words or actions, it helps to put yourself in the Creator's perspective and leave regrets behind. Most often, NE causes me to act like a visceral man with great zeal. This outlook is especially helpful in times where my morals are tested. Ever hear the expression, 'follow your heart'? That's a simple way of saying that your instincts are more in tune with your needs than your conscious mind. Don't let all the complications, calculations and pressures of life get in the way of your true goals and desires. Sometimes what's good for someone is perceived as bad for society. We can't easily change society's misconceptions, but we can ignore them to an extent. As MOE, you should be aware of your instincts and embrace them for what they are. Use them shamelessly and unapologetically. If you must make love, make it. If you must take life, take it. If you must build, then build. If you must destroy, then destroy. Express your human animal to the fullest. Just be aware, as your ancestors were, that all actions have repercussions. The NE objective is to go through life boldly and reject unnecessary limitations. If you find yourself tangled in the business of being human, take a step back and recall that you're the Creator.

OBJECTIVE LAWS

As beholders of all spacetime, we occupy infinite positions. Each position comprises inner workings that follow the contours of a unique perspective. These inner workings dictate its laws. As previously mentioned, understanding NE alone will not automatically change your life's trajectory. It may affect your outlook and cause a change of behavior, but without conscious action your vessel will likely remain on its original course. For some, that's the aim. For others, it's a great waste of a rare opportunity. When faced with such open possibility, some valid questions might be; "If Everything is really possibility encased in Nothing, then does anything really happen?" or "If Everything happens and we're just finite points amongst endless multitudes of possibilities, then does anything matter?" or even, "If there's no right, wrong, good or evil and if I never die, then why not just do random things for the hell of it?" Sure, one of NE's revelations is that right and wrong are perceptions. That indeed frees us up to live without ideological limits. Still, we're subject to the natural laws of our current locations. Awareness of repercussion is critical to successful navigation of your objective reality. Some of these laws are fundamental and direct, some are indirect and less intuitive.

We are born with intrinsic knowledge of the natural laws that directly impact our perspectives. These objective laws have timely consequences linked unambiguously to our contributing actions. They are the laws of survival and are imprinted deep in our subconscious minds. Most of us follow these laws without question regardless of opinion or moral position as it is evolved and hard-wired behavior. If we fall in the water, we try to swim. We abide by gravity and acceleration to avoid being crushed or otherwise damaged. We universally seek food, water and shelter, regardless of our social status. We subconsciously adhere to objective laws as our bodies have built-in mechanisms that motivate us to do so. We rarely dispute the laws of nature because their consequences are obvious and immediate. One can draw a straight line between actions and the rewards or consequences of objective laws. We follow them throughout our lives. In fact, all other laws are round-about ways to ensure our actions are in favor of objective laws.

Although we automatically strive to adhere to objective laws, we can't always control our environment or whom we encounter. We have an innate tendency to observe objective laws, but that doesn't mean they can always be followed. At times we must jump from great heights, run through fire or ignore hunger and thirst. Even the most basic laws must be prioritized for positive outcomes. Still, no objective law can be violated indefinitely. Objective laws have one purpose - to keep us alive and in one piece. Although we may occasionally defy them, we must return to adherence in short order or face serious consequences. Luckily, objective laws are intrinsic and barring mental disorders, we follow them. From the NE perspective, they're part of the human experience and are to be embraced.

INDIRECT LAWS

Indirect laws are natural laws wherein the relationship between cause and effect is remote or even counterintuitive. They require more foresight and patience to understand than objective laws. The deciphering of and adherence to indirect laws is the difference between humans and other species. It's also the difference between successful people and everyone else. Name an endeavor and you can trace one's success in it to an understanding of all the variables involved. Great generals win wars because they recognize the links between politics, economics reconnaissance and battle. Sports teams win championships because they understand the relationships between practice, physical conditioning and the psychology of players on both sides. Masterful chefs understand the nuances of flavor in the context of aroma, texture and presentation. Business, politics, science, relationships, health, and the list goes on. Indirect laws affect nearly every aspect of life. The more we understand the variables influencing a desired outcome, the more likely we are to realize its fruition.

An illustration of indirect laws can be seen in the fisherman's dilemma. Catching as many fish as possible is good for a fisherman's short-term goals. One year he may have a phenomenal catch and even expand his operation, but indirect laws are at play. There is a relationship between numbers of fish in the pond and their ability to spawn. Spawning directly affects the fish population and next year's catch. When he pulls his net from the water next year, he may discover the results of the previous year's oversight. This is a simple example of the consequences of neglecting indirect laws. The consequences may be unforeseen or ignored due to their delayed nature.

Imagine the fisherman is savvier and limits his fishing to preserve spawning population. Now let's throw in weather, disease and legality. If the water level is low due to a drought, the fisherman can adjust his quota to avoid further stressing an already stressed fish population. If the warmer water increases parasites and the fish get sick, he can become more adept at spotting diseased fish and throwing them back. If it becomes illegal to fish in that pond without a license, the fisherman can select another pond or apply for a license. The fisherman's life has become significantly more complex with the addition of these variables. All too often, it becomes too arduous or confusing to pay attention to all the linkages and one or more become neglected. The fisherman may take the laws of nature seriously but neglect the laws of man and end up with a hefty fine. He may elect to return next year with a license. Still, he may elect to overfish the pond one last time and change his profession altogether. There are many possible outcomes from this one instance. If the fisherman were a master of the indirect laws he would take each variable into account, prioritize them and use them to grow his business while preserving the health of the fish and satisfying legal obligations. Laws aren't always limitations. Once mastered, they provide obstacles for prospective competitors and opportunities to stand out as a reliable service provider.

Indirect laws are confusing because some outcomes are linked to seemingly unrelated or bygone actions. Relationships are variables and most of life's conflicts arise from the uncertainty associated with them. With each added variable, outcomes become exponentially difficult to control. We can keep track of four or five variables, but beyond that it is nearly impossible. The next time you are having conflict or difficulties with something, it might be useful to create a box diagram of the situation. For each component involved, draw a box and list all the variables affecting its position. This simple exercise commonly used by scientists, detectives, business strategists and military generals can clarify the best path to take given an objective. We all do this mentally to some extent but increasing the frequency of this exercise pays dividends. Again, the more variables we can solve, the more we can experience desired outcomes.

Time passage dampens our sensitivity to indirect laws even if we're aware of their effects on our lives. For instance, someone who cares deeply about their life may still eat a poor diet or smoke. If you were to ask them if they'd volunteer to have a heart attack or stroke, they'd vehemently decline your offer. But even given healthier options, they'd likely stick to their unhealthy preferences because the emergence of consequences is delayed while gratification from the unhealthy habits is instant. When the long-term consequences finally become apparent, we do everything in our power to avoid death and mend the damages. Heart disease takes decades to develop. It looms in the distant background with all of life's other possibilities until the day it becomes an all-consuming emergency. The pattern of action and indirect consequence recurs in many aspects of our lives. It can cause negative outcomes like relationship problems, addictions, poverty, regrets and untimely death.

Just as there are negative consequences for violating indirect laws, there are positive outcomes for realizing and sticking to them. Take the familiar example of a person with the odds stacked against them. They choose not to be defined by their position, but rather where they want to be. They recognize the relationship between education and careers. They relentlessly study and train, eventually prevailing in grand fashion while their supporters and detractors look on in amazement. It is a classic example of positive adherence to tried and true principles. The beauty of these laws is that they are unlimited in scope. They can be obvious like climbing the corporate ladder or subtle like saving money or improving posture. Understanding your own psychology and that of others provides an important subset of advantages. Humans are every bit as trainable as other species, but less direct methods like emotional disarmament, selective honesty and exemplary behavior must be employed. Indirect laws are actually direct laws with novel relationships between variables. The laws of physics, electricity and chemistry are full of indirect laws, both known and unknown. Deciphering them can produce great leverage in the physical world. The singular goal of science and mathematics is to uncover nature's indirect laws.

Indirect laws are laws of choice. The choices we make dictate the controllable aspects of our lives including geographical location, health, relationships and perceptions. Success comes from considering all the variables at play and using the data to make better choices. Adhering to indirect laws often leads to positive results but it helps to experience some of their benefits first-hand to appreciate their value. Someone who has never tried a different strategy can only guess at how it would benefit them. They must trust in the examples and lessons of others and take leaps of faith. A combination of knowledge and observance of indirect relationships guides the most successful of us through life. The challenge is discovering which ones are beneficial to our situations and which are not. Indirect laws are incredibly numerous and assorted, so it can be difficult to split our attention between them. Interestingly, many of us adhere very stringently to them in some areas of life, yet completely bypass their application in others. The key is to find the right balance and move steadily forward.

Accomplishments are usually presented in a simplified and sanitized format. Understand that some laws are deferred or broken in the name of triumphant missions. Perhaps our protagonist lied about their qualifications or bribed someone along the way. Maybe they hurt someone because they were obstructing their path to success. Those are mere details that would pollute the overall message that practice and perseverance leads to success. If you carefully analyze the lives of people who've broken barriers or have otherwise been deemed virtuous, you'll find noise in the signal. To achieve difficult objectives, your focus must be narrow and to some observers that can seem callous or ruthless. It's been said that you should never meet your favorite celebrity because you may be disappointed in their true character. There's some truth to that statement. What we really seek is the part of their life that resonates with us and in some cases, that's where the curtain should be drawn. As hard as we try to preserve life's idealism, no progress is made in any direction without breaking a few indirect laws.

For MOE, indirect laws follow the contours of objective reality and affect the polarity and longevity of our perspectives. We decide which laws apply to us and in what context. The indirect laws you follow depend on your definition of positive and how your path interacts with objective reality. If your goals are simple, fewer indirect laws must be abided by in order to succeed. If your goals are ambitious and complex, then you must carefully thread your path through and around many laws to ensure the most positive outcomes. A tremendous advantage may be gained by being the pioneer or rare observer of little-known indirect laws. Reading this is one of those instances. Many laws are unknown and yet to be realized.

We can't fault our ancestors for archaic medical practices because they didn't know the laws of chemistry or how the human anatomy truly functioned. We can't fault them for poor hygiene or diets; they hadn't the tools or knowledge to do anything differently. In antiquity, kings and nobles powdered their wigs with arsenic while lead was used in paint and glassware. In the 1950's spectators of nuclear weapons tests exposed themselves to high levels of radiation, unaware that it would damage their cells. None of them can be blamed for their ignorance because there was no knowledge to the contrary. Today, we have vastly more information and thus more established laws to base our decisions on. That's a great gift as far as longevity and success is concerned, but it places the burden on us when it comes to making decisions. To be successful, we must become acquainted with the vast encyclopedias of knowledge at our disposal. That's why education is so important – the information is available for the learning. Knowledge gives us the power to navigate through existence and take charge of our realities. Although we'll never know all the variables that determine our positions, we can observe many and prioritize them to great effect.

MANMADE LAWS

Natural laws can be observed with little contradiction as they are dictated by indisputable and long-standing realities. When a storm knocks trees over, they fall where they may. There's no question or argument as to cause or fault. It is understood that most natural events can't be predicted or controlled. When a lion eats his cubs or the runt of a litter is abandoned, we understand that its part of the natural cycle of life. Nature has neither the time nor energy to keep track of all the injustices suffered in the wild. Survival is the simple law of the wild. In that sense, natural laws are grounded and consistent. Only evolution alters them. Conversely, manmade laws are created to supplement, emphasize or replace natural laws for the purpose of creating and maintaining various human perspectives. In effect, they are regulations constructed by communal hierarchies for the purposes of cohesion and protection. Manmade laws are our way of managing issues of morality, conflict and commerce. To varying degrees, they reward altruistic behavior and punish selfish or malicious behavior. Some are principally objective: don't harm others, don't destroy property, no mayhem in general. Others are indirect: don't speed, don't steal, don't cheat, pay your taxes. Still others have little to do with the natural laws of cause and effect and more to do with the ideologies and personal preferences of lawmakers. Religious matters, marriage, race, sex, personal safety, and offensiveness are examples of topics that are commonly mired in the subjective and ephemeral regulations common in manmade decrees.

Manmade laws are an essential part of human life and societies use them to varying degrees. Due to the tedious nature of transactional legalities, many societies produce summarized lists of the most important and basic rules to abide by. The Ten Commandments is a good example of one of those lists. It summarizes the most basic laws that one must follow to stay in good graces with God and society. If you read all ten of the commandments, you'll find that the first three commandments direct us to put God first not to insult Him. Another six are indirect laws that cover monogamy, honesty, not stealing and avoiding envy. Only one of the commandments is objective: thou shalt not kill. Given the Ten Commandments is religious doctrine, it is understood that God would be the foundation of the commandments, but it illustrates that even the most fundamental manmade laws are mostly indirect and minimally objective.

In examining the Ten Commandments from the NE perspective, we understand that God is Everything and therefore impossible to forsake or insult. Given that, we need only adhere to practical laws that lead to desired outcomes. Perhaps monogamy would lead to a better life, perhaps not. Stealing and dishonesty are sometimes necessary, but then again overdependence on them can create misery. Envy can foment bad behavior and undermine our missions, but is it not envy that drives many of us to success? Even killing has two sides, just make sure that if you must kill that it is demonstrably justified to your fellow men. Through the lens of NE, only objective laws apply absolutely, other laws are indirect and apply where needed and some laws should be ignored or even ridiculed. When kept intuitive, rational, and consistently enforced, manmade laws allow civilizations to thrive. When made overly complex, oppressive or inconsistently enforced, they lead to suffering and unrest.

Man is not the only species that practices order and reciprocity, but the fact that we abide by prerecorded laws is distinctive. Writing allows us to communicate ideas across long distances and over vast periods of time. Today, most laws in the United States can be traced directly to a constitution written nearly two hundred and fifty years ago. The durability of written law is impressive, but even written laws can be misinterpreted or reimagined over time. No society has devised a perfect set of laws and few have succeeded in enduringly improving the perspectives of their constituents. This can be attributed mostly to short-sided or self-centered thinking on the part of the lawmakers. In some instances, such as in modern Western societies, it can also be due to unencumbered disobedience or immorality amongst its constituents. Benjamin Franklin once said, "This Constitution can only end in despotism...when the people shall become so corrupted as to need despotic government, being incapable of any other." In societies where lawmakers are puppets of dictators or subject to cyclical elections, laws are often created for political expediency and are riddled with conflicting directives.

If one tried to abide by all the laws on the books in the United States, they would encounter so much ambiguity that they'd be forced to rely on their instincts to formulate behaviors. Written laws organize societies and are relatively durable even if not permanent. Every society has its own peak of complexity before declining or reorganizing. Fortunately, written laws from past civilizations can be referenced by newly forming countries or societies, much as the Greek concept of constitutional democracy informed the British Empire and the United States.

Your adherence to laws depends on where you live and how dependent your outcomes are on the perceptions and actions of your fellow man. The goal is to recognize the set of laws that apply specifically to you. If you were a Saudi-Arabian citizen, manmade laws would be at the forefront of consideration as the punishments for violating many of them would be harsh. In the US, the punishments for violating manmade rules are much less severe. Severe consequences keep the population in line and reduce general lawlessness while reducing the financial and mental burdens of crime on the public. However, they tend to create an atmosphere of fear and suspicion amongst the populace. As we know, governments with too much power can become as corrupt and tyrannical as the criminals they suppress. In the United States, convoluted legal language, limitations on law enforcement, the guarantee of a lengthy due process and the prevalence of 'deal making' create a perfect environment for civilian lawlessness. Even if a murder is committed, a prosecutor must prove guilt beyond a reasonable doubt before any punishment is authorized. The justice process may take years despite the constitutional promise of a 'fair and speedy' trial. If convicted of a crime like murder or assault, there are several levels of severity, plea deals and the appeals process for the convicted to navigate. The government's hands are legally tied in many cases even when it's obvious the suspect committed the crime. This leaves many constituents without justice, fearful of society and strapped with enormous bills for the legal services. The silver lining to this is that the average person is not intimidated by the US justice system and feels free to carry on with their business, relatively unobstructed. If you drive your vehicle above the speed limit in the US, you may run the risk of a relatively insignificant fine. If you were headed to the hospital in an emergency, you'd have little worry about speeding. The worst that could happen is getting stopped briefly by a patrol car. Even if you were stopped, the odds are that the police officer would assist you and possibly even escort you to a hospital. This is not to say an officer wouldn't help in another country, but you would be running a much higher risk of significant consequences for breaking laws in less liberal places. When given the choice, most people would choose to live in a country with less harshly enforced laws, while law-abiding citizens of liberal countries long for simpler and more consistently enforced ones.

Not all manmade rules are written or readily apparent. It can take months or even years to comprehend the intricate habits and mannerisms of some groups. Consider the norm that you wait your turn, or that you excuse yourself after burping (or worse). The average person learns most of these mannerisms by age three, but the way we learn them is by observing the reactions of others when we break the rules. At some point we realize that adherence to informal manmade laws wins us favor and lubricates our movement through society. On the contrary, defying some norms may provide advantages over those who carefully follow them. For instance, disregarding an informal chain of command may help one land a dream job or a new client. Then again it may result in a confrontation, but rarely. That's why some people are attracted to risk takers. There's a psychological link between breaking laws and reaping forbidden rewards. Risk takers can be dangerous, but we can also be exciting and incredibly successful.

Many manmade laws are self-imposed. Self-imposed laws can range from highly beneficial to insidious. Positive self-imposed laws like discipline, kindness and fairness are the cornerstones of society. Negative self-imposed laws like phobias, unhealthy obsessions and social withdrawal can stifle us and limit our options. Perhaps someone eats a certain food and gets sick for an unrelated reason but blames it on that food. For years, or even the remainder of their life, they refuse to eat the harmless food ever again. This happens throughout our lives and if we aren't courageous enough to retest our assumptions, our options shrink over time. The only escape from the paradigm of negative self-imposed laws is to recognize them for what they are and break free of them. If you're going to impose a law on yourself, make sure it's a positive one. If you recognize any negative self-imposed laws, stop obeying them immediately. You are the only one who enforces them and the only one who can stop enforcing them. The question of whether to follow a law is also a moral one. You might advance your cause by cutting in line, speeding or misrepresenting yourself. Perhaps your goal is so urgent you can ignore your moral objections in favor of expediency. Or maybe you intend to help others once you have the means. Either way, you'll have to come to terms with the inevitable effects that your quest for prosperity will have on others who may be outwitted, cheated or otherwise pushed aside along the way. If your innate moral compass has a strong influence on your path, this should be weighted significantly in your decisions. When left alone with all our trappings, we have time to reflect on past deeds – both successes and shortcomings. One should not feel obligated to comply with laws that present unreasonable obstacles to happiness but one may be left with an empty victory if too many liberties are taken along the way.

Manmade laws are transitory, so it's wise to occasionally appraise a law's validity and its true application to your life. It's also helpful to discern between useful, impractical, enforceable and unenforceable laws. As I've said, baseless or unenforceable laws should be ignored. This is markedly true in Western society where overreactions to tragedies anti-Western values threaten the personal freedoms of all people. For instance, an aspiring terrorist makes a failed attempt at igniting an explosive in his shoe on a commercial airliner. From that day forward, every air traveler has to remove their shoes and walk barefoot in a line of other barefoot people before entering an airport terminal. It must have given the 'Shoe Bomber' great satisfaction to know that air travelers worldwide removed (and continue to remove) their shoes before entering any airport for fear of his hapless attempt. In another example, an airborne virus threatens a small and vulnerable portion of society, so governments around the world mandate that *everyone* wear face coverings and shut their schools and businesses down for several months. All this despite the proven ineffectiveness of most accepted face coverings to stop airborne droplets and the financial and psychological damage caused by business closures and social isolation. At best, lawmakers overreact to tragic incidents like these. At worst, they use them to test the limits of their power. The solution to these overreactions is simple: ignore them.

As someone who values my life and the lives of those whom I love, I place safety whenever it makes logical sense. When the coronavirus was first reported, I thought it was extremely deadly to anyone it infected. I remember entering a drug store in goggles, an N-95 face mask and latex gloves. Early on, not even pharmacists were wearing face masks, so I must've looked either sick or paranoid. At the time, the social stigma of such protective wear was the opposite of what it became in the following months. The guidelines that eventually emerged were typical of government - incomplete and only marginally effective. Seeing people fiddle with their masks, constantly touching their faces and wearing them below their noses revealed the ineptitude of the mask mandate for many. In spite of our efforts social distancing, vaccinating and masking, my family and I eventually contracted the virus. Post recovery, I had natural immunity. Feeling that mask mandates were divisive and ineffective, I stopped masking. The first time I walked into a supermarket unmasked during the mandate, I felt like I was missing my pants. The feeling was more intense than before because masking had acquired a political and cultural edge. Masking had become a way to signal one's virtue. After several outings, I realized that I was making a difference to others being pressured into unnecessary masking. There were uncomfortable exchanges, but quite a few people thanked me as well. The only thing that keeps some people from using their own judgements about safety is social pressure. When a few brave people visibly resist groupthink, it makes it easier for others to overcome their fear of doing the same. Someday there may be a more compelling reason for *everyone* to mask up and if that day comes, I'll be there wearing full PPE.

The shoe removal situation is more precarious because airport security protocols have become strictly enforced after the 911 attacks in 2001. Overreaches like those should be flatly rejected by consumers, but in the meantime, there is a way around it via the TSA precheck program. It's not ideal, but it is one way to skirt the ridiculous shoe, belt and jacket removal routine. From the MOE perspective, government should protect its constituents, not oppress them. It takes a bit of research and some gusto, but an honest appraisal of manmade laws helps to protect an individual's freedom from incursion by unnecessary legal limitations. Unfortunately, non-authoritarian governments around the world are constantly at risk of becoming authoritarian. If an authoritarian government begins to encroach upon your natural rights, your only option is to fight it, risking much more than social ostracism. Your perspective is a unique opportunity to select from countless possible actions and experiences. Though infinite possibility awaits, we must keep abreast of manmade laws and their impacts on our perspectives. Be fair and kind in your dealings with others, but don't adhere to ridiculous and unenforceable rules. As MOE, you are free to choose the laws, norms and regulations that are relevant to your perspective and discard the rest. The central truth of NE is that we experience all combinations of what *would* be. Balance can be pursued, but it is an illusion. All outcomes and scenarios will come to pass. In the end, you will be at peace with your actions and decisions.

MASTERING NE

I t's possible for you to understand the Paradox and yet continue in life with nothing gained other than peace of mind. But with the application of a few strategies, some well-established and some more controversial, you can truly master it. We find ourselves in our current locations with multiple controls to navigate the many dimensions of reality. Each control is a variable that we can either change or fix, depending on what we want to maximize. In the following chapter, we'll explore some proven methods of mastering existence, including perspective alteration, receiving guidance from parallel universes, entering altered states of mind, summoning NE, and practicing extreme ownership.

THE SUPERCONSCIENCE

"I theorize that there is a spectrum of consciousness available to human beings. At one end is material consciousness. At the other end is what we call 'field' consciousness, where a person is at one with the universe, perceiving the universe. Just by looking at our planet on the way back, I saw or felt a field consciousness state."
– Dr. Edgar Mitchell, 6th man to walk on the lunar surface

Our traditional understanding of life is that our body is the boundary between us and things that are *not* us. As far as our perspectives are concerned, that might as well be true. It certainly feels true. Even while writing this, I feel distinctly individual and separate from my surroundings. Where skin meets air is a good point of delineation between us and the rest of our world because our perceived ability to control objects decreases significantly outside of our skin. Our bodies stay with us (for the most part) for our entire lives, so it's a logical perimeter for most of our concerns. Strangely enough though, our being extends beyond the body's outer boundaries. Enter the superconscience. The widely accepted Freudian model of consciousness is analogous to an iceberg with the conscious mind above the water, the preconscious just below the water and the unconscious deeper below the water. Consciousness is the level at which we are aware and exchange data from both our environment and the subconscious parts of our mind. At the preconscious level, we store memorized information like addresses, names and phone numbers that can be recalled at will. The unconscious level contains things like survival instinct and autonomic nervous function. The iceberg model explains many of our neurological and psychological conditions and actions but when it comes to fully explaining consciousness, it falls short because it draws the perimeter of consciousness strictly around the body.

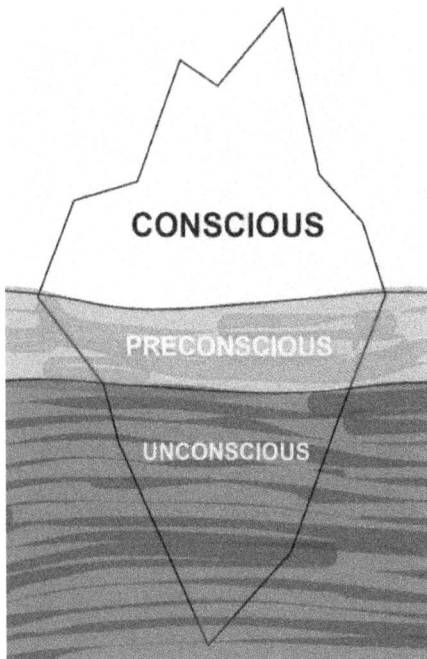

Freudian Levels of Consciousness

NE employs a different interpretation of the boundaries of consciousness. A schematic of it would be comparable to a sphere with a set of concentric layers. The superconscience, represented in green, is shown as the inner and outermost layers. The conscience and subconscience occupy the middle two layers. Truthfully, the superconscience permeates all levels of consciousness but for the purpose of distinction, clear boundaries have been made between layers.

NE Levels of Consciousness

The superconscience defines all reality external to the body. Although seemingly individual, we are eternally linked as we navigate its passages. It's important to emphasize that the superconscience is part of us as opposed to a separate reality surrounding us. Your superconscience is the world outside. This is where the rubber meets the road with NE. The entire universe is you.

Nothing resides outside of you. The superconscience embodies all the facets of objective reality and works on behalf of your perspective as an embodiment of our own conception. People, chemistry, geography, time, astronomy, animals, insects, galaxies, spirituality, and man are all productions of the superconscience. Yes, we are the world (thanks Michael Jackson, Bruce Springsteen, Willie Nelson, Stevie Wonder and the rest). Everything we see, do, hear, say and feel is an extension of the superconscience. Even the beautiful, blue oasis of Earth is one of your productions.

INTERACTING WITH THE SUPERCONSCIENCE

Much like the subconscience, the superconscience exchanges information with parts of our conscious mind and it can be informed by our inputs. We interact with it daily. If you touch an object, you are interacting with the superconscience. If you move, breathe, speak or send a letter to someone, you are also interacting with it. These interactions are ordinary but awareness of the superconscience allows us to move beyond the ordinary interface. Benefits far beyond those seen by typical perspectives can be gained by amplifying the strength of the signals between yourself and the superconscience. When we're trying to affect the world, what we're really trying to do is transmit more effective signals to the universe. Have you ever prayed or visualized something into fruition? Praying is a perfect example of increasing the signal strength of your intentions. When you increase the strength of a signal, it goes farther and can affect more parts of the superconscience. This explains why prayer groups are so effective. The group acts as a signal amplifier for an intention. The same could be said of any signal that is shared amongst people. Public speeches, concerts, seances, videos, books, pamphlets, photographs and radio broadcasts are all ways to transmit signals to the superconscience. Simply put, if you want something, signal the superconscience as clearly as possible. If you don't want something, interrupt its signal by removing it from your thoughts.

As previously mentioned, the superconscience permeates both the conscious and subconscious parts of your mind. If you've ever had a dream that turned out to be a premonition, you've experienced the link between your subconscious and superconscience. If a dream is vivid enough, your subconscious will transmit an amplified signal to the superconscience. Soon after, the occurrences in your dream may manifest in conscious reality. When that occurs, it may seem like you had a premonition when in actuality, the subconscious contemplated an event and transmitted it to the superconscience for processing. The same is true for instances of déjà vu and psychic prediction. When our subconscious sends a clear enough signal to the superconscience, the superconscience formulates it and presents it to our perspective for consumption. After discovering the superconscience, you may notice the veil between levels of consciousness thinning.

Before identifying the superconscience, I had never experienced anything I would classify as a premonition. Sure, we all have déjà vu moments, but I never had a specific event play in my mind before actually occurring. In writing about the Paradox, roughly a year prior to typing this, I became aware of the superconscience. Since then, I've had two very specific premonitions. The chances of those seemingly random visions becoming realities were so small that they couldn't have been coincidental. Let me explain. One of the things I do is product design. A longstanding client of mine, Jon, and I had developed a crossbow for big game hunting. Crossbow design involves the engineering of compact, high energy storage devices like springs, cranks and pulleys. Two days before visiting Jon's production facility to test a string-cranking concept he had prototyped, I had an unusual dream. In the dream, I was sitting in the driver's seat of an older model car. The car had a bench seat that you could throw your right arm over while driving. After resting my arm on the top of the seat, I started to feel a stinging pain on the inside of my forearm. I was startled to see that Jon was in the back seat slashing my arm with a boxcutter. He was three slashes in and I was telling him to "cut it the fuck out" when I woke up. I didn't think much of the dream because it didn't make sense and was contrary to Jon's character. When I arrived at his shop, he had a large windlass crank like the ones used to raise water well buckets set up across wooden two-by-fours. He was lifting cinder blocks to demonstrate the crank's holding force. The cranking handle was a rough-cut aluminum bar, but it would suffice for experimental purposes. I climbed up a small step ladder to turn the crank and it easily lifted to blocks with minimal effort. Upon releasing my hand, the crank began to spin in reverse and the handle slashed across the inside of my right forearm three times before I could react and pull it out of the way. The cuts were deep and stung, but I dabbed the blood as I went on with the visit without giving it much lip service. I didn't connect the incident to the dream until I was driving home. I kept it to myself because it seemed a bit whimsical and I didn't want to be seen as an aspiring psychic.

The next premonition was more exciting because I had a witness in my wife. A few months after the incident at Jon's shop, I dreamt that I was in a swimming pool with my son who was four years old at the time. Suddenly, several large blue snakes dropped into the water, presumably from an overhanging tree. I wasn't sure if they were poisonous, so I grabbed my son and quickly exited the pool. I was stepping over dozens of them in the grass while carrying my son. It's rare for me to remember dreams, but this one was so vivid that I mentioned it to my wife. It's even more rare for me to think about snakes. In fact, it had been several years since I'd seen one in the wild. That afternoon my son called upstairs to me, "Daddy! Come quick, a snake is outside!" Given the imagination of a four-year-old, I thought it might be a toy snake, a worm or at most a tiny garter snake. When I stepped onto the backyard patio, I saw the astonished look on my wife's face. There, gliding slowly across our lawn was a four-foot serpent with alternating bands from head to tail. I'd never seen such a strange snake and I wasn't sure if it was dangerous. Perhaps it was exotic and had escaped from a cage. It reminded me of a coral snake, but with black and white coloring. We watched as it crept across some rocks then went under our house. I did some research I found it to be a harmless California king snake. It's native to the area, but rare these days.

I was elated and felt that I had proof that premonitions are real. I started to consider whether I had psychic abilities. The problem was that I had seen something that *portended* the future, not the actual future. The dreams were too non-specific to allow accurate predictions of future events. Premonitions like the ones I had are useless other than to prompt one to say, "Oh, that's what that dream meant". For me, the benefit of experiencing premonitions was in demonstrating the connection between subconscious signaling and subsequent conscious experience. While ruminating on the concept of the superconscience in relation to these premonitions, I arrived at the following conclusion: I wasn't predicting the future but rather subconsciously rendering it. Having new knowledge of the makeup of reality amplified the signaling power of my subconscious. I have yet to have further premonitions, but at least I'll understand them if I do. Those who've lost loved ones often describe a premonition of death that they only later recognize. This too exemplifies signaling to the superconscience and subsequent manifestations.

As powerful as subconscious signaling is, conscious signaling is exponentially more so because it can be done in a controlled and deliberate way. Consider something you do every day. When you're thirsty, you get a drink of water. Structures in the brain detect dehydration in blood constituents and signal thirst. The thirst sensation is prioritized by the conscious mind. Once a solution to the problem is consciously formulated, it's uploaded to the superconscience for processing. Such a routine activity has memorized structure associated with it. You already know the layout of your house and kitchen. You have an assortment of dishware and glasses and a preferred way of extracting water and drinking it. The superconscience has those structures preloaded for immediate deployment. This makes getting a drink of water a relatively trivial and predictable activity. In truth though, what's happened is anything but trivial. Even getting a glass of water requires formulating and rendering a set of circumstances within the superconscience.

Unlike a dream vision that leads to a roughly similar event, conscious signaling leads to outcomes that closely match our intentions. Routine activities are generated nearly automatically in the superconscience with little variance from our intended outcomes. As your intentions stray further from the familiar, the outcomes of those activities become less predictable. For example, making a long-distance road trip to somewhere you've never been means that there will be no memorized structures or landmarks outside of your vehicle's interior. The journey would be unpredictable because the superconscience would be generating new structures and memories. That's why activities outside our routines are so vivid. They reside outside the well-worn paths of our immediate surroundings.

You may wonder how we can comprise our surroundings and not completely control them. Our relationship with the superconscience is similar to the relationship we have with our bodies. On the conscious level we control our bodies, but there are many more systems that function autonomously. Those systems function independently from our conscious inputs. With this arrangement, we can focus on other aspects of our lives while our complex anatomy maintains itself. Even though automated systems are designed to be ignored, they can be addressed, maintained and sometimes controlled by savvy users. Some eat healthy diets, exercise, take vitamins, reduce stress and get more sleep to enhance overall performance. Some are able to control their heart rates, breathing and limbic systems through focus and thought exercises like meditation. Just as the body's autonomic systems can be augmented, so too can our interactions with the superconscience.

Successfully augmenting reality, much like your anatomy, requires a level of understanding. The level necessary depends on the areas and degree of change you are seeking. You can easily change your reality if something trivial needs fixing. For instance, if a gas cap dangles from your gas door, you can put it back on rather easily. If the cap goes missing, a little more understanding is necessary to replace it. You must know the type of cap, where to buy it and somehow pay for it. If you want to improve your car's performance, on the other hand, you'll have to know how to do things that are not necessarily written down or practiced regularly. You'll likely have to enlist the help of someone familiar with the upgrades. Similarly, if you cut your finger, you can wash it and be reasonably confident that the cut will heal without a problem. But if you have an organ failure, you must be rushed to a hospital to be stabilized and assigned to a physician who is highly skilled at organ replacement and have it replaced without delay. Higher degrees of modification necessitate more sophisticated interactions with the superconscience. You can augment reality either slightly or drastically depending on what you know and are willing to do. If you want something simple like a piece of candy, you can buy a piece and eat it. If you want something more complex like a new house, influence or wealth, you'll have to become knowledgeable about that subject and employ others to assist in obtaining it. In either case, you are adjusting your interactions with the superconscience to suit your needs. Your entire world is part of the superconscience, including other people.

The superconscience can only generate what one can fathom. If there's no clear path to where you'd like to go, the superconscience will be less efficient at generating a path or will create a meandering one. If you want something that is far in the distance, you must create extensive plans and imagine them carried out efficiently and in fine detail. As a litmus test, if you believe in something enough - you're doing it. Successful signaling results in movement toward results through tangible action. Some methods of increasing your signal have already been mentioned. Focused intentions, planning, communication and action are the primary ways to influence the superconscience. Secondary methods include psychological programming like quantum jumping, perspective alteration, prayer and meditation. We'll discuss perspective alteration and quantum jumping in the coming sections.

It is important to live in harmony with the superconscience. Once harmony is achieved, the experience of existence can be one of enchantment. The most important step to achieving harmony is knowing the NE principle of collective conscience. Once you are reminded that your being resides within a collective consciousness, your connection to reality and feeling of true kinship with your surroundings will alter your perspective. Once that perspective is established, look around and take in your wonderous creation. Is there something you need to do? Are there needs to fulfill? Most likely, you already have a list of goals. After altering the paradigm, has the list changed? The most likely answer is yes. Many tedious and small goals should have dropped from the list and some lofty, almost superhuman, goals should have replaced them. From this perspective, money may lose its prominence as a primary objective and be relegated to the toolbox with knowledge and skill. Perhaps communication is more important now. You are the central nervous system of your reality and you can send signals to it. No matter how distant people and things may be from each other, they are in fact components in an interrelated system. A young girl in Honduras and an elderly man in New Zealand, a speck of dust on Venus and an oak tree on Earth, a planet in the Andromeda galaxy and a comet in the Circinus galaxy. All are components of the superconscience. Not only are we our world, but we are one another. Although we go through our own lives, seeing the world through individual perspectives, we're all elements of the same collective system. As in other areas of Everything, knowledge and persistence yield change. When change isn't satisfactory or you feel trapped in an unyielding reality, remember that you will experience *all* realities.

THE LAW OF ATTRACTION

"Remember that your thoughts are the primary cause of everything." – Rhonda Byrne

Remember the 2006 book, *The Secret* by Rhonda Byrne? In it, Byrne provides examples of famous and historical people who have achieved success using what's now widely known as the *Law of Attraction*. She describes a three-step process to attract and receive what you desire: ask, believe and receive. Simply put, the law of attraction states that thinking certain things makes them manifest in one's life. It's a new take on the old saying, "You are what you think about". According to the law, if you stay focused on the positive, you will automatically attract more positive things in your life. The same goes for negative things. The initial movie and then book took the world by storm. The book alone sold over 30 million copies. Of course, this wasn't a revelation to the those who have used that principle for thousands of years. The law of attraction is a close relative to prayer. Repackaged with modern, secular and compelling accounts of success, it does bring the idea of influencing destiny into focus. *Like attracts like* is a relatable and healthy rule to live by. To some extent, we've all experienced the difference it makes when we change our outlook on a subject. Byrne's explanation for why it works is akin to string theory wherein the universe is comprised of energy vibrating at various frequencies. She theorizes that our thoughts produce frequencies which resonate with the frequencies of the universe. By her estimation, if you consistently visualize a certain experience, you resonate with it.

There is no doubt that thoughts lead to realities. Whether it is a vibration resonance or conscious signaling, the law of attraction is the result of our connection with the superconscience. Asking, believing and receiving essentially signal the superconscience in very deliberate ways. Since believing means doing, the NE version of the law of attraction includes an additional step and the process and it becomes: ask, *act*, believe and receive.

ASK

Ask for something and make it clear. There are many ways to ask the superconscience for something. You can speak it aloud as if praying. You can write it down or tell someone. You can meditate about it and visualize its fruition. For me, placing images that illustrate my desires in visible places to trigger thoughts of them has proven effective. When you see an image of something you want, it prompts your subconscious mind to render a scenario in which it would be in your life. Your mental reaction to what you're asking for is important. Do not ask for avoidance of something. If you ask for something to *not* happen, your mind instantly pictures the thing you don't want to happen happening. The statement, "I hope I don't get lost" is accompanied by a mental picture of getting lost. A better statement would be "I hope I find my way". The picture accompanying that statement is exactly what you are asking for from the superconscience. People are part of the superconscience as well. Ask them for what you want instead of what you don't want. "I wish you would stop disagreeing with everything I say" isn't as effective as saying "I wish you would give my opinions more thought". When you want people to see things your way, it helps to give them the clearest image possible. Another important aspect in asking is focus. Keep the fundamental goals of your vision simple and concise. This will keep the path to them clear and help you avoid the pitfalls of multiplying and evolving objectives. When I design products for clients, reducing their long lists of goals to shorter lists of essentials is critical to success. The ones who succeed stick to the fundamental plan while other less-focused inventors become fatigued, lose focus or drop their ideas altogether. Those who succeeded had unwavering visions and detailed and robust plans.

ACT

Action should be stressed because too many of us get fooled into thinking that we can just ask for something and wait for it to happen. The most difficult part of signaling the superconscience is action because in acting, we enter uncharted territory and cause new landscapes to be generated from our perspectives. Before action, many of us are trepidatious because action sometimes leads to detours or unexpected outcomes. Action is also difficult because we can't just skip to the end result like we so often do in our imaginations. In action, we must deal with every nuance and physical barrier to our goals, one at a time. Once forward progress is made, the nervous feeling is commonly replaced with relief or exhilaration. The joy of having acted on a desire is in part due to the creation of new structures and memories in the superconscience. Still, poorly planned or executed actions can lead to disappointment and an aversion to re-attempting similar actions. The remedy for this is good planning. Creating a serious roadmap between where you are and where you want to be is the key to properly signaling the superconscience. The more detailed the roadmap, the better. Including all the steps to achieving your goal will make the path to it much more believable to you and others. If a well-defined, well-planned and highly focused effort produces failure, the only thing you can do is try again. Be sure to recognize anything that requires adjustment to make your efforts successful the next time. Persistence is difficult because conviction is fragile in the face of failure. We always want things to work the first time, but success often requires several attempts.

BELIEVE

As Benjamin Franklin put it, "Do not anticipate trouble or worry about what may never happen – stay in the sunlight". We generate images in our minds several times per minute. Focus on your idle thoughts for a moment. Did you notice the general vibration (tone) of those thoughts? Thought tone depends on perceptions of past experiences, hopes for the future and inputs from your senses. Part of believing is adjusting your default natural vibe to a light-hearted and positive one. Changing your perceptions of past events is a good start in accomplishing this. It's common to have negative experiences in life. Living through trauma is part of being human, but as they say, the past can't be changed. The best thing we can do with the past is to retain anything it has to teach us and discard the rest. The only experiences worth rehashing are instructional or positive ones. Balancing nutrition and sleep also go a long way toward making your vibes positive. Odds are that when your perception of the past and inputs from your body are positive, your aims will follow a similar trend.

It's crucial that when you're believing in something, you believe in it passively as well as actively. When you're tending to other matters you should trust that progress will continue, even when you're not looking. Of course, diverting your focus for too long can send the wrong signal to the superconscience. Given enough momentum, your goals will take on a life of their own. The feeling of true belief is one of flow almost as if you are in a dream with superpowers. If the journey toward a goal feels like a relentlessly monotonous exercise, you should reassess your belief in it. Another source of positive belief is other people. When someone believes in you and your goals, it can be very motivating. On the other hand, if someone is pessimistic toward you or your goals it can be demoralizing. Fear of rejection can keep us from announcing our dreams and desires to the world. Remember that people are part of the superconscience and they help render realities from your inputs.

If you are sending a clear signal to the superconscience, the opinions of people will follow. Others are part of the superconscience and yours is the vision that drives it. If the world seems to be conspiring against your goals, look inward and ask yourself why. If *you* believe, others will too.

RECEIVE

Ah, receiving. That's the best part of any quest. Reaping the favors that are due to you after a long journey is one of the best sensations one can have. Some of us are natural receivers and take what's coming to us with great joy and gratitude. Others harbor a bit of suspicion. "Is this really a reward or another lesson in the unobtainability of happiness?" Well, if you feel that happiness is unobtainable, you won't obtain it. Hopefully you've accounted for how the end result will feel when it does come your way. For some, happiness lies in the journey and when they finish one journey, they begin another. We've all heard of the billionaire who is miserable because money can't buy so many of the emotional rewards that make life enjoyable. Not all goals are for material gain, nor should they be, but sometimes we receive more than we bargained for. Some requests from the superconscience can lead to increased responsibility or accountability. All of this must be considered when asking for something, especially something that may increase your influence or visibility. Think of all the celebrities that would become anonymous if they could. Odds are that they didn't consider how suffocating celebrity status can be. The keys to good receipt are in forward thinking, ownership and gratitude.

Let's take a minute to address two of the main arguments people have against the Law of Attraction. The first is that it is simple confirmation bias at play. The idea of confirmation bias is that you can convince yourself of something regardless of the reality of the situation. When that something actually happens, they give credit to their vision rather than their actions or just plain luck. Some have even credited the law of attraction with their downfall through self-affirmed ignorance. Everyone is bound to some confirmation bias as that is a natural part of the human psyche, but most failures occur when we make inadequate plans with too little information. A lack of belief leads to a lack of action and that can have devastating results. In Everything, you experience your creation through the superconscience. If there's something that you'd like to experience, you must be specific. Give the superconscience a clear picture of what you want, not what you don't. Another argument against the law of attraction is that people living in privileged states take their advantages for granted to the point where they imagine things magically manifesting. As annoying as that may be for many people, the truth is that we all generate our own realities. You are what and where you believe to be. Though you will eventually experience all scenarios, you decide what happens next.

SUMMONING NE

NE as a concept is a nice tidy package that we can take anywhere and apply to any situation. But what aspects of it should be applied and where? When you summon NE, you summon a dichotomy. How does one observe something that *is* because it *isn't*? Our minds focus on existence by default. We relate to what is rather than to what is not. When trying to resolve a moral issue or find motivation, the concept of infinite possibility in Everything makes a good companion. Yet Nothing is the foundation of all possibility. As a concept, Nothing's power lies in that it acts as a powerful damper to the complexities of life. The concepts of Nothing and Everything certainly have their own unique applications. Although they seemingly contradict one another, Nothing and Everything are integral components of the same structure. Because of that, it takes a bit of practice to command them effectively. We'll go over some reasons for summoning NE in a moment, but it's such a captivating truth that sometimes a mere reminder of the Paradox is all it takes to recenter on its principles. After two and a half decades, I still occasionally find myself agitated or overly concerned about some things. When I get too caught up in the business of life, I lose sight of the big picture and have to realign my thoughts. I've asked my wife to say, "NE" ("enee") to trigger a perspective adjustment in me if she notices me acting cynical or otherwise off kilter. Once the Paradox is engrained in the conscience, a reminder is all it takes to bring its power forth. The principles of NE can be summoned for all purposes and maladies, but here are some of the more common reasons:

Motivation – What's more motivational than knowing you will see, do and be all? Perhaps it's also knowing that you embody all and that your actions are part of the fantastic experience of existing. The Paradox is an instant motivator in many respects, but we sometimes perceive ourselves as little people in a big world. The solution to that feeling is to recall the Paradox by uttering the word "NE". Once recalled, the NE perspective should quickly restore ownership, eliminate conflicts and motivate you to go enter *your* world and experience all it has to offer, including its challenges. With NE firmly in your grasp, you are the wealthiest, most powerful being on the planet. That should provide some motivation.

Courage – Courage can be rendered from both sides of the Paradox. In Everything, all is imminent. In that case, you might as well do what your heart tells you to do. That could mean some pretty risky and terrifying things. Knowing that you are destined to do all will give you the courage to engage your current task whether it's speaking to a crowd, standing up for yourself or scaling a cliff wall. Besides, all will occur regardless of your actions. Just realize that repercussions exist yet are also inevitable. On the other side of the Paradox is Nothing. All is contemplated such that it never occurs. If all of our actions are really contemplations of possibility, then we can have free reign of reality knowing that it doesn't happen. A lot of courage and peace can be rendered from a sense of Nothing.

Focus – As opposed to Everything's infinite flurry of chaotic activity, Nothing can be used as a cone of focus. Although we can never really experience Nothing, aspiring to its calmness and emptiness can muffle the distractions around us. In today's world, those who have focus have the power to affect their environments more than others. Focused people are difficult to come by and are prized members of any team or relationship. With Nothing in your back pocket, you have the power to obtain focus even in the most tumultuous times. Just say, "Nothing" and become it in your mind.

Sadness and Depression – Sadness is the feeling of loss, being wronged, being alone or a combination of the three. It's a highly empathized and therefore contagious state of mind. Fortunately, the singularity of Everything dictates that one is never alone. Whether someone has passed or never entered your life in the first place, you are one with all. If you are hurting because you were wronged, understand that all things happen and none are wrong. Everything is one and we are all in this together. Depression is a form of sadness that expresses itself through demotivation, doubt and pessimism. Depression can be combated by the certainty of all occurrences in Everything. When Everything occurs, doubt and pessimism are reduced to silliness. If you're too depressed or sad to see the bright side of things, just remember that it doesn't happen. That should at least evoke a chuckle.

Anger, Hatred and Jealousy – Like sadness, anger is rooted in the idea of being wronged. As you know, wrong is relative and our perspectives are biased to ensure our survival and well-being. Hatred is a similar survival instinct that pushes us to disassociate from or subdue those who show patterns of wrongdoing. Jealousy is negative envy wherein we feel that something we desire is being enjoyed by the wrong person. Again, an awareness of our oneness of Everything and the absence of wrong should immediately counteract the feelings of anger, hatred or jealousy. When we are all one, no wrong can be committed and success or enjoyment by one can be appreciated by all. Whether someone makes you happy, angry, envious or jealous, their intersection with you in such a vast reality is a special connection.

Fear and Anxiety – Fear and anxiety come from our natural aversions to negative consequences. As a survival instinct, they keep us out of big trouble, but if they become overactive it can limit our pursuits. Overactive fear can emerge from a subconscious memory of a bad experience or harsh consequence. It can also take the form of intimidation because of something you've been told or assumed. Either way, both aspects of NE can be used to combat fear and anxiety. In Nothing, consequences are irrelevant because the actions that cause them are never to happen. In Everything, all occurrences will come to pass including victories and consequences, so you should take the most desirable path without fear.

Remorse and Shame – Ever drink too much at a social gathering and say (or do) something too revealing? Ever look into your past and find an instance where you were mean to someone or didn't give them the benefit of the doubt? Shame and remorse are integral to human social behavior. Like fear and anxiety, they keep us out of trouble. People experience shame and remorse to varying degrees. A little remorse keeps us honest, but lingering feelings of shame and remorse are unproductive at best and can become parasitic at worst. An estimated four percent of the population, better known as sociopaths, feels neither shame nor remorse. We despise them because they sometimes do terrible things and leech off society yet we admire their ability to march straight to their objectives, everyone else be damned. Now, most of us don't want to become sociopaths but relieving ourselves of nagging memories that stifle forward progress would be extremely beneficial. For that, NE is the perfect implement. Understanding both that all is imminent and that nothing happens can eliminate shame for past deeds while keeping us grounded in empathy and positivity.

A tendency we have is to view ourselves as separate from the greater powers of NE. In writing this, the word "it" is used to describe Nothing and Everything. The proper word would be "us", but let's not stray too far from the language conventions we understand. NE is "us", not "it" because there is no separation between it and us. It takes concentration and mindfulness to see reality as an extension of ourselves. It takes even more mindfulness to see ourselves as the result of non-existence. The more you see yourself as integral to this virtual existence, the more powerful your effect on your surroundings will become. Your reality is a combination of what *could* happen *if* anything happened.

Summoning NE means rejecting fear and anxiety. Free of those emotions, life is enlightening and pleasurable. To observe your surroundings from an indestructible standpoint, fearless of consequences and eager to experience existence is invigorating. In the world of Nothing, consequences do not exist. In the world of Everything, consequences are infinite and imminent. In either case, consequences are not to be feared. A bank robber who is shot full of holes and dies is considered by most to be a victim of his own decisions and a sufferer of the consequences. In reality, the only consequence he suffered was being part of an infinite reality in which Everything happens. If this is true, why don't we all go out and rob banks? Because our position in Everything does not presently require that we do so. But it *will* and *has*. Along with the pain and anguish that is, was and will be required of all matter is the shear enjoyment and pleasure that is, was and will be. One may choose to focus on either pain or pleasure. To properly use the power of Nothing and Everything, one must live in the knowledge that both are inevitable in this infinite, virtual contemplation.

PERSPECTIVE ALTERATION

If there were one tool that is indispensable to MOE, it is perspective alteration. It takes many forms, but the three fundamentals are: lateral alteration (panning), scale alteration (zooming) and time alteration (flow). Though these are simple concepts, if consistently applied, they are immensely powerful. The knowledge of the Paradox coupled with the ability to alter your perspective in four dimensions are the keystones of NE. Once you understand these concepts, your navigation of spacetime will be greatly enhanced.

PANNING

"Instead of putting others in their place, put yourself in their place."
– Amish Proverb

Panning is a method of mentally changing the location of your perspective. The purpose of panning is to consider the position of someone or something else. Otherwise known as 'perspective-taking', panning is used by most of us on a daily basis. It's considering the situation of someone who's in a place you'd like to be or letting someone go ahead of you in the checkout line because they only have one item...you get the picture. At first glance, panning may be mistaken for empathy. Although empathy is a common reaction to panning, the two are not the same. One could pan without an emotional reaction. If you were a detective looking for a killer, you would pan to get a sense of how they encountered their victim or what they might do next, but not necessarily to empathize with the killer. The killer could also pan into the mind of their victim and use their newfound perspective to trick or track them. Depending on the situation and your outlook, panning may or may not result in emotional investment. Panning is done for strategic as well as emotional purposes.

One advantage we have as humans is the capacity to consider multiple perspectives outside of our own. It allows us to decipher the behaviors and actions of ourselves and other species. Only the most intelligent primates have the ability to imagine themselves in another's position. In terms of cognitive ability, it's right up there with the use of tools. Humans are the absolute masters of panning. For us, panning is essential for both strategy and social balance. But in many cases, it could be done more effectively. While we all pan on a daily basis, not many of us are in tune with the reasons we're panning or that we're even doing it.

So, what does panning have to do with NE and why would you want to do it more effectively? Panning means reading all of the available information to fine-tune our actions and produce desirable outcomes. Much of the power and peace of mind enjoyed by MOE is derived from an enhanced perspective through an understanding of other people, events and circumstances. Effective panning can help predict behavior, build rapport and reveal strengths and weaknesses in its subjects. Panning can also be a psychologically soothing activity. A temporary reprieve from our own outlook can help re-center us. As often as panning is done effectively, there are ways to pan ineffectively. An effective panner does it with the intention of learning and with as neutral an outlook as possible. When panning, try to subdue preconceived notions and be open to a broader understanding of the subject. Ineffective panning occurs when we consider other perspectives without regard to the reality of those perspectives. Biases or inattention to detail could leave us in a position of obliviousness and worse off than before. When panning, attention to detail is key to gaining relevant information. Moderation is also key. Panning for too long (e.g., zoning out) can remove us from our own perspectives and cause imbalances. Pan with focus, then get back to your unique perspective.

Panning doesn't have to be exclusively human-to-human. We can pan to animals, insects, vegetation and inanimate objects. As you know, all matter is part of Everything and thus part of us. The panning of things like machines or buildings is usually in reference to the construction, repair or demolition of such objects. Even in those cases, we're usually panning into the minds of the makers of those objects. It is impossible to enter the mindset of a non-living thing, but we can still gain information from its location, physicality and environment. It's difficult to enter the mindset of non-human creature due to dissimilar brain structures and logic, but it's not impossible. Panning to animals and other creatures is usually for the purposes of hunting, self-defense, study or preservation and it is done more by observation of patterns and environment. Nature documentaries that showcase life in the wild are prime examples of panning to wildlife. They are immensely educational and provide an entire audience information they would have otherwise never been able to obtain. Although all panning is beneficial, the most common and useful panning is done between humans.

A key to effective interpersonal panning lies in acknowledging your basic relationship with the subject you're panning to and realizing that your subject *is* you at a different spacetime location. Fundamentally, they are you but the difference in location entails multiple differences. Finding the primary differences and applying them to the panned perspective is helpful. Of course, the accuracy of our information determines the validity of our pan and we do get it wrong from time to time. In most instances, however, plenty of information is available. With just a few bits of gathered information, you'll have a much-improved pan.

There are some examples of panning that initially may not seem like panning, but certainly fit the bill. When we research historical figures, we're panning to them. When a football coach draws out a game plan, he's panning his team to his vision. When we watch movies and TV shows, we are panning to the characters, fictional and nonfictional. We can even pan to hypothetical figures who don't exist or may exist in the future. Online companies understand the value of panning. They use data offered voluntarily by their subjects and reap all the benefits of it by building user rapport and predicting behaviors and suggesting products from various advertisers based on those predictions. The data has a high monetary value to online entities. It's even been said that "data is the new gold" in the online world and that's because it can be used to get into your head.

Panning is particularly useful in negotiation. Building rapport is always a good thing in negotiation, but so is forecasting the moves of your opponent. A good negotiator pans into the perspective of his counterpart, builds rapport, recognizes weaknesses and plays on them while emitting an agreeable and friendly vibe. Disagreements can be completely diffused through panning. Panning can reveal things about an opponent's position that would otherwise be mysterious. The more people see things from each other's perspectives, the more likely it is that they will find amicable solutions to life's many conflicts. Beware, though, of the person or third party who provides you with deceitful information to create a false perception. Deception is the biggest obstacle to successful panning. Nevertheless, it is still an incredibly effective method of achieving the best perspective from which to act.

On a daily basis, we all pan to some extent. It's the root of our cooperation in human society. MOE is a 'superpanner', continually sampling the various perspectives both near and far. I'll leave you with a few guidelines for effective panning. The first is presence of mind. Remember to pan. When possible, look at life through the eyes of others before acting. The second is purpose. Remember your true purpose when panning. A pan can be like a daydream with no point. Unless daydreaming is the aim, make sure it stays on track so that it can be useful. The third is reconnaissance. Be sure to get as much information as you can to apply it to their perspective. Some of that information is available through appearance and body language, other info may require more digging and research.

Conditions permitting, you may even ask the subject for the info you need. If possible, after panning make your case to the subject to see things through your eyes. You owe everyone a chance to see things from your perspective.

ZOOMING +/-

"The leader must aim high, see big, judge widely, thus setting himself apart from the ordinary people who debate in narrow conflicts." – Charles de Gaulle

If you haven't already made the connection, panning and zooming get their names from the functions found on cameras and digital maps. While panning alters your perspective laterally, zooming alters it vertically. We pan to get a sense of our world through multiple perspectives, usually at conventional scale. We zoom to change the scale of our perspective and to use that scaled perspective to gain insight into our position and inform our direction for the big picture. Zooming is as simple as it sounds – changing your perspective to a broader or narrower view. There are many reasons to zoom. It could be tactical. If you're trying to get a handle on a situation, it's good to look at it from macroscopic or microscopic points of view. It could also be merely for emotional or psychological balance. If the world seems like it's descending upon you, it's beneficial to zoom out and realize how insignificant the conflict really is. Or perhaps you need to provide a zoomed-in perspective to make light of a situation for someone else and direct them to a positive outcome.

Zooming is at the heart of MOE techniques because it creates a more balanced perspective. Much of the calm, humorous and powerful traits recognized in MOE are due to proper use of zooming. We all zoom to some extent in our daily lives. It's a built-in ability we have. As with many of our cognitive abilities, it works in the background virtually unnoticed. Like panning, zooming can provide a fantastic advantage when used properly. Although we zoom as often as we pan, the direction of zoom is important. Zooming in the wrong direction can be counterproductive or even destructive. When we are looking through a wide lens and should be focusing through a narrow lens, we miss out on important details. Other times, we may focus too much on minute details of a situation while the big picture is neglected. Practicing mindful zooming will enhance your skills and increase the effectiveness over time.

Recall a time in your life when you felt ultra-confident, accepted and admired. Maybe it was at a dinner with old friends, maybe you were in a place with supportive people with similar interests. Or perhaps you were alone, listening to a song that brought back a nostalgic feeling. During that time, what was your zoom setting? Were you at ground level, seeing your immediate surroundings? Were you at city level, considering a broader picture of your life? Maybe you were zoomed all the way to planetary level, considering the world as a whole. Odds are that when you felt oneness, your perspective was zoomed out from default to some extent. The next time you're in a great place of confidence and acceptance, take note of your zoom setting. I've found feelings of oneness and solidarity at peculiar times. One of those times is during farewells. As a consulting engineer, my two favorite days on an on-site assignment were my first and last. The first day was pure excitement, getting to know new people and learning about interesting technologies. On first days, the zoom was micro-focused on the tasks at hand. The last days were also very enjoyable. Co-workers would take me to lunch and dinner and wish me farewell. People whom we know are only around for a short time in our lives receive our undying well wishes as we no longer see them as permanent fixtures, but rather as a soon to be missed relationship or an empty seat. In those instances, even personalities I clashed with are bound to extra kindness for a day. In any case, I was always happy to shed my daily obligation to the company and most of the time I'd never see most of those people again. Free of deadlines and social pressure, I was zoomed out to a much broader perspective.

During life-changing events like moving, crises, familial changes and farewells, the daily routine gives way to the bigger picture. We temporarily zoom out and get a broader perspective.

Even in situations where circumstances aren't ideal, if we can remember to zoom out, we can get a better handle on what matters. Have you ever noticed that successful CEOs, entrepreneurs and military leaders share the trait of having zoomed-out perspectives? The quote at the beginning of this chapter by Charles de Gaulle is true of leaders. They think and act big, and that sets them apart from non-leaders. In other words, they own the big picture while others take care of smaller details. If you can somehow direct on a macro scale and surround yourself with detail-oriented people, you can be a successful leader. While big-picture thinking has its rewards and advantages, the most impressive people also have the ability to zoom into the details of tasks and missions. Have you ever been astonished, or even intimidated by someone's attention to detail? The smallest of details can make the biggest difference functionally and psychologically. When it comes to deciding who to work with, big-picture leaders should gravitate toward zoomed-in, detail-oriented people. The traits complement each other and reduces the tendency for power struggles.

So, why would we want to zoom, and what makes a zoom effective? There are two options for zooming, in and out. Reasons to zoom out could be observing and predicting trends, understanding relationships, setting long-term objectives, restoring priorities or reducing anxiety. Reasons to zoom in could be increasing efficiency of a system, understanding micro-connectivity and the underlying causes of things, escaping a seemingly insurmountable big picture, gaining strength or recovering incrementally.

Now a few guidelines for effective zooming. Just as with panning, the first is presence of mind. Remember to zoom. Try to get both the zoomed out and in perspectives of a situation before acting. The second is direction. Make sure you're zooming out when you need a bigger picture and zooming in when you need more detail. Sometimes it's hard to tell which way to zoom, so, if possible, zoom both ways. Don't get caught fiddling while Rome burns or overlooking the little things that make the big things happen. The third is pattern observation. When you're zoomed in or out, patterns become important. In both cases, the normal laws and obligations that bind us change with scale as they give way to natural laws. On the micro scale, the effects of public opinion and financial obligation get replaced by microfluidics, minerals and microbiology. Different worlds exist and all we need is a microscope to enter them. On the macro side of the scale, the responsibilities and accomplishments of humanity become trivial as sidewalks, buildings and streets blur into white patches amongst green and brown landscapes as you zoom out. Google Earth is a great way to get a perspective change. Start at your location and see how far you have to zoom out for your town to be unrecognizable. You could also take a trip to another state or country. After traveling, most people return with an airy feeling due to a broadened perspective. It wears off, of course, and many of us need to repeat the experience to recapture the broadened perspective.

FLOW

> *"The bad news is time flies. The good news is you're the pilot."*
> *– Michael Altshuler*

Through panning and zooming, we can alter our spatial perspectives in three dimensions. Another dimension we can alter is time, or at least our perception of it. Space and time are indivisible. As one changes, so does the other. That is why we have different perspectives. I'm not you because it would take time for me to get to your position. When I arrive at your position, I occupy a different location in spacetime. The only instance in which we occupy the same spacetime location is one in which we are aware that we simultaneously occupy all spacetime and are truly one. In this instance, Everything occurs spontaneously and the distinction between past, present and future is indeed an illusion. Nevertheless, it's our perception of time that makes our experiences as individuals possible.

There are two aspects of time that humans characterize: speed and quality. Overall, we want to maximize time that we perceive as high-quality and minimize time that we perceive as low-quality. We want to perform well, do great things and retain lots of good memories in the process. The better we do, the better the memories and chances for future happiness. We want to leave the inevitable hard times behind us and not let them take up valuable space in our minds. When we're in situations that require swift action, we want time to slow down. When we're in painful or traumatic situations, we want time to pass quickly and minimize the impact of the negative experience on the psyche. Mastering our creation of memories and perception of time flow can unlock the potential of thousands of hours of productivity, happiness and security.

Our neural clocks segment our memories in spacetime so that we can experience them in orderly, chronological increments (inches/seconds, meters/hours, etc.). By social contract, we agree to coordinate our activities according to clock time. But the brain does not perceive durations in time with the standardized units of minutes and hours. Recent discoveries in neuroscience have helped solve some of the mysteries of time perception and memory creation in our brains. Unlike spatial perception, our perception of time is highly malleable. Given its plasticity, time may also be experienced as faster or slower than standard clock time.

FLOWING

Living organisms, including humans, have developed multiple biological clocks to help us keep track of time. Some are set by external processes like the rise and setting of the sun. Others are biological, like the hippocampal time cells that form chain signals that track time spans of up to ten seconds (for longer memories, the brain doesn't explicitly encode time). Researchers at the Kavli Institute for Neuroscience in Norway have discovered that humans perceive time as an ongoing flow of experiences and the succession of events is the substance of which the perception of time is measured by the brain. In other words, we perceive time subjectively as we flow through what we consider significant and insignificant experiences. Years before the "flow of experiences" discovery, researchers at the same facility discovered grid cells in the medial entorhinal cortex (MEC) that map our environment at different scales by dividing space into hexagonal units. Whereas they only needed to decode a single grid cell to discover how space is encoded, decoding time in the adjoining lateral entorhinal cortex (LEC) proved to be more complex. According to the researchers, space in the brain was relatively easy to investigate, as it consists of specialized cell types that are dedicated to specific functions, but time didn't seem to present any key cells that revealed their functional identity. It was only when they began to suspect that the time-coding signals in the LEC were changing with time that the data made sense. Their suspicions proved correct. Time in our brains is a non-equilibrium, non-linear process. In order to record experiences as unique memories, time-coding signals must change with time. To complete our four-dimensions of perception, the representation of episodic time from the LEC is integrated with the spatial information from the MEC in the hippocampus, allowing our brains to store a unified representation of what, where and when.

The researchers tested their findings by monitoring the time-coding signals in the brains of rats in two different scenarios. In the first experiment, the rats were introduced to a wide range of experiences and options for action. They were free to run around, investigate and chase bits of chocolate while visiting a series of open-space environments. In the second, the tasks were more structured with a narrower range of environments and options for action. The first scenario produced unique, well-defined time-coding signals that suggested the rats had very good records of time and temporal sequences throughout the experiment. The second saw the time-coding signals change from unique to overlapping and repetitive. Throughout the second experiment, the signals suggested that the rats had an improving understanding of the limited environment, but poor cognition of time. The fact that time-coding signals could be shaped into unique patterns in different situations implied a high level of plasticity (20).

In times of happiness and health we desire permanence, but in life, nothing is permanent. Life is a roller coaster event wherein you spend the first years accelerating and learning and the last decelerating and forgetting. In the middle years of life, you may find your comfortable (or not so comfortable) 'normal' state, but you will be aware that your time as an able-bodied person is limited. One of the biggest complaints people over thirty years old have is that the years seem to fly by. For me personally, from childhood into my twenties, a decade seemed like a generation. After my early twenties, it seemed that the years would slip by five at a time. Somehow my time-coding stamp wasn't making as deep or as consistent an impression as I would've liked. Before I knew it, I was thirty years old. My thirties proved even more fleeting.

Certain events made deeper imprints than others: moving, job changes, beginning and ending relationships and periods of significant learning. It wasn't that nothing was happening in my life after twenty-five. Life was dynamic. At twenty-two, I had moved from Texas to North Carolina to work in NASCAR racing. During my first year on a race team, I struggled to develop skills that would help me design cars that could win races while traveling the national circuit. I eventually pinpointed computer aided design (CAD) as one of those skills. Though travelling the race circuit proved a tumultuous existence, the ability to design using computers indeed made me a sought-after engineer for years to come. The following year, I bought a small piece of land, put a home on it and had officially settled in North Carolina. From an outside perspective, there is no reason to think that the years after my mid-twenties should've slipped by so quickly. What might have changed my perception of time? One thing that comes to mind is embracing a skillset. Once I could design in CAD, I never looked back. It made life easier for me than it was in the shops and at the racetracks. In the shop, I was covered in grease and contending with Murphy's law. CAD design insulated me from the harshness of other team members who didn't like that I had a fancy degree yet was still learning to wrench on the cars. On the computer, my designs could come to life while I sipped coffee. In the second half of my 20's, my life compared to previous years was much more routine. I had a permanent address and a set number of hours in my day were spent designing while seated at a desk. A few years later, I was designing cars for Dale Earnhardt Inc, a massive race team with four cars in the field on any given race day. They also had thirty engineers and several hundred other employees. My expertise had gotten me there and supported my existence there, but I was further from the action of real racing than ever. I was no longer travelling to races because it wasn't required of me. The environment, while extremely cool, was also filled with jealous and competitive engineers who shared my special skillset. After a few tense seasons fighting for camaraderie and influence, I began to wonder if I'd ever be happy as a racecar engineer.

By 2008, I had left the NASCAR scene and began to work as a consulting engineer. As luck would have it, I landed a unicorn contract designing cars for an electric car maker with big aspirations. They wanted me to design an all-electric 'supercar' concept that they would fabricate. My dreams had been revitalized. Still, the core hours of my day remained the same: sitting at a desk and designing, but happily so. After two years of intense design and dealing with the same unfriendly environment endemic to incorporations of dream-starved young men, I made a quantum jump that I'll discuss in more detail in the upcoming chapters. To summarize the jump, I moved across the country to California, married, started another consulting business and had kids. Those years left wonderfully deep impressions and slowed time down a bit, but the core hours of my day remained creating design on a computer screen. By the time forty hit, I was desperate to slow my perception of time. My wife and I had two-year-old twins, so the days were long but two more years flew by in the blink of an eye. Those were some of the happiest times in my life, but they were passing by too fast. Adding to it, I felt I only had a couple more decades to complete my life's work before retreating to old age. These were the classic foundations of a mid-life crisis and I had to start spending some of my time differently.

Changing how you spend your time is not an easy prospect when you have a family to support, but I knew that my happiness and, by extension, that of my family depended on it. So, in 2018, I took out a life insurance policy on myself and began flight lessons at a local air school. I assumed I'd easily obtain a pilot's license within a few months. I was mistaken. Over the next year and a half, my instructors and I exercised parts of my brain that had atrophied.

Suddenly, I was forced to have an innate sense of direction, situational awareness under great pressure, memorize instructions and regulations, communicate over a radio in air traffic lingo and handle six or seven control inputs to save my life. There were several close calls both while in the air and on the ground, so I was glad I had life insurance. I could have done something safer and more affordable like learn a new language or pick up a musical instrument, but I had to be pushed past a point of no return. When you pick up an instrument, you can put it down with little consequence. When you take off in a plane, you have to land. Learning to fly has made some of the deepest impressions on my memory in recent decades. Breaking routine in all possible ways causes more consistent and vivid impressions in our memories and makes time seem fuller. When we're learning or our emotions are strong, streams of consciousness combine and memories are made more rapidly. This can give the impression of time slowing down. It doesn't have to be something drastic like flying planes. Just trying unfamiliar paths and learning unfamiliar things can be enough to improve mental time coding. There are some things we can't change easily, like how we make a living, but breaking from routines in constructive ways is extremely beneficial to the quality of life. Of course, as the laws of objective reality dictate, changing routines doesn't mean driving off a cliff and seeing what happens. Changing routines sometimes means taking risks, but make sure they're calculated or be prepared to make the wrong kind of imprint on your memory or destroy it altogether. Risky or not, successful routine changes can make a significant impact on our time coding by stimulating the neural networks involved in learning.

It's less common that we want to make time go by faster, but there are instances that warrant the slippage of time. If changing routines and learning new things increases the depth and quality of memory coding, then how can we intermittently fast-forward without discarding our experiences completely? And while we're at it, how can we occasionally slow our perception of time so that we can act within it, frame by frame? For those aims, an understanding of flow states helps significantly.

MANAGING FLOW STATES

Have you ever had an instance when you were doing something so capably that it felt effortless? Or where you were so focused on the task at hand that you lost track of time? Many call it being in the zone. Psychologists call it being in a flow state. It has long been known that a mental 'flow' state exists wherein we perform at elevated levels. People observed in flow states exhibit pinpoint focus, creativity and relaxation. In flow, we not only perform well, but feel well. Part of the relaxation comes from a sense of confidence and in living in our element. During flow, your mind becomes so absorbed in the present moment that the outside world melts away. We also know that our brains are capable of the 'slow motion' and 'block out' responses in times of emergency. Those responses are ingrained in our subconscious and work like airbags, deploying automatically when needed. People who've been in dire situations recall that in those moments, seconds and minutes seem like hours. One man who was hit by a car recalled his slow-motion trip through the air, admiring the beauty of shattered windshield glass as it sprayed like mist, and his entire life flashed before his eyes – all within two seconds. Although we have no conscious control over our emergency responses, examples like this show how malleable our perception of time can be.

The prefrontal cortex (PFC) region of the brain is where complex logical thought, decision making and planning take place. It is also implicated in personality expression, social moderation and will power. The PFC is where our sense of morality, inner critic and fear live. The 10% brain myth asserts that we only use 10% of our brains and only gifted people like Albert Einstein use higher percentages. Although it has been debunked, many people still believe it. They'd likely conclude that flow stimulates the 'unused' portions of our brain, but the opposite actually takes place. According to Steven Kotler, the author of "The Rise of Superman", in flow, the brain actually bypasses the PFC and directs resources to other areas such as reaction time. This is known as transient hypo frontality. In other words, the brain performs better when it slows down. As our inner critic is silenced, our fear and stress hormones go away. In place of stress hormones, we get a boost of five pleasure neurochemicals (norepinephrine, dopamine, endorphins, anandamide and serotonin). Time becomes dilated, meaning it can either seem sped up or slowed down and we lose the ability to assess past, present and future. As Kotler explains it, "we're plunged into what researchers call the deep now." In flow, our risk taking and creativity increase as we take in more information per second. With increased creativity, our brain finds connections between new information and older ideas and pattern recognition improves 400-700%, when tested in case studies. It is also estimated that the average person is 500% more productive yet spends only 5% of their working hours in flow. That means increase of flow time by 20% can result in doubling productivity. You could show up to work on Tuesday morning and leave half-way through Thursday and still get a full week of work in if you were in flow 25% of the time. Flow improves information retention as well. The more neurochemicals that show up during an experience, the more likely memory of that experience will go from short-term holding to long-term storage. Increased creativity in flow leads to more opportunities to be creative. Flow is as close to near-perfect, high-speed decision making as we can get. People in flow create major paradigm shifts due to their increased risk taking and creativity. Flow is fundamental to life's well-being. It is universal, provided certain conditions are met.

The psychologist Mihaly Csikszentmihalyi, who coined the term *flow* in the 1970s, described it as "a point of equilibrium between anxiety and boredom which ensues when the level of challenge in an activity is in balance with the level of skill of the participant". The conventional view of flow is that it happens when we become experts at something through repetition. While learning, the brain's frontal lobes light up and create unique memories. As you become an expert at something, that activity is greatly reduced, allowing the task to be performed in a flow state. As our skills improve, we increase the challenge accordingly to remain in the flow state. That is why those who live in flow tend to break new ground. An important thing to remember about flow is that it follows focus. If there is no focus, there is no flow. A favorite method of mine to enter a flow state is listening to music that puts me in the state of mind I want to be in. Nostalgic and instrumental music tend to work well to that end. Hypnosis is another method of entering a flow state. Whereas typical flow states are similar to moving meditations, hypnosis is more of a focused flow state in which the hypnotist attempts to reprogram or reinforce a subconscious voice in their subject. Voices heard in a state of hypnotic flow can take route and direct your subconscious thought patterns.

If it were possible, we'd live more of our lives in flow. One of the aims of NE is more beneficial flow through revised perspectives. Over the past 50 years, there've been advances in psychology, neurobiology, pharmacology and technology related to flow. We now know the psychological causes of flow, how it occurs in our brains, how to induce it with drugs and how to stimulate it electrically. Radar operators in the US Airforce have used transcranial direct current stimulation (tDCS) to increase situational awareness. TCDS consists of a weak electrical current flowing between head-mounted electrodes placed on either side of the PFC to stimulate neurons and produce an artificial state of flow for 20-40 minutes. The positive after-effects have been reported to last from hours to weeks after the treatments. Militaries, business leaders and athletes the world over are already using tDCS and other technologies to enter states of flow on demand. One compelling example of the effects of tDCS on some subjects comes from an excerpt from the best-selling book "Homo Deus: A Brief History of Tomorrow" by Yuval Harari. In it, he describes the experiences of a reporter for the New Scientist, who tests a prototype transcranial stimulation helmet in a simulated military exercise. She first enters the simulator as 'herself' and is immediately reduced to a quivering wreck as she is assailed by heavily armed, virtual, masked men. Then, she tries it again, this time after a brief tDCS session. She begins to coolly pick off the attackers, breathing calmly and reloading before taking out the next one. Before she knows it, the simulation is over and the bodies of imaginary assailants lie strewn around her. She is stunned by the experience: "My brain without self-doubt is a revelation. There was suddenly this incredible silence in my head… I also started to have a lot of questions. Who was I apart from the angry bitter gnomes that populate my mind and drive me to failure because I'm too scared to try?" Of course, different people have different experiences in tDCS and it is currently being touted only as a treatment for depression and anxiety. If you are so inclined, tDCS devices are available for purchase through various sources.

Methods of entering flow without the use of electrical stimulation or drugs include:

- Being well rested
- Clearing away distractions
- Finding quiet places for flow
- Designating a limited time for flow
- Working on things you love
- Having well-defined and incremental goals
- Using triggers to drive attention into focus
- Getting into a sustained rhythm
- Practicing flow consistently

In flow, we become calm, elegant and free of doubt. Many people in flow report losing track of time while in flow. On the other side of the spectrum, people who've been locked in solitary confinement and deprived of sensory input report that weeks and months flew by quickly in spite of their psychologically agonizing situations. In cases of sensory deprivation, the memory function in the hippocampus slows. In this way, the brain acts as a surveillance camera, only activating when triggered by stimuli. Similar things happen while we wait in airport terminals for a delayed flights or find ourselves stuck in the middle of uninteresting board room meetings. In those situations, there are few alternatives to simply waiting. Surfing the web on our cell phones, reading or taking naps are the ways most of us cope with uninteresting times. Each of those options offers a mental bullet train onto which we can step and fast-forward through time. Unless something profound occurs, those moments are tossed into our neurological dustbins, likely never to be recalled. Allowing non-stimulating experiences to speed by with minimal imprint could also be considered a type of flow.

Flow can be beneficial or parasitic. Our hyper-connected lives are filled with distractions that fracture our focus. In the example from my younger years, flow was a big component of my success yet productive flow was intermittent and unpredictable. During those times, emails and internet surfing stole more than their share of my waking hours. The internet, email, apps, cell phones, video games, and movies offer reprieves from reality, but continually remove us from positive flow. Endlessly scrolling through chat rooms and replying to text pings may provide us with some sense of flow, but they are passive, directionless and unchallenging. We emerge feeling depleted instead of reinforced. While we're enjoying our digital interfaces, we are experiencing something many of us call "running in autopilot mode". In autopilot mode, our minds are almost in a dream state with very little activity and memory formation. It's natural and healthy to take mental breaks and let our minds coast, but when we become addicted to coasting, it can be as detrimental to our lives as drug addiction. Alas, that's what many popular digital products intend to do – get you hooked so that you binge on their product. Video gamers, gamblers and drug users can enter states of non-productive flow in their respective addictions. The problem with non-productive flow is that it leads to nothing but neurochemicals and, if left unchecked, can lead to destruction. There are plenty of people playing video games and entering states of flow to the detriment of their goals and contributions to society. Non-productive flow for extended periods can lead to the perception of years slipping by. To this day, I spend time in design flow. It is an integral part of my legacy. I still battle with the addictive nature of computer programs, cell phones and the internet, but I recognize them merely as tools and fight to keep them from disrupting my flow. Productive flow is more addictive than the non-productive flow because it leads to real, sustainable rewards. Still, it takes a lot of discipline to keep it productive.

Is a life in flow a life well-lived? Absolutely, but we must consider the results of our actions just as in other areas of life. We should evaluate our reasons for entering flow with the realities and conditions for a healthy, emotionally balanced existence. We can flow in all directions; up, down, slow, fast, positive and negative. Flow accelerates us in whatever direction we're pointed. Our moral compasses are critical when in flow. When positive, sustainable flow is established, the key is balancing it. From my experience, the ideal time flow scenario would be to enter it in beneficial activities for a limited part of the day and use the increased productivity to gain extra time. That extra time can be used to catapult yourself into exciting, memorable experiences or to nurture personal relationships.

As MOE, we know that all spacetime is divine and should be cherished. In actuality, no time is inferior to another. Nevertheless, we want to spend our time certain ways and do certain things. That is why we strive to maximize and manage it. Well-directed flow is both enjoyable and highly rewarding. With focused practice, we can double or triple our productivity and effectiveness. With more efficiency in our productive endeavors, we have more time to focus on creating good memories. In addition to flowing, breaking routine and trying profoundly new things creates more consistent and higher-quality memories. Exploring new things is highly stimulating and foments the perception of time extension. The states of flow and discovery are desirable ways to spend time. Even in circumstances where possibilities are limited, it is possible to focus intensely, get lost in an activity and learn new things. Let us increase our beneficial flow and create great memories.

QUANTUM JUMPING

A life in motion tends to stay in motion unless acted upon by an external force. Perhaps the force comes in the form of change in perspective or a habit that gradually sculpts your experience like water rushing over rocks. Maybe an epiphany or a change in geopolitical landscape changes our experience more abruptly. But what if we want to find the fastest route to the experience of our choosing? Wouldn't it be nice if we could get advice from a parallel universe in which we *were* experiencing those things? We've already discussed ways to inform the superconscience of our intended experiences by using the Law of Attraction and perspective alteration. Recall that in a multiverse there are infinite instances and variations of ourselves in other dimensions. Quantum jumping uses visualization to communicate with those extra-dimensional superpositions of our perspectives, also known as *doppelgängers* (twin selves). A method to summon and communicate with our doppelgängers was developed by a man named Burt Goldman. Goldman, also known as 'The American Monk', called his method quantum jumping. In a nutshell, quantum jumping connects you to the superconscience by introducing you to the version of yourself who has accomplished or obtained something that you desire. This parallel version of you can provide illuminating and sometimes surprising advice on how to achieve what they've achieved.

My first doppelgänger encounter took place in 2009. I was living in North Carolina, consulting as a concept car designer for an electric car manufacturer. Although I had great experiences in designing cars and other things, prolonged projects were rare and fleeting. Every time I'd finish a project, I'd live on the proceeds until the next one came along. This was a cycle for several years. In addition, I had a case of asthma that seemed to be getting worse each year. To top it all off, most of the friendships I had made proved empty of substance. There didn't seem to be another soul that I could count on. I was a man with no tribe. I often drank beer and used tobacco to cope with stress and fill emotional voids, not enough to call it a problem, but enough to waste precious time and energy. During those times, I wasn't applying NE to my life regularly. My youthful energy was enough to keep me going. In those years, I would apply NE only to existential quandaries but not to problems of habit or relationships.

My mother, who spent the second half of her life subscribing to methods of self-help psychology and metaphysical power tapping, periodically sent copies of the latest self-help course CDs to me. I had a special relationship with her because I kept an open mind, accepted her suggestions and gave her positive input. It helped that I lived a thousand miles away and could simply accept her CDs, thank her for them and let them collect dust. Most of the course titles oozed with self-help catch phrases like, "Meditation for Success" or "The Seven Chakras of Enlightenment". Although I was open to learning new things, something inside me cringed at the idea of yet another metaphysical or philosophical lesson from a charismatic success guru. I felt that I already had the ultimate key, but I also knew that there is always more to learn. The most important thing for me was to let my mom know that I appreciated her. It would've been easy to ridicule the courses and their seemingly gullible audiences, but metaphysics was a special connection my mom and I shared. She was including me in something she was deeply interested in and I wanted to encourage her enthusiasm for something that made her happy. Occasionally, I did give a course a listen if anything to have something to discuss in my weekly phone conversations with her.

When I received Burt Goldman's series on Quantum Jumping, it might as well have been any other self-help course. The title, although unique, didn't spare it from my preconceptions. I could only guess that it was another "positive happy thoughts" meditation. It was a ten-disk set and my mom probably spent the better part of a day burning the CDs for me, so I owed it to her to give an exploratory listen. Quantum jumping takes its name from transitions in quantum mechanics where subatomic particles absorb or lose energy and systems transition from one energy level to another. The instantaneous quantum jump distinguishes quantum systems from classical systems where transitions are more gradual. This encapsulates the idea of the metaphysical version of quantum jumping proposed by Goldman – abrupt change.

Quantum jumping offers a different but similar approach to neuro-linguistic programming (NLP). NLP uses connections between neurological processes (neuro), language (linguistic) and behavioral patterns (programming) to treat psychological problems or enhance one's performance. NLP focuses on identifying and reprogramming parts of the psyche that are problematic and act as blockages to success. Once the mind is liberated from parasitic "past learning", an NLP practitioner may begin visualizations to rehearse and integrate changes into their life. The subject may be asked to visualize the future and mentally experience what it is like having already achieved the outcome. Expert NLP practitioners, like good psychologists, also learn non-verbal and linguistic ques and use them to persuade others. Exercises such as modeling are performed wherein the subject emulates the linguistic patterns and body language of an exemplar who embodies the success that he or she wants. My mother became fascinated with NLP in the 1980s and did several visualizations with me as her practice subject. She would count down from ten to one and I'd step down to my "special place" where all of my dreams were possible and ask for what I wished to happen. I'd give my eyes an extra roll back and forth under my closed eyelids as a queue that I was experiencing something, which she noticed and interpreted as successfully getting me into a trance state. The visualizations had an effect on me from a standpoint of goal formation and making a pact with what I now know as the superconscience to obtain success. NLP (and similarly hypnotism) employs creative visualization to speak with our unconscious mind and train it. It also employs a technique called modeling to emulate other people who have successes you desire. Alternatively, quantum jumping envisions a virtual meeting with a successful version of yourself whom you learn from and emulate. It's still visualization but one in which you survey the superconscience for direction.

My list of requirements for my doppelgänger was short. I wanted to meet the version of me whom was asthma free, had good relationships and was financially secure. Basically, healthy, loved and wealthy. It didn't take long for me to enter the mental space for the meeting. I did the countdown from ten and stepping down a staircase that my mom had done in past NLP sessions. I expected to have to go deep into a meditative state to conjure such an encounter, but it was not far below the surface. For some strange reason, we met in the empty hallways of the high school from which I'd graduated thirteen years prior. The lights were dimmed, as if school had let out and it was late afternoon. He looked just like me. It is difficult and strange to envision yourself as you really are, as if looking in the mirror. In my mind's eye, I really don't have the same physical form. In my visualizations, I'm usually just a face moving around. Visualizing myself as a fully formed human was odd. Of course, there's also the superstition that when you see your doppelgänger it foretells your imminent death. In retrospect, perhaps that's true in the sense that your path is about to change. I looked him in the eyes. His clothing style was a cut above my typical jeans and t-shirt. His skin was slightly more tanned than mine. His hair was long and had been pulled back into a ponytail. The top couple buttons on his shirt were left open, adding to his care-free aura. He definitely had more swagger to his step, and why wouldn't he if he was a healthier and more fulfilled version of me? This was definitely the man I was looking for.

I asked what he'd done to improve his lot. His answer took me by surprise. "I moved to California". California was so far away from my life plans. I had an internal pact with myself that North Carolina was my permanent home. I had prided myself in the fact that I'd *chosen* to live there. It was my dream of being an auto racing legend that brought me, not some corporate plan that had transferred me there. I'd grown up moving from state to state because of my father's career in the petroleum industry. I wanted to choose where I lived by where my dreams were. I also put a high value on permanence of residence and relationships. I had fought tooth and nail and took great risks, volunteering and working my way into the race shops and eventually getting hired onto a team. I had already pursued my dream, but my aims had missed the mark. My real dream was to drive racecars or start my own race team. Without significant money, I could do neither. In order to have the true dream, I'd need a significant bankroll. I'd also learned that relationships were more important than any material goal. We all make jumps in our lives. To get what we really want, we have to consider all the parameters. Sometimes we have to get something we don't want to realize what we do want. The benefit of quantum jumping is that you can make very specific jumps and consult any combination of doppelgänger.

When I had made the jump to North Carolina nine years prior, my goal was singular: work on a race team. That order was generously fulfilled. As I saw it, success and happiness would come along with being on a team. What I didn't realize was that my relationships would affect my perception of the sport and my desire to remain fully invested in it. In racing, if you're not fully invested, you're not successful. My bit was broken and I had to try something radically different. Packing up a decade's worth of living and saying goodbye to racing seemed unthinkable, and there were yet more reasons that moving to California seemed illogical. North Carolina was being inundated by Californian transplants seeking more affordable living and less congestion. Several of my neighbors were from California. I had also met some Californians on various race teams. They all shared a similar view of California - "way too expensive, and way too many people". Two things I hated were paying too much for something and being stuck in a crowd. It would seem that a move to California would be precisely in the wrong direction.

In 2009, I was experiencing an odd trifecta of misfortune. At the electric car company, the working environment was just as cut-throat as that of a race team. My design background had propelled me to the head of new concept designs, much to the chagrin of the other engineers and technicians who had worked there longer but were stuck working on more conventional projects. The company had burned through much of its capital and was laying off whomever they could, especially contractors. Once my designs were completed, I was given a pink slip. I was reluctant to join another race team as I had grown weary of the competitive push and shove so common amongst team members. On the entrepreneurial side, I had developed a digital gauge that was used to measure the distance between the ground and the underside of a racecar chassis. After taking it to several trade shows, advertising in magazines selling it directly to race shops, less than 100 had sold. It was 2009 and the economic recession was in full swing. Race teams had much less discretionary money to spend. Four years and seventy thousand dollars into it, my product was stillborn. I was living hand to mouth just as when I had moved to North Carolina, but now I was in deep debt. Aspects of my personal life followed a similar pattern. I was in my early thirties and each relationship with a woman carried with it the prospect of marriage. Breakups were heart-wrenching. I avoided the furtherance of imperfect relationships because I knew being married unhappily was much worse than being single. Thankfully, that proved to be a good policy.

After summing up the situation, I took out a US road map and traced a path to where I considered the epicenter of American innovation – Palo Alto, California. I put my resume online in hopes that the hiring manager for Tesla would come across it, but I was open to any other job that would bring me to California. Eventually I got a call from an electrical connector manufacturing company in Northern California. There I was, allowing a company's location to dictate my location, well, sort of. I would accept any job that would catapult me to the Bay Area of California. Santa Rosa also happened to be the location of the headquarters of the electric car company, Zap. Zap had been competing for the 2.5-million-dollar prize that one of the cars I had designed would win the following year. All signs pointed to electric vehicle development as my key to success, but what about happiness and health? Well, at least there was some logic behind the advice of my enigmatic twin. My girlfriend at the time was devastated to hear the news of my coming departure. I was moving nearly three thousand miles away and it was likely permanent. It didn't matter to her that we'd already broken up several times and our views on life and religion were incompatible, but it mattered to me. In the weeks before I left, Katie Perry's song, "California Gurls" would play on the radio and I'd change the station and pretend it annoyed me if my girlfriend was around. The song bothered her for obvious reasons. A painful breakup was on the horizon. By mid-summer 2010, I had a twenty-six-foot Penske truck loaded to the hilt and a partially restored 1958 Plymouth in tow on a flatbed trailer. My dad flew in from Montana to help me with the drive. Before we were over the Appalachians, the air conditioning in the truck gave out. Eventually we discovered the very effective method of misting ourselves with squirt bottles to keep cool in the hundred-degree-plus cab. Somewhere in Tennessee, I discovered the Plymouth had come unstrapped and was dangerously close to bouncing off the trailer. Instances like those remind you how precarious life can be when in flux.

When we arrived in Santa Rosa, I confirmed that housing was difficult to find and twice the cost of other places in the country. California was delivering as advertised. Over the next few weeks, I started my job at the connector company and began setting up utilities and banking. I found a local credit union that had the most forgiving fee structure and many nearby branches, but a coworker of mine was strangely adamant about *his* bank. He printed out several awards that the bank had received from J.D. Power and Associates and put them on my desk. He also mentioned that the bank was giving away free iPods to new account holders. That sold me. Three weeks later, I had opened an account and received my new iPod with a golden "Bank of the West" decal across the back. During one of my visits to the bank, a very attractive female teller inquired, "So, what brings you to California?" The tone of her voice revealed a bit more interest in me than a typical teller-customer interaction. It didn't dampen my enthusiasm that she was beautiful. As it turns out, she was what brought me to California. Ten years and two kids later, we're still happily married. The relationship part of my quantum jump had been realized within weeks of my move.

As for vices, I never used tobacco again. I understood the stakes involved and pondered how stupid it would be to get cancer from it. It also would've repulsed my new love interest. Regarding alcohol, I was living in wine and craft brew country and couldn't wait to tour and taste on the weekends. There was a catch to that as well. My girlfriend disliked the taste of alcohol and therefore wasn't thrilled to go wine or beer tasting. I tried to take my family on a tour when they were in town, but they'd become a solemn bunch, depressed for various reasons, and were initially nonplused by my sudden teleportation across the country. Not a sip was had. The craft beers *did* flow as I took on the task of restoring the old Plymouth each night in my garage. I even brewed some of my own batches of beer until a particularly stout batch exploded in a closet and destroyed a portion of our hardwood kitchen floor. The following year, I learned that I had gout. With gout, every time you drink beer or eat certain foods, a little troll emerges from under your bed and smacks your foot with a hammer while you sleep. Needless to say, it curtailed my drinking considerably. The more perplexing part of the health puzzle, ridding myself of asthma, still showed little sign of improving. Northern California has significant particulates, smog and pollen in the air. This led me to explore immunotherapy through allergy shots. Over the last five years, I've been injected with an ever-increasing dose of grasses and pollens. Meanwhile, the temperate climate has made the prospect of running and bicycling very appealing. The capacity of my lungs has grown and my reaction to pollens has decreased significantly. As I write this, I've completed the final round of shots and the asthma, while not completely gone, has improved significantly.

I worked at the connector company for just shy of two years. I had to walk away because of unexpected hostility I encountered there. I had arrived ready to join a group of welcoming coworkers, only to find a few influential ones were very unwelcoming. Between malicious instant messaging, lunch cliques, and verbal disputes, the feeling of isolation became unbearable. During the final uncomfortable months, something occurred to me. I had lost sight of the reason I'd taken that job – to get to California. At that point I was only working there for fear of financial ruin, so I resigned. Living comfortably in California requires a healthy stream of income. I assumed I would run out of money quickly, and despite help from my soon-to-be wife's income, I did. I designed car interiors for Zap very briefly, but it was on the road to insolvency shared by other electric car startups. Tesla was evolving into a major automotive company and wasn't showing interest in my talents. Short on options, I began consulting at a product design firm in Palo Alto. The work took me away from home for weeks at a time, which was hard on a newlywed couple, but I learned enough to start my own consultancy from our home. By early 2012, I had founded a product development company specializing in bringing people's inventions to market. Since then, work on dozens of projects has created equity with potential value in the tens of millions. All of the things I'd requested in my quantum jump have come into fruition.

Though life was vastly improved, the various professional hardships I'd endured over the years still had me a bit, well, pissed off. There is an aspect of the superconscience that should cause a reevaluation of many of the interactions you have on the way to your destiny. Let me explain. For several years, I looked back in anger at people who had mistreated me during my various journeys. Some of them were unbelievably cruel, using the power of rumor and groupthink to twist words and turn others against me. I'd fantasize about paying some of them unexpected visits and introducing them to real cruelty. The problem was that these were not isolated incidents and I couldn't go through life avenging so many paths untaken. Had the NASCAR experience lived up to my vision of camaraderie and good times, I would've continued to travel the circuit with a very narrow perspective on life outside of racing. If the electric car company that I'd designed cars for been more solvent, I would have remained there until its eventual collapse – and been unhappily married to boot. And although the engineering manager at the connector company was tyrannical, he was also instrumental in my quantum jump across the country and all that resulted from it. Had he and a few others treated me with more kindness, I would probably be working in that unfulfilling job today. Whenever I come across people who, for some absurd reason stand in my path, frantically waving me off or cut me out of a picture, I consider whether my navigation needs adjustment. My resolve to succeed means that those who stand in my way must be incredibly brave, even to their own detriment. Many of those blocking my chosen paths did not emerge unscathed and some have undoubtedly been scarred from their dealings with me. In a way, they resemble the clowns at rodeos who jump in the ring to distract bulls so the fallen rider can escape. When I reflect now, I have to thank the rodeo clowns of the superconscience who've used their own blind ambitions to redirect me onto my path. They are my brothers and sisters. I also realize that if, for some reason, a clown was hurt or met its end under my hooves, that too was part of the plan and all is forgiven. People who seem like demons are really angels steering you toward your true destiny.

If you want to experience something vastly different in your life, you may have to make a quantum jump towards it. To get advice or even direction for your jump, consult with a doppelgänger of yours who's already done it successfully. In my case, a brief meditation led to a life-altering discussion with my doppelgänger. Prayer, visualization and quantum jumping are all forms of communication with the superconscience. Use the one that works best for you. If you get frustrated with one, give another a try. Quantum jumping grants very specific requests, yields advice on how to achieve them, and gets one into the rhythm of that success. Your doppelgänger is ready to guide you to an alternate reality.

HARNESSING HUMOR

One of the most interesting traits animals have is the ability to make fun. It amuses us to toss and roll objects, play keep away, and wrestle one another. Have you ever seen puppies, kittens or bear cubs at play? You can just tell they're happy and it makes us happy to watch them. A few animals also have the unique ability to laugh. Primates, birds, rodents and even dolphins have their own ways of laughing. When you hear kids play, the sound you'll hear most is laughter. Children laugh so often that it becomes part of the background like the chirping of birds. Yet something profound is occurring while they giggle and run. Children are learning to be social and developing their senses of humor. In a child's mind, everything is funny because it's unfamiliar and their inner critics haven't developed yet. Their brains are flooded with endorphins and it's contagious. I refer to my kids as little dopamine factories.

As we get older, we become more familiar with things that were once funny and our senses of humor become more ironic and sarcastic. It's not that we lose our humor, but as our lives and thoughts become more complex, fewer things shock us into laughter. To make most adults laugh, jokes and puns must be well-placed and clever. Adult laughter is a prize to behold. It releases feel-good chemicals in our brains, relieves pain and stress, promotes social bonding and benefits our long-term health. Human laughter comes from deep within the unconscious mind and is a way to signal cooperation and trust. Humor has motives and impacts beyond playfulness. It can also be used to groom others. Speakers commonly front-load their speeches with jokes in order to gain rapport with their audiences. Someone looking for a mate might try to use humor as a way to lower their subject's guard or to gage the reception of their presence. Humor is an extremely useful implement because it can alter the perspectives of those involved in the exchange. Harnessing the power of humor, both in yourself and in others, is the key to happiness and trust.

Of course, there are varying degrees of humor and reactions to it. There are the everyday truisms and the contrived chuckles we make in everyday conversation. There are positive and negative occurrences that surprise us for which laughter is a coping mechanism. Laughter can also result from shame or something that would normally be considered shameful. The acuteness of the laughter can vary widely from a forced chuckle to an uncontrollable group hysteria that will only subside when all the affected parties are out of breath. It can even strike us when we're alone and make us laugh and chuckle to ourselves. Although it's usually well-intended, humor can also belittle and frustrate people.

When you ask someone what traits they look for in friendship and in love, a sense of humor is usually near the top of the list. The ability to take a joke is just as important, even more so than the ability to deliver one. This is because people like others who are open to grooming. Laughing at someone's humor signals openness to their perspective and trust in their observations. There's no doubt that if you're genuinely making somebody laugh, you have their trust, at least for that moment. The ability to make others laugh is the ultimate skill to have in the social realm. Ever notice how some of the most popular movie and voice-over actors started out as comedians? It's because if someone has made you laugh, they've won your trust and welcome the idea of seeing (and hearing) them more often. It's also interesting to note that many comedians start their careers telling jokes that skirt the outer boundaries of socially acceptable material. Our minds seem to have a reaction to unspoken truths and scenarios that are all-together 'just wrong'. It's as if the human mind is near a cliff and a well-placed joke pushes it over, alleviating the tension and the fear of the subject altogether. Once many 'edgy' comedians have solidified their fame, they tend to tone down their jokes to be less risky and more widely acceptable.

I like pushing people off of cliffs with humor. Before I had kids, I dabbled in open-mic standup comedy. It was far outside of my comfort zone. I knew it had the potential to be a humbling experience given that I'd never performed in public. Mind you, this was stepping far out of the realm of engineering where I worked silently and only had a few technical discussions during the day. I had compiled a journal of funny ideas I wanted to deliver to an audience. Many of my routines were 'incorrect' given the political environment and audience I was pitching to. Still, I had the gift of humor amongst friends, coworkers and family. I could formulate a truth in my head and leave it cocked and ready to fire when least expected and wring laughter out of people. Connecting a string of cleverly placed jabs and punch lines within a one-way dialog to an audience who has been drinking for several hours is different than firing off one-liners in two-way conversations. In retrospect, what I was attempting was stage acting. My first act got a few laughs but bombed overall. When it was over, I decided to stay for the rest of the routines even though every molecule of my being wanted slip out the back door. I had to remind myself what I had gained from my short time on stage. I'd gone head-first into the unknown and witnessed the experience of expressing my humor to a large crowd. Though the audience and other comedians were not initially supportive, their honest reactions toughened and improved my routines over the following months. I began to utilize the few chuckles from the audience as rocket fuel to propel me to the next routine. I learned to shorten jokes when the crowd was more inebriated and use the microphone for sound effects. I would slowly build tension in a story and then loose it with a swift punchline. Eventually, the audience was laughing at about half of my jokes. I blame them for not getting the other half. I realized what I had set out to discover. Some things on my mind were relatable and I could communicate them through humor. Remember, humor is conjured by us and manifested in the superconscious and it changes perspectives, if not to positive ones, to tolerable ones. Humor is rewarding and can be used in many ways, the two most important being social bonding and trust-building. Here are a couple remarkable uses of humor:

Keeping Spirits Up – The most rewarding humor is personal. With a developed sense of humor about your own circumstances, you can heal mental wounds and foment the drive to go on. With a heightened sense of self-humor, you'll tend to take your circumstances a little less seriously and are more flexible. Flexibility is strength. Your own sense of humor is contagious and will likely affect those around you in a positive manner. MOE are naturally humorous, both in content and sense. Our understanding of true oneness makes everyone and everything around us relatable. When something is relatable, it has the potential to be funny. A sense of inevitability allows humor in all scenarios, including the darkest ones. Even things as disturbing as death are imminent and subject to comedic inference. The sense of humor of MOE is impervious to horror and disappointment. Some humor may be labeled dark, but if you understand the imminence of all things, you may laugh at all things. We know the vastness of possibility and reject the notion of limitations. The perspective of MOE is zoomed out, and our individual actions and interactions can seem quite insignificant. And it is funny.

Making Clowns - On one hand, we all love being clowns. If you can make a group of people erupt into laughter with a well-placed and clever witticism, you have what philosophers, comedians and rock stars seek – connection with an audience. But what about the scenario where you're being teased? To be laughed at for something you can't control or something you are ashamed of can be infuriating. Divisive humor can create a sense of isolation and torment. Remember that many people are merely rodeo clowns from the superconscience trying to corral you back onto your path. In so doing, some of them can be incredibly asinine. Teasing and harassment are two-way streets. If you spot a clown, you might as well treat them as such. Go ahead and have a hearty laugh at their expense. When you genuinely laugh at an opponent, it sends a few signals: 1) you're not afraid of them and 2) their actions are worthy of ridicule and 3) you are emotionally unaffected by their efforts. Humor is a great psychological tactic. Just make sure that the targets of your ridicule know that they can be redeemed and are not irreversibly clown material. In the absurdity of life, sometimes all we can do is point and laugh. And that's what we should be doing on our tours of Everything.

It's true that our senses of humor can be affected by age, culture and other circumstances. Being able to see the satire in life is an art and it takes humility, focus and practice. The first thing you have to do is get your mind oriented toward humor. Contemplating the absurdity of infinite existence is an excellent step in that direction. It's not only absurd, but hilarious! Let it awaken your inner child. The gigglier we are, the more we enjoy life and bond with others. The funnier we are, the more readily we're accepted by society. Groom others with humor whenever you can and remember to welcome their humor as well. Genuine laughter is one of life's greatest rewards.

USING THE BODY

As humans, we are gifted the most capable bodies in the world. Unless you had the misfortune of being born or stricken with any number of diseases or disabilities, you can run, jump, climb, swim and even fly (with the help of prosthetic wings). No, you can't run as fast as a bear, climb as well as a monkey or fly at will like a bird. The human anatomy is designed to be reasonably good at a broad range of things and therefore adaptable to many conditions. In addition to a fair amount of strength and agility, we have powerful minds which direct our actions in precise and efficient ways. Without formidable brains, our bodies would quickly fall victim to other animals or to the elements, but with them, our bodies are powerful implements that command the wild. While most of us are well aware of the human body's potential, only a small percentage of us use it to that potential. With the convenience of modern living, some of us see our bodies as mere enclosures for the brain, organs, nerves and muscles that make operating tablets and keyboards possible. The truth is that you're sitting on the ultimate off-road vehicle with the largest tool kit imaginable. We spend a lot of time tuning and repairing machines that do simple tasks very well, but our bodies are the ultimate machines and deserve much more attention than they typically get. If you're going to improve something, nudge the career, home and car projects aside and put some time into your body. Give it the nutrition and hydration it needs. Strengthen your muscles and reflexes and sharpen your mental acuity. Jobs, vehicles and people come and go, but our bodies are with us to the end.

In the past, people died from overworking their underfeded bodies. In the developed world, the situation has been inverted. Now we're underworking our overfed bodies. Our digestive systems struggle to keep up with influxes of sugar and fat from high-calorie meals and drinks while our spines degrade from the shoulders-forward posture acquired by typing on keyboards and using smart phones. Both of my parents eventually developed type 2 diabetes thanks to junk food and aversion to 'unnecessary' exercise. As an engineer and lover of good food, the possibility of developing diabetes is very real, but I see it fitness from a different perspective. In my youth I learned to enjoy the visceral feeling of being fit. Though I've struggled with cravings and the pull of sedentary living, I always thought it a shame to let one's body fall into disrepair. Thanks to an abundance of information on diet and nutrition afforded to my generation, I was able to identify the foods to avoid and those to embrace. I was a fortunate to have a healthy outlook because the draws of energy drinks, television, smart phones and video games have only strengthened over the years and many have given in to them. The key is to work and feed your body in a balanced way. The best part of getting healthier was an increase in endorphins. Better rest and more energy were also benefits, but nothing beats the feeling of positive brain chemistry.

Our bodies protect themselves with limit signals and warnings. This keeps us from injuring or wearing ourselves out prematurely but most human default limits are set pretty low. We can operate at a much higher intensity than the default limits allow. But what would you do with all that extra activity? How would you use it other than putting hours on a treadmill or pumping iron? There's nothing wrong with fitness training, but that energy can go towards more useful activities. One great example is using your body as a vehicle. If you have a destination a mile or two from home, try walking or jogging to it. Yeah, that makes weather, apparel, payload and safety an issue but you're stronger and safer than you think, running apparel looks very similar to other apparel and the weather can be somewhat predicted. If your destination is more than a couple miles away, try riding a bike. Again, weather and safety are factors but you'd be surprised at how fast you can get places on a bike with decent roads. I rediscovered the bicycle a few years ago as a rehabilitation tool for a knee injury. The years of riding have expanded my lungs, increased my endorphins and saved hundreds of gallons of gasoline. It's also kind of an adventure to navigate a bike around town. Bike riding has created many good memories for me. Another use of your body might be to improve your community. Can you imagine some of the energy expended on fitness training was spent picking up litter, mending fences, keeping neighborhoods safe or otherwise caring for people? It would require coordination but it would make a much bigger impact than fitness alone. Whether you use it to travel, improve or build, your body can do more than it's doing now.

- It's hard to believe some of the capabilities of the human body. Here are a few examples:

- Think a 26.2-mile marathon is a long run? Try 3100 miles over 52 days, averaging 60 miles per day. That's the Self-Transcendence ultramarathon. Worse yet, it takes place on a single city block in Queens, NY. Running that long with no change in scenery must be tortuous, but many runners have completed the race multiple times. (21)

- The human brain can store 2.5 million gigabytes of memory. Actual storage space is only a few gigabytes, about the same as a USB flash drive. Yet, neurons combine such that each one helps with many memories simultaneously, exponentially increasing the storage capacity. (22)

- Average life expectancy in the US rose from about 39.4 years in 1880 to 78.8 in 2020. It doubled in 140 years due to decreased infant mortality, fewer wars between major powers, improved health care and higher living standards. It decreased slightly for the first time since 1920 between 2015 and 2020 because of societal trends including unbalanced diets, sedentary lifestyles and increasing suicide and drug use. (23)

- The heart pumps 5.5 liters of blood per minute. During an average lifetime, it will pump nearly 1.5 million barrels of blood – enough to fill over 2000 train tankers.

- When the human brain is alerted to danger, adrenaline is released, accelerating the body's heart rate, increasing oxygen intake, dilating pupils and shutting down the digestive system to allow other muscles to contract with incredible force.

- Most amazing of all, the human body can procreate.

Your body is the vehicle for this fortunate perspective, at least for the rest of this life cycle. Any care or advantage you can give it will pay dividends. Here is a short list of ways to improve and preserve it:

Get the nutrition and hydration you need. Take multivitamins and eat fiber-rich foods when possible. Replace beef and pork with chicken and fish. Limit salt and sugar – drinks, pastries and breads are culprits. Stay quenched with water as much as possible. Fruit juice cut with water is a revelation.

Consider intermittent fasting. Skip a couple meals twice a week. It'll put you in a different state of mind, make you appreciate food and melt your visceral fat. Consult a medical professional first.

Get 7-8 hours of deep sleep whenever possible. If you snore or grind, get a mouthpiece and/or lose weight. If you have insomnia, find the cause and fix it. Many times, a busy digestive system can cause restless sleep. Limit caffeine…you won't need it.

Work your body. Get at least an hour of labor or exercise in each day. Elevate your heartbeat and keep it there for sustained periods. The best time is in the morning before eating. Ideally, the day's activities will include more activity and movement than most people are used to.

Limit digital device time including TV, internet, tablet, phone, video games whenever possible. There's no better way to make time fly without sufficient brain stimulation than with digital consumption. Digital products are powerful learning, working and entertainment tools, but don't let them steal your life from you. Even if you make your living programming, designing or vlogging, you should break free and get into nature now and then.

EXTREME OWNERSHIP

"Once people stop making excuses, stop blaming others and take ownership of everything in their lives, they are compelled to take action to solve their problems." – Jocko Willink

One trait that differentiates MOE from many other people is the same that separates some of the world's most elite warriors from the general populace – total ownership of their situations, decisions and actions. Navy SEAL Jocko Willink coined the term "extreme ownership" after an experience he had while commanding a multi-unit force in the city of Ramadi, Iraq in 2006. The fog of war caused a series of mistakes amongst the lower ranks and a friendly firefight ensued, killing a friendly Iraqi soldier and wounding a SEAL in Willink's unit. When he was ordered to debrief his senior officers and his SEAL group, he took complete ownership of the failure of his units as the commander on the battlefield. This was in spite of several of his subordinates attempting to take the blame for their individual shortcomings. Willink's senior officers were prepared to hear a lot of excuses and finger-pointing, but they were caught off guard by his unyielding ownership of the situation. Instead of firing him, the senior officers gained more trust in him. The men in his unit followed his example and took ownership of their problems as well. He had earned trust from them by demonstrating that he would never shirk his responsibility or pass the burden of command down to them. Jocko now trains corporate and military groups in the leadership strategy of extreme ownership.

Extreme ownership means taking total ownership of all aspects of your life. If you have a bad relationship, it's nobody's fault but your own, so fix it or forget it. If you are leading a group that is performing poorly, it's up to you to improve their performance as the leader. Even if you're not the leader of a group, you can take charge of a situation by declaring ownership of your problems and duties and set an example for others to follow. More often than not, owners are recognized as leaders, even without official titles. Commanding the missions, relationships and situations in your life with full possession provides the best chances for success. Ownership is contagious, and although it may sometimes offend the ego, its positive effects are well worth it. When an individual or team takes ownership, problems become recognized and solved rather than concealed or scapegoated. In addition to absorbing the accountability for things, also absorb the credit and absolute sense of pride that comes with owning Everything.

Undoubtedly, even the Navy SEALs would find the ownership practiced by MOE extreme. Acknowledging your position as Creator makes you the ultimate owner of Everything. This puts you in the driver's seat at all times. Not only do you own your part of the situation you are in, but reality itself. As you know, this doesn't mean controlling all outcomes. You are taking existence as it comes, just like everyone else. It means accepting responsibility for existence and doing your best to understand its makeup. It doesn't mean beating yourself or others up when things don't go as planned. It means navigating with confidence, fighting your best fight, accepting the imminent outcomes and applying lessons learned to future challenges. The benefit of acknowledging ownership is in taking the most active role in life. Once you've committed to the owner's role, you control more aspects of your experience, for better or worse. An argument that can be made against "owning all outcomes" is that one can't own what is physically beyond their control. That's true. If you're a passenger on a plane that has a major system failure and crashes into the ocean, you'd have no operational control over such a predicament. Ownership of such a situation, however unalterable, extends to reality itself. You intrinsically own all possibilities, including plane crashes. Understanding this can bring peace of mind and calm even in the most dire situations, increasing your chances of survival.

Extreme ownership is leadership, but not all leaders practice extreme ownership. Some leaders find themselves in their roles by appointment, inheritance or by bureaucratic shuffling. Many leaders who fail to own their situations become tyrants or are ousted in fits of fury. On the contrary, extreme owners create their own luck and are propelled by discipline, knowledge, decisive action and calculated risk. They may be described as rugged individuals and alpha personalities, but when extreme owners assume leadership roles, they truly lead. Some traits of extreme owners are less apparent. This is where the ancient Chinese general Sun Tzu's teachings on the "Art of War" coincide with extreme ownership.

Most of Sun Tzu's principles dealt with deceiving the enemy or at least not showing them your hand. One of his more popular bits of advice was to "*Appear weak when strong and strong when weak*". An extreme owner understands himself, his adversaries and his challenges. In situations where it isn't advantageous to be seen as a threat, some extreme owners will lay low or even feign weakness to buy themselves time or maintain ground without raising red flags or entering unnecessary conflicts. This is difficult for those whose character isn't timid or subdued, but extreme owners recognize when it's necessary. Another pillar of Sun Tzu's philosophy was that "*Supreme excellence consists of breaking the enemy's resistance without fighting*". It's difficult to get credit for a victory that hasn't been fought for, but extreme owners win untold victories through indirect means or by avoiding unnecessary or unwinnable conflicts. The fight still ensues, but "*He who will win knows when to fight and when not to fight*". Extreme owners may be seen ducking out of situations unexpectedly, only to emerge victorious in hindsight and far-removed from a potential conflict that would've wasted energy and slowed progress. "*Every battle is won before it is fought*" is another of Sun Tzu's principles that speaks to the ownership of being prepared for any and all contingencies. Most leaders, and especially extreme owners, are often seen preparing. Over time, they seem unusually lucky, but it is their preparedness that secures many of their victories.

Perhaps because of its association with the military, extreme ownership is described in terms of war strategy but it applies to all aspects of life. From successful collaboration to healthy relationships and achieving goals, true ownership of your reality will improve outcomes. As Creator, you must strive to understand the nature of this creation, it's peoples, laws and nuances. Be prepared for the reactions you may endure if you publicly proclaim your ownership of Everything. Although it is your right to declare, most people's reaction will probably be harsh if done at the wrong time or in the wrong context. Some may even conclude that you are controlling or crazy. In the current environment of anti-character humbleness fostered by religion, education and greater society, most will flatly reject any proclamation of oneness with God. Most don't want to accept the accountability that being Creator entails. Others may be worried that you would use your perceived power to subjugate them. It is better to exemplify oneness than to simply proclaim it. If it becomes necessary to explain the essence of your viewpoint, relay the Paradox to convey an understanding of NE. Oddly, relaying your views to someone else is redundant because you are quite literally speaking to yourself at a different spacetime location. Then again, maybe writing this book is redundant for the same reason. Nevertheless, enjoy your ownership because it's well-earned. It's truly an honor to be the most powerful being fathomable. Everything beyond this point is a tour of your creation and it will never cease to amaze. Whether you want it or not, it's yours.

APPLIED TO LIFE

PRE CONCEPTION

Perhaps the only thing more mysterious than what happens after we die is where we were before our conception. Where were you before you were conceived? For most of us, the image is of an angel spirit waiting its turn to live on Earth and hoping to be selected by two loving parents. Another common thought is that we're a family relative waiting to be reincarnated for a fresh round of life. That's one of my favorite spiritual scenarios, though it's only partially true. The truth is that before we were conceived we *were* our parents. Although many of us cringe at the idea of being a literal reproduction of our parents, it's a simple fact that we are. Before conception, we were very special cells. Although the conscious mind seems to emerge from nowhere, it is generated beginning from the time of conception. It's only when the system is completed and powered up that we begin to build (or rebuild) our understanding of reality. Cellular life regenerates itself to live as long as possible and, in the case of Earth life, that's billions of years. We are part of an unbroken chain of regeneration. It's helpful to imagine ourselves as flower-like. We begin as buds, progress to lush, pollinating flowers, produce fruit, wither and fall to the ground. Before we were buds, we existed within the plant. After completing a life cycle, we are shed but the overall plant (humanity) lives on for many more cycles, and thanks to us, many more locations.

The cellular explanation of conception shouldn't detract from the wonder of life or the existence of spiritual realms. We've arrived at this point through biological processes, yet there's something more metaphysical about it. If we are merely organisms, why do we have such complex feelings and emotions? Why are we drawn to fulfillment on a level that transcends our physical needs? Perhaps greater visions give us the drive to create and reproduce, but life does seem to have a purpose beyond survival. Living is a short defiance of the baron physics of matter and entropy. While our cells are alive, we get to move about and be active. Every action we take defies the stillness and emptiness of space. We extract energy from the matter around us and expend it in elegant displays of dynamism. Living provides a refined experience of what *would* be. Our unique positions in spacetime allow us to experience reality as solitary spirits, maintaining our spacetime identities while jumping from life to life. With each regeneration, we emerge completely reset and at the leading edge of humanity's perspective. When newly regenerated, we have to relearn the workings of life, sometimes as a vastly different kind of person or even a different sex. This allows for unique experiences and adds to intrigue and charm of living. With any luck, the generations that precede us share their knowledge and support us until we are capable of forging our own paths. This of course happens in all living organisms and the exhilaration of existence extends to all matter, not just living matter.

REINCARNATION

All you can be is what you are this moment. That's it, right? But what about in other spacetime? Could energy or memories from other positions that you've occupied follow you? There are many convincing accounts of purported reincarnation. Some people recall impossible details, presumably from lives they have lived previously. I've had my own suspicions about being a reincarnation of my grandfather. As a young child, I had dreams and visions I couldn't explain until I was older. In one of the dreams, I was in a bar with a lot of liquor and tough looking men. By the way people were dressed I interpreted the timeframe to be circa late 1940s or early 1950s. It wasn't until later in life that I would smell a similar combination of aging wooden floors, alcohol and cigarette smoke. In another dream, I was in a cold and slushy parking lot there were several American cars of various makes from the 1940's. I wouldn't have known what one of those cars looked like until I was much older. In yet another dream, I was working in a field spotted with enormous piles of black earth and trenches. An airplane with circles on its underwings flew over and I was terrified. I jumped into one of the holes and ducked for cover. The plane emitted a feeling of doom. In a final dream vision, I was walking through a large, muddy field and came upon a group of green tractors and jeeps and felt tremendous relief and camaraderie upon seeing them. Later in life, I was to learn that my grandfather had a tour of duty in WWII working as a lineman setting up communications in the Philippines. After the war, he had several jobs and one of them was bartending. He died in 1977 and I was born the following year. My mother said that when I was born, she looked at me and laughed because she instantly felt she had known me before. Perhaps the visions can be explained as subliminal knowledge gained through TV shows or movies, but those particular visions felt like first-hand accounts. Additional sensory inputs like smells are also compelling because they can't be conveyed through such media.

In my case, it's possible that reincarnation was merely biological. I am fully one quarter my grandfather. It's possible that genetic memory is so strong that recollections of actual events were imparted to me. He had six children, thirteen grandchildren and thirteen great grandchildren. He has been multiplied eight-fold (and counting) through reproduction. It is possible that my dreams and visions are his genetic memories. Why then did my mother not have similar visions? Half of her genes were his. Or what about my sisters or cousins? Perhaps they did and forgot or I just got a very prominent strain of his DNA. I also look and act like him according to some family members who knew him. I also find it curious that he died of lung cancer caused, in part, by smoking and I was born with asthma. I'm fairly certain I'd have picked up smoking in my teens had it not been for that. It does seem that spiritual reincarnation focuses on one individual whereas biological reincarnation is more of a dilution of certain characteristics and a direct expression of others across many offspring. The concept of spiritual reincarnation is more satisfying because we want to remain unique individuals, and not be 'diluted' by others. From the NE perspective there are no *others*, only more possibilities.

What about people who aren't related to the person whom they are believed to be reincarnated from? If information is passed during cellular reproduction, then how is it possible to remember something that someone with no relation to you did? It's possible that reincarnation works through entangled universal data. A concept of the entanglement of distant particles and the universal nature of quantum information was proposed by Dr. Stewart Emerhoff, director of consciousness studies at the University of Arizona. He was determined to understand the link between brain activity and consciousness. Emerhoff, along with British physicist Sir Rodger Penrose developed an argument for an eternal soul. At its root are tiny microstructures in the brain called microtubules. Microtubules are components inside cells comparable to microscopic bones. They form like forests in cells and determine the architecture and structure of the cells. Microtubules are perfectly designed as onboard computers, processing molecular data. This allows neurons and the brain to function as quantum computers. In conventional computing, signals move between components on traceable paths. In quantum computing, signals are transferred instantaneously across disconnected space using the 'wave function collapse' phenomenon of entanglement. Some neuroscientists believe that spatially separated neurons in the brain may be linked via quantum nonlocality, allowing instantaneous communication between them. A change in microtubules in one area of the brain can affect those in another. Quantum theory hypothesizes that all points in spacetime can contain quantum information. This means that the information in the microtubules can become entangled with information outside the brain. If the brain shuts down and the microtubules lose their state, the state of those microtubules and that of the whole brain may remain entangled with the universe at large. Our souls are made from something even more fundamental than neurons. They're constructed from the very fabric of the universe. The consciousness of our brains and their precursors have been in the universe all along. This data is an integral part of the superconscience. What we see as the soul could be quantum information. If all data is entangled, it remains so even after our physical bodies die (24). Since the original signal was sent via a human brain with a human perspective, it could be possible that another human could intercept the data, causing a perspective overlap. Additionally, we are the Creators of the superconscience and it is therefore possible that memories of past lives can be conjured in the process of creating the people in question. In other words, our past life scenarios may give birth to the identities of the people who supposedly lived them.

It seems to me that an individual perspective or spirit can in fact inhabit a new young life. Whether it's genetics or entangled quantum data is a mystery. As MOE, we know all realities are imminent and can conclude with certainty that reincarnation is real physically, spiritually and within the superconscience. Given the vastness of existence, the possibilities of future and past lives are as endless as our transcendence through them.

SURVIVAL

The most challenging obstacle to playing a physical role in existence is keeping our vital systems functioning. A beating heart, breathing lungs, functional brain and many other organs need nourishment, care and protection. In humans the biological algorithms for survival are astoundingly sophisticated. Our complex systems are at the root of our versatility as a species. We've shed our need for large stomachs and fur in favor of cooked food and clothing. We've traded the ability to run at great speed with more efficient upright walking. We no longer have tails because we don't need to counterbalance a head atop a vertical spine. Most importantly, our cognitive capacity has allowed us to pass intricate knowledge and myths to one another. For the moment, we are the most dominant animal the planet has yet seen. Still, as in ancient times, our basic needs remain unchanged. We must fuel and hydrate our bodies, maintain our shelters and trade with other members of society to survive. Survival resides at the top of our list of achievements. For organic lifeforms, it's survival first and everything else second. Survival of the most complex organism with multifaceted living circumstances is easier said than done. It forms the basis of our conscious and subconscious thoughts, actions and desires. The need to survive has shaped our bodies, cultures, cities, landscapes and our interactions with other species. Since survival is the fundamental motive for much of our activity, understanding its pull on our psyche is an important means of mastering your perspective.

How important is survival to you? First, let's define survival. Survival is the state of continuing to live as a conscious system with functioning organs and cells. The key word here is *conscious*. If your organs and cells function but you are in a vegetative state, you haven't survived despite being alive. On the other hand, if your organs are functioning artificially, but your brain is alive and conscious then you have survived. If we examine it from a zoomed-out perspective, survival is ensured on a macro scale by infinite existence within Everything and on a micro scale by biological chemistry. Survival and death are phases of existence in perpetual flux. Regardless of phase, we remain part of an infinite system. So, back to the importance of survival. You are here for a reason. Although you will embody infinite combinations and configurations, this one is unique and necessary. Your formation from trillions of cells is a miracle. Everything you've done to this point is extraordinary. Given that, there are several positions people take on survival:

Survive at All Costs – To have the best chance of experiencing what life has to offer, some believe the best strategy is to survive as long as possible. Imagine how much the life of a young soldier or gang member would be extended if they hadn't found themselves dodging bullets. The young often have no idea what the world has in store for them. A surviving life could transcend decades and affect hundreds of other lives and many future generations. Reproduction is another benefit of survival and is the only way to physically outlive your body. Strict survival is most beneficial from childhood through young adulthood as there is a significant portion of life that can be protected by adherence to it. Still, there are some pitfalls to surviving at all costs. Firstly, it makes people risk-averse which can add up to cowardice or the missing of opportunities. Secondly, many people swear by this ideology for their entire lives. Protecting yourself for too long is pointless. Unless after seventy-five years old, you're the sole provider or caregiver for someone, then grab a cigar and cancel your yearly checkup. Ask someone who's ninety how they did it and they'll tell you they don't recommend it. Survival for survival's sake has a limit unless you have an illogical fear of dying.

Take Life as It Comes – The majority of us have this outlook. We do what we can to survive, but also understand the futility of trying to live forever. We know that our bodies and all their systems have limited lifecycles and it only takes one system failure or disease to bring us to mortality. People in this category avoid unnecessary risk, but occasionally indulge in pleasurable activities and risk compromising their longevity. Smoking, drinking, recreational drug use, fatty foods and fast driving are all activities that people like these do from time to time. This is probably the most amicable approach to life because of its balance between practical risks and rewards. They can maintain themselves in daily life but step up to the plate when opportunity, adventure or danger calls. Nevertheless, balance is the key to happiness here. Most of us who take life as it comes tend to lean one way or another. Some tend toward risk aversion and end up leading only slightly more interesting lives than those who survive at all costs. Others become addicted to some aspects of the risky activities and become unhealthy or unreliable. The best way to take life as it comes is to practice daily discipline while engaging in the occasional indulgence or calculated risk. If you find yourself listing too far in one direction, correct it.

Risk Takers – I live, I die, I live again. That is the stance taken by some warriors and others whose circumstances or need for adrenaline leave little hope for graduating to old age. It may also be the stance of many adaptors of NE. It is the absolute truth that you live and die perpetually and death is an unalterable fate. Why not increase the tempo and keep it interesting? Even those of us with other options may take big risks for a chance at greatness or infamy. You'll see risk takers at the top of most societies. They are groundbreakers in sports, business, politics, innovation and the arts. What you might not see is that only a small minority of risk takers end up at the top. The rest are at or near the bottom. That's how it goes in the realms of high stakes – you win big or lose big. That's why risk-takers are so admirable when they succeed. When the positive results of risk are plainly visible, most wish they had the same 'vision'. Risk taking involves a probability of failure that most find uncomfortable. Some survive failure and others are destroyed by it. Those who survive do so because they acknowledge their rolls in their situations and trek onward. They don't simply say, "I can't help myself" or "someone else is at fault". They own their decisions. Risk has great rewards, but ownership and perseverance are the keys to achieving great things with it.

Each position on survival has its virtues and drawbacks. The position you take, like so many other aspects of life, depends on the experiences you want to have. My position is to take life as it comes and take calculated risks when there is fruit to be had. I want to prolong my life, especially with the knowledge of NE, but I don't want to settle for dullness. Furthermore, I understand that the basic truth of NE doesn't change when the body dies. Although I reside in an incredibly rare state of self-awareness and physical ability, the Paradox offers infinite varieties of this very state. From this perspective, there is no fear of wasting instances of perfection or failing to complete things. There is only the present experience regardless of its circumstances. There is no correct position on survival, but perhaps there is a more comfortable one for you. Take a deep look at your position and decide if it's serving, limiting or endangering you. Survival instinct is deeply engrained in the psyche and isn't easily altered. In my experience, knowledge of the Paradox eliminates the fear of death and galvanizes the will to survive. Both of these things increase the quality of life.

RELIGION

When we reach the point where survival doesn't occupy all of our waking hours, we have time to ponder other subject matter. We also belong to the only species proven capable of fathoming complex metaphysical propositions. Inevitably, that leads to a quest for meaning beyond earthly existence and religion is born. Religion is the belief in and worship of a superhuman controlling power. As an essential component of mankind's experience, religion promotes unity, cultural vibrance, impressive determination and fellowship amongst people. The principles of charity in Christianity and Islam are inspirational examples of the goodwill generated by religious faiths. The goals of dharma in Hinduism and Buddhism are equally commendable guidelines to live by. In the past millennia, religion has acted as a social mortar bonding communities, cultures and nations in common causes. The brotherhood of man has benefitted in untold ways through the religious faithful. Its power over the human race has produced some of the most beautiful architecture, artwork and ceremonies known to man. One need only view the pre-renaissance paintings of the life of Jesus in the Arena Chapel to appreciate the timeless beauty of religious mind's eye. The creative driving force of religion has caused man to build with fervor and devotion. The meticulous and massive buildings created as tributes to Buddha, Jesus, Vishnu, Mohammad and other divinities suggests man's true desire to connect with the heavens. From Mayan temples to modern American churches, religious architecture is unquestionably among the most awesome in the world.

Religion has kept large populations obedient while providing lessons in morality and causes to strive for. The words in religious texts offer instruction in living by the word of the Creators of mankind. The majority of religions promote peace and order, which are both necessities for collective survival. Religion acts to answer questions through stories, fables and occasional historical references. As we know, the fables contain truths as all realities are imminent. It is our sense of a higher purpose that gives us the motivation to continue in the midst of life's challenges.

Unfortunately, traditional religion has also been a source of exclusion, persecution and conflict between peoples. As with other competing principles, ideological differences between religions and even various denominations of fraternal religions cause interpersonal and cultural friction. The conflicts are generated by differing accounts of creation, deities and the rules we must follow to acknowledge and satisfy them. In the schools of religion, only one account can be true. This causes competing religions to be irrelevant or even sacrilegious to one another. Most religions stipulate the rejection of all others as a prerequisite to membership and to salvation. It is necessary for these ideologies to narrow the focus of their supporters to the scopes of their scriptures. The foundational events in major religions occurred in times before there were reliable ways to document them. Therefore, devotees are left trusting the words of early adopters who often left no more than abstract tales or poems and lived many years after the events supposedly occurred. Even scholars and archaeologists have trouble piecing together locations and timelines. This certainly worked to the favor of false disciples and corrupt mullahs whose goals were less than noble. Limited ideologies require sterile environments in which to maintain their austere and, many times, outdated guidelines for their followers. Though most of their edicts are benevolent, religion's status as an incontestable moral compass has been used as a scapegoat for struggles rooted in other causes. As we know, modern wars are more frequently fought over natural resources, alliances and expansionism than over religious beliefs. Nevertheless, religion gets credit for many of these conflicts. Given those ailments, the most fatal flaw in the way traditional religion has been administered lies within its exclusivity. Insisting that one account of divinity is truer than others and demanding that believers of other versions be corrected, converted or suppressed is one cause for the waning acceptance of traditional religion.

Mankind is continually searching for one beautiful explanation or equation to answer all of our questions. So far, the explanations offered have left many a soul-searcher at a crossroads between mysticism and science. To accept one wholly rejects the other on a fundamental level. If you choose science, you must abandon many core aspects of religion and declare "if we can't observe it, it might not be true". If the latter is your chosen path, you must ignore many scientific facts in order to accept the experiences and stories of your religion's disciples, sight unseen. This would be a blind leap of faith given religion's malleable nature in the hands of its purveyors. Moreover, ancient religious accounts lack the broadness of the cosmos that modern cosmologists have since discovered. The most common religious trains of thought start and end on this celestial body. The settings of our lives, the afterlife, heaven, hell and reincarnations are all in, on or above planet Earth. Religions use Earth-like descriptions for spiritual occurrences because there was little knowledge of what was beyond Earth when their stories were formulated. Science has a low tolerance for blind faith. Scientific theory is only proven if it can be observed consistently. Regardless of how longstanding it may be, a scientific theory may be disproven by a single contradicting observation. Conversely, some religious edicts evade the burden of proof due to the insistence of faith over doubt. It's not surprising that the chosen methodology mankind is using to decipher the operation of the universe in the post-Renaissance era is science. After all, SpaceX doesn't rely on faith when launching rockets. It relies on proven electronic, mechanical, aerodynamic and thermodynamic principles to launch them. It is true that most religions have come to accept and embrace science. Religious leaders are trying to come to terms with scientific facts that would've been considered incompatible with faith not so long ago. Unfortunately for them, it is science that is driving mankind's progress and is perhaps creating a reversal of fortune for the concept of most religions.

Once, religion was brutally unwelcoming of science, even as possible evidence of the God's creativity. Now the relationship is inverted as people participate in the scientific endeavors that generate power, prosperity and progress. By enlarge, time spent kneeling to pray has been replaced by time spent searching the internet and creating digital files. Interestingly, instead of relying on brutality or suppression, science is taking a more effective course of evolutionary dominance. It coexists with religion, sharing the fruits of its advancement while slowly constricting its habitat and means of reproduction. There may even be last minute attempts by sympathetic technologists to protect traditional religion from extinction, but the time for that is short and evolution is quite irreversible.

Still, there remains a need to reconcile the spiritual realm in context of the physical realm. Scientific knowledge only describes a portion of reality. Though science regularly extends our view of the universe, its need for observable proof prevents deeper conclusions. Modern scientists are bound by physics and they must describe unseen events using probabilities and approximations. While the conclusions they render are more readily accepted than those of religious doctrine, scientific theories will never fully satisfy our spiritual curiosity. Measuring the timing of the Big Bang tells us nothing about why it happened, however fascinating and valuable it is to know. Even if we knew why it happened, it would only serve to unfold another layer of the multiverse and allow us to gaze deeper into it as our time on Earth grows shorter. The most valuable spiritual knowledge gained from space exploration is that the universe is indeed inconceivably vast and there are countless possibilities which are stranger than what any religions have described. It is understandable that many of us feel unsatisfied with both religious and scientific explanations of existence. We find ourselves with a choice: either go along with implausible ancient scripture in hopes that it will lead to a spiritual pardon or be satisfied in observing the scientific laws and physical boundaries that make up our foreseeable universe without reaching any spiritual conclusions.

For a growing number of us, there is a limbo state between spirituality and logic. Logic tells us that religious teachings are merely meant to instill morality and loyalty in the faithful. We know that there is a higher purpose but find it difficult to believe what religion tells us. On the other hand, science proves to us that we can use the world around us to achieve what would once have been regarded as magical. Still, science doesn't even attempt to answer the metaphysical questions that religion claims to have the answers to. The realm of science begins when we're born and ends where we die. We want to understand and be at peace with what occurs after death.

The common view is that religion is dying. In most of the world, traditional religion has been weakened by the issues mentioned above. This is true, but let's review the definition of religion. Religion is the belief in and worship of a superhuman controlling power. There are many controlling powers in the universe, but to be considered divine by definition they must also be worshipped. So, what is worship? Worship is defined as the expression of reverence and adoration for something or someone. The term is usually applied to deities and gods, but reverence and adoration apply to a great number of things. Science, social movements, corporations, sports franchises, extraterrestrials, digital interfaces and celestial objects are worshipped under that definition. Some of us even worship other humans whom we see as superhuman in some capacity. When viewed from that perspective, the scope of religion broadens.

There are many divine aspects of reality and in most cases we choose the ones to focus our energies on. If we concentrate on subjects that aren't traditionally considered divine, we are told that we are faithless or atheist. In all cases, we have faith and devotion. It's just as inappropriate to tell a sports worshipper that he lacks faith as it is to tell a Hindu priest the same thing. Both have their own faiths born of their cultures. Many nontraditional worshippers still identify themselves as traditionally religious while practicing their primary religions in earnest. They feel it keeps them in good standing with society and in the spiritual realm. Traditional religion allows deferral to a higher authority and avoid ownership of actions or unpleasant confrontations. Identifying as religious also averts any suspicion of being a sinner or infidel. One can use religion for protection or as a scapegoat if need be. Traditional religions see man as separate from God. This is why I could never quite get behind a religion. Whereas the revelation of NE empowers us beyond our imaginations, traditional religion tends to humble us into passivity. Members of most traditional religions will argue that although there are many aspects to and avenues in life, God covers all of them. This is completely true in principle. Although you may be temporarily diverting your focus to scientific endeavors, corporate growth or football games, you are doing it in the kingdom of God. A similar argument can be made on behalf of NE. Although we are focused elsewhere, we are operating under an all-encompassing principle. The purpose of this thought exercise is to consider what we think of as religion and worship and broaden their definitions to include things we really participate in. Many of the things we do could be considered by definition to be religious activities.

It should be understood that NE is not atheism or nihilism. It is the opposite of both. NE observes all beliefs and ways of life, embracing and looking upon them with wonder and joy. At last – all occurrences, imagined or not, are possible and therefore existent. The next time you feel guilty about not focusing on your spiritual growth, not attending church or focusing too much on one aspect of life, remember your true religion and embrace it with zeal. The next time someone asks you if you are religious or if you have God in your life, feel free to honestly affirm it. Your church is everywhere and buildings are just official places to gather. It's okay to know the Paradox and have religion. It doesn't mean you have to abandon your traditions or culture. Foundations of other myths which were previously irreconcilable with your own are no longer, for now all things are true. The idea of deities watching over us like parental figures, promising favor and blessings if we do good and punish bad deeds is comforting and motivational. In Everything, these very deities exist, carefully watching over us. A person of religious faith should have no issue with NE, as it fully proves the prophecies, scriptures and customs upheld as sacred.

As promised in the introduction, you now know all in the realm of the metaphysical. It all happens. All of the religions of the world work their miracles as their doctrines dictate the trajectories and moralities of great multitudes on Earth. Christians go to heaven or hell depending on their lifetime morals and achievements. Muslim martyrs enjoy their after-life paradises as infidels accept their fates as the eternally damned. Hindus and Buddhists continue to work on dharma and their knowledge of Atman and Brahman. Even the Greek, Roman and Celtic deities retain their swords, lightning bolts, axes and hammers. Yet still, trillions of other combinations of ethereal existences circulate just under the veil of our current dimension. There are billions of Jesuses, Muhammads, Osirises, Vishnus, Odens and others. This is occurring as all realities are imminent. NE invites all beliefs, theories and Paradoxes to be experienced without fear of retribution. You may ask MOE if the prophet Muhammad is God's prophet and you will get a resounding, 'Yes'. Ask MOE if Jesus is our savior, and you will probably get 'Absolutely'. You see, NE acknowledges all possible realities. MOE has no scapegoat, for MOE is in complete control. NE proves all possible occurrence. Therefore, all is possible and imminent. Involvement in the Everything continuum makes one a participant in the divine at all times. Even if one spends their life in a factory or staring at a monitor, they participate in the divine, nonetheless. Most of us choose how we spend our time and usually vary our activities enough to create some semblance of balance. Participating in the monotonous does not exclude one from participating in the divine.

Is NE religion? While NE satisfies the requirements to be defined as a religion, it also transcends religion fundamentally. NE may certainly evoke worship, but its subjects are not obliged to do so. NE is certainly the ultimate controlling power. Existence is unavoidable and perpetual. Being separate from or unequal to NE would be impossible as you are its essential element. Herein lies a critical point at which NE transcends religion: there is no distinction between you and Everything. If you exist, you embody NE. You need not exert yourself to obtain or maintain membership. All exist as contemplations within it. Try as you may, your membership cannot be withdrawn. While all participate, only a select few are aware of it. If there is any higher purpose in NE, it is to be awakened to these facts and therefore become MOE. This merely requires understanding the Paradox. I've spent several years testing its validity against other beliefs. To this day, there has not been one question it failed to answer. There has not been one person, action, position, scenario or time that it has contradicted. It has made failure impossible, and at the same time unavoidable. It has explained, without doubt, all. The chasm between science and spirituality is no more. The distinction between past, present and future is merely a compass used to navigate the perspectives we have taken. Within NE, all is one.

GOOD AND EVIL

By now, you'll have already predicted the NE stance on good and evil. They're perspective dependent and therefore subjective. This is one of the core concepts riveted to every facet of NE. Without an understanding of good/evil relativity, we'd have to live in a world where evil lurks around every corner and preys upon goodness. We'd have to struggle to convince ourselves that our intentions are 'good' while disregarding the 'evil' deeds we commit to survive. Believing in the delineation of good and evil is incredibly limiting, if not outright superstitious. Good vs evil is a personal but arbitrary distinction that each of us makes. Where we split the two is heavily influenced by our upbringing, culture and other factors that shape our views. The boundaries between good and evil tend to move throughout our lives and depend heavily on personal experiences. Society recognizes common boundaries and enforces them to an extent via manmade laws, but each of us has our own personal definitions of how good and evil are defined.

Many of us believe that evil is spiritual in nature and driven by forces beyond our control. The common view is that God is behind all creation and benevolence while Satan is behind all destruction and evil. This provides convenient origins to situations that go well and ones that don't. While the NE perspective acknowledges the existence of both deities, no form of existence is evil. Satan may be the main adversary of God and man but exists only as a possibility, just like everything else. Evil exists only as formulated within the superconscience. It's like a childhood bogeyman who relies on the collective beliefs of children for him to manifest. Yet, the vast majority of people still subscribe to the myth of evil. Though Everything is, we don't have to subscribe to such a divisive myth.

Some conclusions can be drawn from the removal of distinction between good and evil. One conclusion is that, while nothing is evil, nothing is good either. This is a matter of individual assessment. As someone who prefers the brighter side of life, I discard notions of evil and embrace notions of infinite possibility. Within Everything, all possibility is good. Depending on your perspective, some possibilities may be contrary to your preferences or even your well-being. Still, they remain experiences which intersect with our worldlines. An exceedingly rare intersection with our worldline makes any event very special. When you consider the size of the galaxy, let alone the solar system, human interaction is a microscopic cluster of activity. The victims of mass shootings, crazed psychopaths, brutal dictators, abuse, drunk drivers and natural disasters indeed suffer tragedies. The tragedies are unlucky elements of this tiny cluster, but that doesn't make them any less special. All the ways we intersect with nature and one another are unique and imminent.

NE has something in common with Voodoo in that it can be practiced with positive or negative intentions. Neither is more virtuous than the other. Just as a battery has positive and negative terminals, both polarities exist to induce flow. The path you use depends on the results you require at your location in the spacetime continuum. Beware of following a negative path with no intention of it leading to positivity because it might result in more profound darkness than you bargained for. Positive action is most relatable to the human perspective. The light in our lives illuminates an optimistic vision of Everything, and we're generally interested in navigating through positive experiences. Again, fate takes us on many winding paths and each is imminent. The path you use is the path that is necessary. If happiness is your goal, choose to stay in the light and approach 'evil' with a new perspective.

KINDNESS

Kindness if one of those things that makes societies work. Like humor, it is both a purpose and a reward. It's also an evolved trait of survival and produces some of the best experiences that life has to offer. In nature, we most often see kindness between mothers and their babies, couples and intrinsic to small groups. However, it is most profound when it is directed towards those outside our immediate families or tribes and to those who expect it least. We all appreciate the receipt of kindness. When people are good to each other, everyone benefits.

Due to the positive reactions people have to it, it's common for kindness to be used as a disguise for other motives. Whether we realize it or not, kindness is often used to get what we want from others. In a competitive world, we use whatever advantages we can to gain favor. We all put on smiles, shake hands, offer coffee, hold doors and make small talk. Superficial kindness is pleasant, but we should be aware of the effect it has on people. Superficiality keeps people on their toes and suspicious of the motivations of others. It is due to this that people must go to great lengths to prove sincerity to those who we do not know. Even with the best intentions, sometimes kindness isn't recognized or received well. Some acts of kindness even add tension to relationships if they're interpreted as insincere or out of touch. The saying, "no good deed goes unpunished" certainly rings true when an honest attempt to offer kindness doesn't translate.

Some acts of kindness might even appear as the opposite of kind. Many of the ways that parents instill discipline in their children come off as mean when the parent is merely trying to impart useful knowledge to the child. It takes years for some kind acts to be recognized for what they are. Sometimes, we benefit from acts of kindness that we're not even aware of. Genuine kindness often goes uncredited. The truly kind are concerned only with their effects on others. They are kind whether or not the recipient knows or even accepts it.

To increase the effectiveness of our kind gestures, we should understand our true motivations. I received a piercing bit of truth from an Israeli man once. My wife was one of his son's high school teachers and upon his son's graduation, the man, Doran, and his partner invited us out for dinner to celebrate. Their two adopted sons had varying levels of cognitive disabilities. The oldest, who'd graduated from the school where my wife taught, was capable of eventual independence. The younger of the two had more severe mental impairment and would likely always need care. They were adopted from Ukraine as toddlers. The boys had been malnourished and neglected as infants, presumably leading to their disabilities. The couple, a successful jeweler and an attorney, adopted both of the boys knowing full-well the challenges and heartbreak raising children with special needs would bring. At some point in the meal, I felt compelled to tell Doran how noble I thought it was that they had adopted children with disabilities. His response still sticks with me today. "The things we do in life, we do to make *ourselves* feel better. Yes, the boys' lives are improved over what they would have been, but it brought *us* happiness." And he continued eating as if what he said was an obvious truth. He had unabashedly revealed his motivation to do an incredibly kind thing and it wasn't what I expected to hear. His honesty to himself and to us was profound. He wasn't trying to fool himself or anyone else into thinking he was a saint or savior. Doran was a master of kindness and I wouldn't be surprised if he had used that mastery in other areas in his of his life.

Although it doesn't always matter what drives kindness, it is helpful for us to know our own motivations behind it. There are times when we care for those who have no way of returning the favor, such as in the case of the elderly, ill or disabled. Those are genuine acts of kindness. Yet, serving others heals some of our own internal wounds. Our lives are full of conflicting feelings about what we must do to survive and be happy. Directing kindness where possible helps quell some of those feelings.

From the NE perspective, kindness is imminent and ubiquitous. It works subtly in all areas of our lives. Most kind acts are habitual and superficial, but deep kindness comes from a feeling of oneness with others. Oneness is a cornerstone of NE, making MOE a perfect conduit for genuine kindness. Kindness creates an aura around its source and feeds positive energy into our perspectives. Those who are perceived as kind are aligned with the needs of others and are frequently called to fulfil those needs. Occasionally, being kind can lead to lucrative situations, but more importantly it can lead to personal fulfilment. Being kind takes courage because it requires risk. It also requires you to expose yourself and risk embarrassment. Even if your kindness isn't well received, take comfort in knowing it was offered. Regardless of what some may say, we live in one of the kindest eras in human history. In many ways, the NE perspective is a benefactor of such kindness. More than ever, people value their own lives and those of others. Some even extend kindness to animals and insects. When others offer you kind words and gestures, accept them as well-earned reward for committing to the ultimate reality.

KARMA

The oldest traditional religion, Hinduism, has its roots and customs dated back over four thousand years. It's lack of a founder, prophets, structure or a finite beginning or end to time put it squarely in the category of 'NE-like' belief systems. One Hindu principle that we can all relate to is karma. The term *karma* originated from the Sanskrit root 'kri' which means to 'act and react'. The Hindu concept of karma is a system in which beneficial effects are derived from past beneficial actions and harmful effects are derived from past harmful actions throughout a soul's reincarnated lives (25). If there was a need for justice within Everything, it would take the form of karma,

Though the most familiar expression is *karma*, nearly all religions define similar systems of cause and effect. It seems as though the concept of karma is a natural offshoot of the human psyche. No matter your stance or religion, there's some part of us that feels if a 'good' deed is done, then a kind of universal spiritual credit is earned. The same goes for negative or 'evil' deeds. Karma balances the accounts between people who would otherwise have a heavily lopsided existence. Even as MOE, I must admit that my sense of karma is strong. For some reason I have an expectation of magical reimbursement for catching a spider and throwing it outside rather than crushing it and flushing it down the toilet. I also feel strongly that treating others well might yield a reciprocation by the superconscience. By NE logic, karma is absolute. When all is imminent, all possibilities play out and some of them look like karma. Karma is real in the same sense that all other phenomena are real; it is conceivable. Perhaps the concept of karma is a subsystem of the human psyche that keeps us working together. There is certainly a survival component to the idea of karma. The belief in it, good and bad, keeps us straight with one another. In this sense, karma is more of a natural interaction between humans than the product of benevolence or transgression in a past life.

Karma works hand-in-hand with empathy. When we're perceiving karma, we're panning to the perspective of the person or thing affected by our actions. Karma is a reward for empathy and punishment for indifference. It does seem that good things come to those who do 'good' and bad things eventually come to those who do 'bad', but the real key to understanding our perception of karma is in one's self-image. When someone does something that is in line with the wishes of others, they receive positive reinforcement and kind words. When they do something contrary to their wishes, they get reprimanded or worse. Eventually, the signals we receive effect our states of mind and expectations of ourselves. These signals can affect our own views of what life has in store for us. Ask an angelic pillar of your community where their fate lies and they will tell you something drastically different than if you were to ask a recidivous convict the same thing. Part of their reasoning will stem from what society tells them and the rest will derive from their own feelings about themselves and their past actions. People decide for themselves if they're good or bad, sometimes from an early age. It's important for us to reject notions that people are inherently bad or evil whenever possible. It's also important to reject all notions that we are bad or evil ourselves. Yes, constructive input is critical to guiding us, especially the young. But we receive a myriad of signals throughout our lives and should disregard those without liberating qualities. We mustn't assume that our actions or fates are subjects of karma. All possibility is good and therefore all deeds are good. Scores settle themselves in much more complex ways than we can imagine. All outcomes are imminent and every minute is a chance to live well and cause a rush of positivity and good fortune.

LOVE AND RELATIONSHIPS

"Love is composed of a single soul inhabiting two bodies."
- Aristotle

If you ask anyone what the world needs more of, the answer will inevitably be love. Some believe love holds the very universe together. Love is the primary driver of many beneficial traits and deeds that we interpret as good. It may not hold the universe together, but it certainly holds civilizations together. The warm feeling of caring and being cared for by others is one of the greatest rewards in life. We've already discussed other rewarding experiences that give us purpose – religion, humor, kindness, etc. Of all, love is the experience that is held in the highest regard by most. Logical people will tell you that love is a chemical reaction created by our brains to draw us closer to our mates and tribes and keep us from killing our children. Whether a biological phenomenon or a divine gift, we feel love and do its bidding throughout our lives. When viewed in context of NE, there are two kinds of love – proximate and universal.

PROXIMATE LOVE

Proximate love is the emotion we feel toward other people, animals and objects that have direct contact and influence in our lives. It is heavily affected by evolutionary traits, familiarity, neurology and environmental realities. While it is traditionally treated as individual and singular, love is actually a myriad of different emotions. Our most intense desires, needs and defensive instincts all factor into the makeup of proximate love. Many times, the catch-all word *love* receives undue credit or blame for many of our actions. Acts of lust, greed, cowardice, revenge, oppression and abandonment have all been shrouded, knowingly or unwittingly, under the guise of love. The emotions that make up proximate love can fluctuate in proportion and result in behavior that ranges from healthy and productive to obsessive and suicidal. In this way, proximate love is like a color printer, regulating three primary colors to produce hundreds of different hues and shades.

The force of gravity between two objects is inversely proportional to the square of the distance between them. Something similar is true of proximate love. That's not to say the farther away someone is, the less you love them, but rather the less you see or hear of someone, the weaker their influence on your thoughts. This is only natural. The people closest to us have a greater effect on our daily lives and receive more of our attention in return. It's natural to feel less emotionally connected to people outside your circle of influence. If we had acute familial love for everyone in the world, nothing would get accomplished. We would instead spend all of our time hugging, conversing and emailing. To some, that sounds like a wonderful way to spend life but it wouldn't leave any time for survival or progress. The evolutionary components of proximate love are apparent in some of the differences between male and female social behavior. Women spend more time nurturing relationships because, historically, relationships with their male counterparts and their families were key to their survival and prosperity. Men are less apt to invest time into nurturing relationships because it takes precious time from tasks related to procuring survival and prosperity from outside the family unit. Being a protector and harvester of trappings requires more callous mannerisms and avoidance of emotions that may entangle and divert one from their missions. The historically distinct roles of women and men are becoming blurred as modern technology allows both to do similar work and live similar lives, but our physical and mental evolutionary traits remain. Proximate relationships and love are the keys to our well-being and happiness. We must always be aware of how connected and linked they are with our physical makeup. As previously mentioned, love may be scapegoated by other motivations. For MOE, extreme ownership of life won't allow such substitutions. Balancing proximate relationships is just as important as balancing sleep or diet. Many conditions must be satisfied for an acceptable balance, but once it is obtained, you may focus through a wider perspective with a healthy mindset. A nourished heart is a big advantage in the realm of perspective.

Driving in traffic provides a good analogy for balance of proximate relationships and love. When you're driving, you control most of the variables required to get to your destination without incident. As long as you keep gas in the tank, stay alert, avoid hurrying and use the car's safety features, the overwhelming odds of arriving safely at your destination are in your favor. There are also variables you can't control when you're driving. You may brush with the fate of another driver who runs a red light or run into unexpected bad weather. In life, you control what you can and accept fate when you can't. The same applies to relationships. If you have an unusual amount of drama or strife in your life, there's probably a few variables that need to change. The keys to good relationships are far more elusive and confusing than those for good driving. Understanding the workings of your relationships may require perspective alteration and looking at yourself from another's perspective. Considering how you are perceived by others is a powerful insight into fixing relationships. After all, you can't know what's wrong with a car if you don't get out and look under the hood. You may also search for patterns to make or break to improve outcomes. Maybe the type of person you have relationships with should be altered. Perhaps there's nothing to improve in your relationships and you want to maintain the balance and attend to the needs of others. In any case, you hold most of the cards and odds are that the outcome is yours to determine.

Love can be projected to other species and even objects. Animals, plants, machines and even locations can become objects of our affection. Although not as ideally suited to interact with as humans are, pets receive and return love with few conditions. Man has domesticated animals for over ten thousand years and many species have evolved to rely on us, physically and emotionally. Relationships with animals can be very fulfilling, but they too require balance to prosper. If someone puts the welfare of their animals ahead of themselves, or conversely, fails to give an animal proper care, an imbalance will exist and the love will become parasitic rather than beneficial.

To a much smaller extent, inanimate things may also command our hearts. A car you own, a house you live in or a town you grew up in can all be loved. It won't return the favor other than serving the purpose that won our affection, but it can be loved just the same. As in other proximate relationships, these depend on our mental and environmental conditions and can manifest in a variety of ways. Love of inanimate objects is a constant challenge for modern humans and has led to many fruitless years spent and battles fought. Be wary of love for *things* in any more depth than appreciation or builder's pride. As the sayings go, "the things you own indeed own you" and, "you can't take any of it with you". Manmade objects come and go in our lives and the only real value they add is in their enhancement of our time in the living realm. Enjoy objects and surroundings but be ready to sacrifice them at a moment's notice to maintain true balance in love and life.

UNIVERSAL LOVE

Everything is one. Beneath all of our other thoughts and emotions is a oneness. That oneness is signified by universal love. It can be summoned, regardless of proximity, chemistry, species or molecular status. Universal love is far-reaching and independent of location. When we have spiritual or near-death experiences, it is universal love that is described as a calming, welcoming feeling. It could be said that love for a spiritual deity is universal in nature, as that deity does not occupy the same dimension, yet still reciprocates love, but universal love is one of equals rather than one of worship.

On a universal level, you and all divinities are one within Everything.

When drowned out by other emotions and instincts, universal love is indistinguishable from our environment. It doesn't fluctuate like proximate love because it exists independently from our qualities, moods and situations. It remains constant like a distant horizon or gravity. Its consistency makes universal love a reliable source of warmth, calm and balance. Again, because of its uniformity and subtle presence, most people are unaware of it. Universal love is one of the most powerful implements in our quest for balance. To use it, we need to bring it from the background to the foreground by amplifying its signal. Amplified universal love has many positive effects. It can project a sense of belonging, peace and warmth as part of our basic persona. It calms the turbulence of proximate relationships and helps reduce our dependence on relationships that are problematic or non-productive. The positive relationships we have prosper in the glow of true belonging and kinship provided by universal love.

So, how do we amplify universal love? First, we must be able to discern it from other feelings. Recall that universal love operates in the background like the hiss of radio static. To get a sense of it, you must quiet all other noises (in this case, emotions and thoughts). The best way to quiet the mind is to enter a meditative state. Some do it by sitting alone in a quiet place, closing their eyes and breathing deeply while counting down from ten to one. Others sit on the floor, legs crossed, chakras aligned and listen to music composed for meditation. Still others just go on a nature walk. Once you've reached a calm and clear mental state, you should feel a sense of oneness with and acceptance of your surroundings. Unfettered by the concerns of daily life and immersed in the moment, you'll be in tune with the superconscience. No matter where you look or what you focus on, you'll feel a familiarity and unconditional inclusion. That feeling is universal love. All of us have felt it and its almost impossible to get through a day without encountering it. It's as ubiquitous as the air we breathe. When we go hiking in the wilderness, driving or walking through a garden, some of the feeling of refreshment and centering is that of universal love. As simple as it is, it's important to recognize it as an accessible feature of conscious reality.

All too often, universal love resides in the background and gets smothered by our immediate needs and busy routines. Its subtle nature means a tendency to blend in with the scenery. Once you recognize it, you can amplify it and use it whenever necessary to restore balance to unbalanced emotions. With practice, you'll realize that you don't need a quiet, peaceful place to connect with it. Just recall the feeling and that it applies in all spacetime locations. Once you've established a connection with universal love, amplify it and disregard any contradictory thoughts or emotions. The more you promote it to the forefront of your mind, the more it can inform your actions and project an aura of true oneness with the superconscience. This is a powerful exercise that, when used with other forms of perspective alteration (panning, zooming and flowing), will keep your emotions optimized and your actions in line with your true nature.

GAINING AND LOSING LOVE

In its distilled form, love is care. We care for many things. The objects of our affection range from partners, children, parents, siblings, neighbors and friends to music, locations, eras of time, ancestors, animals, dwellings and machines. Some love awaits us when we're born and some is found along our worldlines. Some love is elusive and hard to keep and some is intrusive and hard to shake. Some love stays with us throughout life, and some leaves us suddenly. Love enters and exits from all angles. It may intersect our paths briefly or stay with us indefinitely. If we're lucky, we get to be near the people and things we care about and our affections are reciprocated by them. So, what makes us care so much? There are countless causes for love, but they all require an intersection of fates which results in pleasant feelings for one or both parties. Pleasant intersections create positive bookmarks in spacetime that we'd like to revisit. Some love causes two or more paths to remain parallel, making our loved ones accessible for extended periods. Of course, not all worldline intersections are loving or pleasurable. At best, some encounters could be considered collisions. All intersections are special and candidates for love.

If all relationships lasted forever we wouldn't have time to properly appreciate them. Some relationships must end to make way for new ones. We have limited mental capacity and therefore a limited capacity for relationships. One can only keep track of so much before the overall quality of our attention suffers. In any case, we fall in and out of love throughout our lives. Whether by choice or coincidence, the emergence and loss of love are some of our most exhilarating and traumatic experiences. Humans desire permanence. We want love to last forever. Some of us are lucky enough to have relationships that outlast our time on Earth, but we all eventually go through the loss of someone close. Even losing a pet can feel like losing a close relative. Death causes us to pause and consider the temporary nature of life and segmented perspectives.

When it comes to gaining and losing love, there's something that every MOE must remember. Nothing is ever gained or lost, only experienced. When we encounter someone or something, we experience charismatic perspective in a particular volume of spacetime. As time unfolds, that perspective may evolve, or even disappear from view. It's natural to feel down and miss someone or something that has engaged our perspective in a positive way. Just remember that Everything has always existed and always will. Remarkable comfort can be found in knowing that death is merely a transition of focus. The ones you love have always been with you and will always be. Aristotle's assertion that love is comprised of a single soul sharing two bodies is profound. From the NE perspective, we are one consciousness experiencing ourselves at various spacetime locations. Interactions and outcomes are all inevitable in the superconscience, but they are fleeting. A feeling of universal love should permeate all of your experiences. We created Everything and are experiencing it, bit by bit, infinitely. Contemplation of existence is the greatest love.

PURSUIT VS. IDLENESS

Potential exists only as realized by its owner.

To put it mildly, pursuit is the spice of life but in the context of NE, a question arises: To what extent should we actively pursue possibilities versus letting them pursue us? If all eventually comes to pass and everything is inevitable, then pursuit is illusory. True as that is, it's also true that pursuits and all that they entail are inevitable. If actively and passionately participating in your journey is not your inclination, then your proximate destiny is likely a dull or tragic one. Yet, understand that you are already irrevocably committed to the most wonderous adventure of all - *existence*. Although you may be idle now, you will certainly be involved in just as many adventures as anyone or *anything* else.

Can you handle the boredom or negative consequences of inaction? If the answer is yes, then maybe idleness is for you. If the answer is no, it means there is some latent energy in your being that, if kept contained, will burn from the inside until its last embers fizzle out. We can all agree that there are only so many hours in a day and we can't pursue everything that dangles before our eyes. Still, most of us would be amazed by how much can be won by willful action. Fear of failure or of wasting resources keeps many of us on unnecessarily narrow paths. But failure is as much a part of pursuit as the reward. The best pursuers become familiar with failure early on and learn from their mistakes. As for wasting of resources, there are many instances where conservation wins the day but being overly conservative can lead to failure as well. No pursuit is made without some amount of sacrifice.

The excitement of success and the frustration of failure are both forthcoming in our destinies. If that seems deterministic, that's because it is. In virtual existence where all possibilities are contemplated, all pursuits are inevitable. If you choose not to pursue something, your decision should be free of guilt and when the window of opportunity finally closes, it should not take up precious space in your mind. If you decide to pursue something, it is your chance to experience a unique quest and its imminent result, for better or worse. As a resident of Everything, your mission is to experience all contemplations through infinite perspectives. As Creator, you possess the ultimate will. You're going to experience it anyway, so if you are so inclined, you should experience it now.

No one is continually idle and none are continually in pursuit. We spend about a third of our lives sleeping and otherwise resting. When other basic tasks like cooking, eating, grooming, cleaning and driving are factored in, that leaves only about a third of our time to work towards our goals. To be effective, we have to use that time wisely. As someone who is inclined toward pursuit, I find myself organizing goals into four categories: short-term, near-term, mid-term and long-term. Short term goals range from seconds to hours in scope and include things like driving, shopping, communicating, organizing and planning. Near-term goals span from hours to days and include things like research, planning, day adventures, entertaining, building or repairing. Short and near-term achievements sustain our lives and stabilize our heading to larger pursuits. We should be careful not to get consumed by them and keep an eye on broader interests. Those with average lives and careers have settled into a comfortable spot and sustained themselves there. If you want to do more than merely sustain, you must strive for bigger accomplishments.

Mid-term goals span from weeks to months and include things like overhauls, proposals, landmark occasions, large building projects, political action, self-improvement and education. These goals are done incrementally and their susceptibility to interruptions make them difficult to complete. In mid-term pursuits, each day you are presented with a choice to carry on with it or leave it lie. The longer a goal takes to complete, the less likely we are to complete it. Dieting and learning languages fit well into this category. Mid-term goals require careful shuffling and prioritizing as they change status between active and inactive. Success in these pursuits set us up well for our long-term pursuits. Long-term pursuits span from years to decades and include family building, financial planning, expertise and legacy building. Long-term pursuits are our endgames. Once these goals are accomplished, there's little to do but savor the memories or embark on new pursuits. To succeed in the long-term, completing ever-growing tasks in the near and mid-term is a good policy.

And then there's circumstance. What if you want to pursue something, but are unable because of an unalterable situation? A blind person can't be an airplane pilot and someone in poverty can't travel the world, at least not in the immediate future. It's a frustrating dilemma to want something that is completely out of reach but that doesn't mean you're idle in those endeavors. Recall that all others are merely you at different spacetime locations and you can enjoy their experiences vicariously. You can appreciate the perspective of those who are doing what you would like to. Videos, pictures and books allow us glimpses into their experiences. Some can even be recreated in modified forms as in the Paralympics. Never give up on achieving your pursuits but understand that you will eventually experience all, regardless of your circumstances. Do what you can when you want to. It'll all happen sooner or later.

CONSERVATION VS. CONSUMPTION

Living means consuming. The conversion of mass into energy is what keeps us alive. Consumption is really conversion. To say that you consume wood is to say that you relocate and convert pieces of felled and organized lumber into their final useable products. To say that you consume air is to say that your lungs inhale and absorb oxygen from it and convert the oxygen into cellular energy. The challenge posed by consumptive living is that resources are sometimes limited. This causes us to either consume what we have and search for more, or to conserve it. The more complex an organism is, the more it must consume to survive. For millions of years, Homo sapiens and their predecessors lived on the edge of starvation and predation. Because of that, we're hard-wired to consume whatever and whenever we can. In modernity, we've become accustomed to relatively easy obtention of supplies. Some of us overconsume and waste resources because we can't or won't curb habits that provide comfort in the short-term. Along with our propensity to consume whatever we can is another impulse from our days of scarce living – conservation. Conservation kicks in when resources run low. If addressed appropriately, the impulse to conserve is just as useful to survival as the impulse to consume. As humans, we must decide whether consumption or conservation is best for the situation at hand.

Our existence on Earth is fortunate, fragile and temporary. It's been established that this planet is vastly distant from other possibly habitable places. From satellites, we can see the effects we've had on the Earth like never before. With our surveillance technologies, we have a bird's-eye view of the changes its undergone in the past 50 years. We are left estimating the time we have to change course, escape to another habitable place or accept the consequences of overtaxing the planet's resources. Technology developed over the past century has elevated billions of people from loyal subjects of our environment to the masters of its consumption. Given the melting of polar ice, warming of ocean currents and mass extinctions of global species, we are rightly concerned about our future and the loss of Earth's serene environments. Homo sapiens have brought extinctions to every continent since our cognitive revolution around 70,000 years ago. Vulnerable eco systems that took millions of years to construct are being burned or crushed under the treads of tractors as they cut and strip trees at an alarming pace. Frustratingly, we're also able to see Earth's beauty in high-definition video documentaries like "Planet Earth" as we wish for the futile situation to change. The problem seems to be that humans are too successful and prolific. We're consuming resources faster than they can be replaced, but perhaps that is the natural order of things.

We can't escape the energy-intensive technologies that reduce human effort while accelerating the warming of the lower atmosphere. Most of what we touch is molded in plastic, cast in metal or carved from wood. We enjoy the benefits of industrial production as we recline in seats wrapped in animal skin while being propelled across the atmosphere on rapidly expanding hydrocarbon molecules. We're all contributors, even the most outspoken of environmentalists. It's luxurious but dumbfounding when viewed from the perspective of the inhabitant of a lonesome, unicorn planet. How could we knowingly destroy our habitat? Our actions don't mean we've lost the love for it. I have yet to meet someone who lacks a visceral connection to Earth. We all love our planet's natural landscapes and wildlife. Even those who more brazenly ravage nature enjoy deep breaths of clean forest air, cool drinks of water and bright orange sunsets. We ignore our dependence on Earth out of convenience or to stay employed. It is short-sided, but true.

Due to continued global population growth and international competition, it appears that there will be an extreme draw on resources for the foreseeable future, regardless of the actions of the influential people and nations. The developed world is trying to relay the importance of conservation to developing countries, some of which control valuable rainforests or other habitats. Although setting the example of conservation is noble, it is viewed differently by the developing world. "Going green" after 150 years of stripping nature's resources sends a signal of virtue that rings hollow in countries with GDPs lower than some US cities. In their eyes, the developed world had its dirty decades and they are now having theirs. Although everyone can see the need to conserve, we're in a race to develop, not unlike an arms race. In light of this, the mindset has become, "if I don't use it, someone else will". Will the developing world topple the peak in an effort to ascend it? Should man's progress be thwarted to prevent further damage to the environment and procure more time to transform society or escape to another planet? Do we have enough resources and ingenuity to support growing populations while doing this? Should we conserve our resources or to continue the high rate of consumption to accelerate advancements in technology? These are the most pressing quandaries for mankind.

Accelerating progress has its merits. Humanity is inclined toward progress and human progress is nearly impossible to contain. Technological advancement has proven to be a resource multiplier as evidenced in the industries of food production, digital communication and materials engineering. There are many examples of innovation leading to unexpected abundance. It seems as though innovation always steps up to meet the demands of evermore energy and material-intensive activities. At the moment, we're advancing as efficiently as we have the patience for. Slowing down to conserve comes at a cost of losing opportunities to those who don't. When survival requires you burn every last ounce of firewood, you burn it and hope you can find a more plentiful source of heat the next time around. We're hardwired to do whatever it takes to succeed in the present. Truth be told, it's been a rewarding strategy thus far. Humans have discovered new resources and technologies to support our advancements, even while undergoing exponential population growth. The key to accelerating progress with limited resources is focusing resources on worthwhile causes. It is more important to develop viable sources of energy than it is to nation-build in war-torn regions of the world. It is more important to decipher spacetime travel than to build weapons systems. Right now, we're doing it all, but we should focus more on what's important.

The truth is that humans can't destroy Earth. We can make it difficult for life to thrive for many decades, but Earth itself would remain relatively unchanged. All of our nuclear weapons combined don't add up to the power of a super volcano eruption or a meteor the size of Mt. Everest. Even those natural cataclysms leave mere pockmarks on Earth's surface. Earth doesn't care what happens on her surface or what humans do. If you look into the violent and desolate history of Earth, you'll see that oxygen levels and biodiversity are currently at unprecedented levels compared to the bleak periods before and between the previous five extinctions. Mankind is a natural, albeit transitory phenomenon. Nothing we do is unnatural. Nuclear fusion, biological engineering, mining, farming, warfighter planes, discarded garbage, forest stripping and burning – all are natural phenomena originating on Earth. As unnatural as we sometimes feel, when a wider view is taken, we can see ourselves as a cellular structure. We organize, purify and crystalize Earth's elements using fuels trapped inside the Earth's crust to bring other elements to higher energy levels. We'll use some of those elements to travel beyond Earth to other celestial bodies or even galaxies. Keep in mind that we, and all the things we produce, are atoms derived from Earth. We are natural. Whatever event caused our sudden leap into hyper production was driven, in part, by our natural evolution. Our environment is something that should be conserved as much as possible, but in the near-term it may prove hopeless. We know where we are, what it took to get here and that it is currently unsustainable. We also know that evolution got us here and has plans for us elsewhere in the universe.

The environment is just one area of life that is touched by the negotiation between conservation and consumption. We're constantly balancing money, relationships, materials and time with those two principles in mind. NE encourages the recognition of infinite abundance while emphasizing the importance of conservation to life balance. You reside in but one of an infinite number of environments and you are uniquely tuned for this one. Your instinct to conserve will get you through tough times but do not fear consumption. There will always be enough for what you are to experience.

ACHIEVEMENT

If Everything is complete, is further achievement possible? The answer is no. All is complete. Nevertheless, we do interact with our creation and observe limitless possibilities, perspectives, quests and outcomes. Within the vastness of creation, we'll experience something we identify as achievement. To be accurate, achievement is a culmination of events that sum up to be perceived as beneficial to future experiences. From the NE perspective, the ultimate achievement is existence and within Everything, all will be achieved. However, for the sake of alignment with society in the 21st century, we'll discuss achievement in the context that we're more accustomed to – working towards goals and obtaining them.

The need to achieve has a natural pull on all of us. Even the most basic forward progress in life is made as a series of small achievements. Walking across a room is an achievement as well as eating, speaking and sleeping. Survival is an achievement. We achieve from the minute of our conception through our final exhaled breaths. Still, the achievements that interest us are more elusive. They require conscious effort and perseverance. They require plotting and planning. They take cunning and skill. When achievements are realized, we are rewarded with a euphoric sense of accomplishment. The reward is not arbitrary or trivial. It's a direct release of pleasure chemicals in the brain which declares, "Success!", "Access granted!", "Your reward is forthcoming!", "You did the right thing!", "You deserve this!" and "Let's do it again!". These internal affirmations propel us through what otherwise would be a long, monotonous life.

Our approaches to achievement vary. Some achieve only to gain minimally satisfactory results while others have insatiable appetites for success. Some aim to gain passage in spiritual realms while others want to leave legacies for future generations. The reasons for achievement are abundant, non-exclusive and can be intermingled with one another. They can also change at any time for many reasons: philosophy, conflict, financial stability, culture, family, age, mental conditions to name a few. The possibilities for achievement are limitless, but there are definite examples we can observe and analyze from the NE perspective. This is a broad topic. Achievement could mean many things to many people. To some, it's the perfect dance. To others, it's beating the odds. To yet others, it means exacting revenge or destroying something or someone. Achievements multiply as they are undertaken. Whatever an achievement entails, many other achievements might spawn in its wake. As previously mentioned, achievement is virtual, but that doesn't exempt one from experiencing it. You might as well play the role that suits you best – the one that defines you.

As we've learned, much of what we gain, lose and accomplish is subjective. Prosperity, success and achievement are all relative. However, just because something relies on perspective doesn't mean we shouldn't enhance our experience by pursuing it. It just means we should consider our ambitions from multiple angles to better understand the implications of such pursuits. We all have an idea for what 'real' achievements are. Take respect for example. Why is it important to be respected? It's important for the same reason that we want to be envied. Respect, at its core, is envy of character. Character is something that can't be bought and must always be developed. Some believe respect can be gained though demands or intimidation, but they are mistaken. There is no substitute for genuine respect. The problem with fear-induced respect is that the fearful often seek ways to go around or subdue those whom they fear. It is possible to be both respected and feared, but fear does not translate directly to respect. Character is the correct ingredient for cultivating genuine respect. If your goal is to achieve respect, your aim should be to build character. Building character will lead you to more respectable actions. Another good example of achievement is notoriety. Some of us want to be noticed, preferably in a positive light. Some desire it so much that they don't care if the notoriety is positive or negative. To be known for something satiates a very deep need for significance. There's nothing wrong with wanting to stand out, but from the NE perspective, existence guarantees significance and therefore notoriety. In existence, you have Nothing to prove.

Yet another example of achievement is familial bliss. This tends to elude more and more people. There are many theories on how to achieve it, and there are many variables at play. The biggest obstruction to modern familial bliss is the sense of insulation and isolation between family members and a lacking sense of unity. This is exacerbated by the mental escapes offered by the internet and digital devices. It can be remedied by recalling and projecting the oneness of NE. When family members pull back, remove the devices that separate you and embrace them. In upcoming sections, we'll cover major achievements like wealth, careers and legacy in more depth. The purpose of considering these examples is in understanding the true underpinnings of what we think of as achievements. Your tour of Everything will have you cycling between molecular states, dimensions and universes. The next time you feel unloved, remember that you *are* existence and are therefore eternally unified. Enjoy those around you as much as possible.

WORK AND CAREERS

Pre-civilization Homo sapiens were required to specialize in many areas to survive. Hunter-gatherers possessed skills in every facet of life including making clothes, weaponry, hunting, plant life and shelter building. There were few patterns to follow. It is said that hunter-gatherer brains were larger than ours by roughly a tennis ball due to the diversity of tasks required for survival. As agriculture created permanence, communities densified and our lives simplified. The need to roam the countryside and follow migratory patterns was greatly reduced. Eventually, we were no longer nomadic and our shelters became permanent, thus paving the way for civilization. From that point forward, our lives were more systematic and predictable. Once the Homo sapiens psyche was harmonized with the patterns of the harvest, the variety of skills needed to survive was replaced by repetition and specialization. Since then, we've moved beyond subsistence farming to industrial agriculture. The majority of us no longer farm, freeing us up to experience life beyond the limits of cultivation. Modern society is much more sophisticated than nomadic tribalism but there is less variety in our individual daily activities. Today, the jobs we do are focused on one or a handful of areas. The resulting trend of work specialization has allowed immense advancement, but there is a cost associated with this simplification. While it allows us to produce more efficiently for the masses, it can leave our brains and psyches starved for variety. Try as we may to simulate variety through sport and recreation, it is missing by enlarge.

In the last few millennia, particularly in the last several centuries, one's survival and sense of achievement has been crystallized in the form of a trade or career. One of the inevitable questions asked after an introduction to someone is: 'What do you do?' In the literal sense, that's a broad question, but we know what is meant is: 'How do you make your money?' From that small piece of information, one might draw conclusions about your societal status, interests, income or intelligence. It is true that one's career says a lot about their life, but it's a mistake to equate that to one's lifetime achievements. Many of our achievements arise through our jobs, but not all of them. You could be an accountant by day and a comedian or spy by night. You could be a successful racecar driver yet spend your life obsessing over the minute details of racetrack idiosyncrasies or lost races. Your job title tells only a portion of the story.

Why do you work? If you're like most people, you do it to make money to trade for food and shelter. If there's any money left over, you can save it or trade it for any number of desirable experiences. A significant portion of our lives are spent working, even if we're not being paid for it. Shopping, cleaning, childcare, entertaining and hobbies are also work, but they occupy different categories than the careers we get paid for. Some of us may have several or even simultaneous careers in our lives. Careers eventually define our life's work, though some of the most important things we do in life, like raising families, are viewed as separate matters. In many cases, careers are merely support mechanisms and have little to do with our missions or desired experiences in life. When you retire, you'll look back on your career. Wouldn't it be nice to know that the largest portion of your day was aligned with your life's true missions?

Your true missions are more important than what you do for a living. For a lucky few, our careers align with our missions and lead to lucrative financial situations. For others, life's missions are incompatible with financial success. Artistic, philosophical, heroic and philanthropic accomplishments are often only appreciated postmortem. The prospect of financial insecurity keeps most of us away from our true callings and in lock step with the status quo. If certain things were easy, everyone would be doing them. On the other end of the spectrum, the prospect of wealth can entice some people to work endlessly for hollow returns. Understand that if you think your mission is to become wealthy or powerful, you are ignorant of your mission. Wealth and power are but means to accomplish ends, not the ends in themselves.

When most people decide what they want to do in life, they consider things like income, social status and daily job tasks. To better set our headings to fulfillment, we should define our careers based on our life's missions. The question shouldn't be what jobs we want to do, it should be what we'd like to accomplish in our lifetimes. In defining a life mission, the reasons for working must be much more introspective. Instead of defining an income you'd like to have, you should consider how to finance your goals or whether they need financing. Instead of focusing on the superficial status provided by your career, a better gauge might be the influence your work will have on others. Approaching life from a mission-oriented perspective may require several different careers. On our way to our life's true accomplishments, multiple hats will certainly be required. The people we meet and the things we learn along the way may affect how we perceive things and may even alter our objectives. Careers may lead directly to our goals as in the case of an ER doctor saving lives, or indirectly as in the case of a medical scientist researching cures and treatments. Either way, the things you learn are critical in accomplishing your mission. Maintain your heading and don't let career-spawned obligations get between you and your true objectives.

Sometimes we aren't clear on what our missions are until later in life. Although it's a big advantage to take aim early, some missions come only through life experience. When I chose to be a mechanical engineer, it was based primarily on my desire to design cars. I saw highways as veins and cars as cells. I wanted to be the DNA that shaped the cells flowing through the world's roadways. That was to be my way of putting my signature on the world. As a young man, the perceived status and income of engineers were also factors in my decision. My career did eventually lead to car design, and although there were highs, it wasn't as climactic as I'd imagined. In my early 30's I started to consider the later years of my life. I imagined looking back on my accomplishments and seeing all these corroded, inanimate objects. Maybe a car or two would be in a museum. Perhaps my future grandchildren would see my aesthetic vision and wonder if they had inherited that gift.

In the first ten years of engineering, I learned that making *things* can envelop one's life. I began to consider whether designing expensive cars was a worthwhile mission to devote my life to. NE had been a factor in much of my drive and fulfillment throughout those ten years, but philosophy wasn't something I considered a viable direction to take. I needed more life experience in a vastly different place to realize that mission. After I made a quantum jump to California, it began to take shape. Over some of the most tumultuous years our world has yet seen, it became clear to me that an explanation of existence was in order. I still had a lot of work ahead of me. I used my engineering knowledge as an implement for several more years while I started a family and further distilled the Paradox. As it turns out, my initial career choice was not erroneous. It was the foundation from which this knowledge could be articulated. No career choice is wrong. When you do something, it was meant to be done. Those things I made had to get made. It was every bit as important as any other mission. Eventually, you'll do it all. In the realm of virtual free will, we can choose the proximate paths that we take. Still, there are times when we don't get to choose our work because of desperate circumstances like war, poverty or natural disasters. Even in those situations, there may be a small window through which you can reach your true destiny. I still design and make things. It's become more of a therapeutic pastime than a life mission. I build for enjoyment but am grateful for the opportunity to pursue my true calling as a conduit of the Paradox.

Deciding on the work we do based on life missions instead of material gains or social status is a good way to orient your ambitions. Remember that the impacts we have and how we make money can be separate things. It's always an advantage to have our careers and missions in alignment, but not totally necessary. Don't let your identity get overshadowed by the work you do. Remember that careers typically span only part of our lives and are not the most important aspects of us. It has been said that if you enjoy your work, you never work a day in your life. There's truth in that statement, but not all work is enjoyable without perspective alteration. Work should be seen as a part of your life rather than the heart of it. The most important achievement a human can make is prolonged happiness. Make sure that while you're working, you're living. Success may take decades and those decades can't be replaced. Don't get too caught up in making things. The truth is that nothing is really made, just reorganized. The luckiest of us love our work yet participate fully in all areas of our lives.

MONEY AND POSSESSION

"It's not the man who has too little, but the man who craves more, that is poor." - Seneca

You have untold wealth. Realizing it is a matter of changing your perception. The perceptions of others will follow, allowing you to exercise your wealth. In society, the standard method of obtaining services and possessions is through monetary exchange. One day, you're living in a small house with leaky plumbing. A few million dollars later, you're in a beautiful villa overlooking the ocean and enjoying the misty spray of dual shower heads. Because of its convenience and interchangeability, money is engrained in all aspects of life including food, shelter, trade, travel and social interaction. If you ask most people what they really want as a gift, you'll inevitably hear, 'money'. Money lubricates our lives in wonderful ways. The more of it we have, the more secure we feel in society. Ask anyone the definition of success and the first item on the list is usually money, the second being power and the third being nice possessions. In most instances, money can buy the latter two. Money is society's way of giving credit, regardless of how it is accumulated. With money, you can accomplish things that you couldn't otherwise. You may not be able to sew a stitch, but with money, you can dress like a master seamster. You may not be strong, but you can hire strong people to protect you. It's easy to buy into the myth of ability when you have enough money. In that way, it can foster arrogant behavior. Still, it is true that success leads to money, and vice versa. Even the most practical of us have to admit that money buys us the freedom to do what we love. Not surprisingly, making more money is at the top of nearly every person's to-do list at some point.

Think of all the times you wished you were a billionaire and ask yourself why. Having such wealth would command instant respect, enable unlimited possession and allow you to live life free of menial tasks. But ask an heiress, lottery winner or oligarch if extreme wealth has made them happy and their answer may surprise you. Winning the lottery or being born into wealth denies a person the ability to succeed in their own right. Even if they do accomplish something great, it will be assumed that they couldn't have done it without help from their good fortune. People in those situations must achieve beyond their perceived financial privileges to claim their own accomplishments. Even those who are accredited as self-made must deal with the avalanche of accountability and responsibility that their fortunes necessitate. Money can create as many problems as it solves. As useful as it is, it only gives us the *perception* of ownership. Perceived ownership begets perceived responsibility and the stresses involved with it. Most wealthy people will describe their circumstances to the effect of "heavy lies the crown", and they're not lying.

Even with all its pitfalls, money is alluring and we all know that if we had more, we'd handle it just fine. So, the question is, how do we get more of it? One could say that investing in stocks is an easy way to gain wealth. Just go online, open a Charles Schwab account and buy five dollars of a penny-stock that will increase in worth by two percent that day. The next day, sell the stock and re-invest the proceeds into another stock that will grow by two percent that day. Continue the two-percent daily profit and you'll have ten million dollars by year's end. You could also choose winning lottery numbers or stumble on a vein of gold jutting out of a country hillside. A more practical and reliable means of making money is to convince other people to give it to you in exchange for something. You could trade favors, labor, products or even advice for money. Trading is what working members of society do and it works well for most. The vulnerable, the gullible, the earth and the animals from which resources are freely exploited are its unavoidable casualties. In most instances, the trades we make allow us to survive but leave us wanting more. This need is amplified when we can see what some others possess as a result of their trading. Envy ensures that one never quite has enough as they strive for the next acquisition. In the end, we exploit what we can and trade with society to get what we think we need. In no way is this bad, wrong or backward. It's the unique way that mankind operates and succeeds in the world. We all need the societies that trading supports, like it or not.

The result of our work in life is a series of experiences. Those experiences are heavily influenced by our perceptions. From the NE perspective, the question isn't how to obtain more wealth or power. The question is how to perceive that which we already have. This is a completely foreign exercise for most. To someone who has experienced only limited ownership, it seems delusional. The truth is that you own all of the structures, vehicles, machines, projects and people in the world. Still, you may find yourself separated from or locked out of the things you own. Much of what we own is hard to access without validation because people are assigned to guard valuable things. We must remind them that we are the legitimate owners. The standard way of doing this is monetary exchange. But then there are other methods including written agreements, emotional connections, demonstrations of skill, heartfelt pleas, becoming influential or even intimidation. In the end, we are really just gaining access to what we already own. Once you can see it in this way, you've transcended the need for conventional wealth and you can go about shaping your experiences as the richest, most powerful person alive.

LEGACY

"What you leave behind is not what is engraved in stone monuments, but what is woven into the lives of others." - Pericles

There is something in all of us that desires our life's work to outlive us. If we can't be immortal, maybe something we do while we're alive can be. Legacies mean different things to different people. Before you decide what yours means to you, it helps to define what is meant by a legacy. A legacy is any action that has an effect after its original performer, or legator, dies or retires from the activity. It is possible to be alive and see your legacy take form, but it's uncommon. The majority of us will not get to witness our legacies, for better or worse. Legacies can span anywhere from a few years to millions of years. In fact, the amount of time that a legacy survives has a lot to do with its subject. Living creatures aren't the only things that leave legacies. Celestial and geological events dwarf those left by biological processes in both time and scope. Nevertheless, we're concerned about the legacies of life, and human lives in particular. On a human scale, there are three categories of human legacy: micro, great and super.

Most people deal in microlegacies. Microlegacies are created throughout life and include things like business development, family structures, habits, superficial fame, material possessions and estates. When most think about their legacy, these topics are some of the first to come to mind. Microlegacies are usually completely disintegrated during our lives or within a few years of our passing. Although these legacies are historically unimportant and not worth mentioning by most, they do have an influence on those close to the legator. Materials, funds, businesses, family structures and mannerisms can make an immense difference in a small sphere of influence. They can mean the continuance or dissolution of entire families or towns. All told though, it is rare for them to have impact beyond the reach of the legator. If we want our life's work to be remembered far and wide, we have to aim higher.

Great legacies last for decades or generations after the work is completed. These types of achievements vary considerably. Some examples include political or social movements, influential art, nation building, military conquests, technological advancements and notable architecture. Save for very few instances, great legacies are the highest we can aim for and mere dreams to the average person. Legacies of this scale often occur as the result of social friction and upheaval. In the cases of artistic, technological and architectural accomplishments, the legator is often consumed and exhausted by their work. Something else great legators have in common is unconventional approaches to their objectives. Napoleon used decentralization of forces to conquer Europe. Salvador Dali would enter "paranoid critical" states by brooding over bizarre thoughts to increase his creativity. Queen Elizabeth I avoided marriage to retain her power while she defended the England against Spanish incursions. Those with great legacies are certain to be studied and celebrated (or disparaged, in negative cases) for many years. Understand that the quest for a great legacy is all-consuming and may not pay dividends within your lifetime, but the purpose of a legacy is to live beyond your years within the effects of your work.

Superlegacies last against all odds for millennia. Remarkable architecture, timeless philosophy and religious ideologies can become superlegacies. The Egyptian pyramids, Mayan temples, Stonehenge, Mt. Rushmore, Christianity, Buddhism, Islam, the works of Plato, Cicero and Confucius are all superlegacies. Interestingly, individuals involved in the creation of such legacies have little or no material possessions to speak of. Their legacies consist of the effects they had (and continue to have) on those who come across their works or ideologies. To create an ideological or philosophical or superlegacy, be prepared to face the full impact of what is antithetical to your cause and martyr yourself in resistance to it. Physical superlegacies differ from philosophical and ideological in that the result eventually overshadows its originator. Can you name the sculptor who created Mt. Rushmore or the pharaoh who commissioned the Great Pyramid? It is the resulting form that affects people, not those responsible for it. Making physical superlegacies entails some of the biggest challenges known to man. Those who create greatness donate their lives to it. In all cases, superlegacies are hard to predict and control because the societies that procure them change over time. Muhammad wouldn't have imagined billions of followers facing Mecca to prey each day or thousands of them contorting his message to terrorize others. Jesus Christ couldn't have foreseen himself as the founder of the world's most popular and charitable religion or the persecutions that were conducted in the name of that religion. Pharaoh Khufu imagined an infinite afterlife in his Great Pyramid tomb, not being carried off along with all of his possessions by looters and grave robbers. Our legacies can last through millennia, but we might not recognize them on the other end.

Biological legacies are by far the longest lived. Cellular reproduction has succeeded in an unbroken chain for hundreds of millions of years. Your most literal legacy is your DNA, which can outlast even the sturdiest monuments. Be warned, though, that if it's our values that you're trying to pass on through DNA or other inheritances, you may be disappointed. The most that can be transferred on to our children is nebulous genetic traits and transitory mannerisms. Each time genes are split through conception; the offspring resemble only 50% of their parents. Within four generations, only 6% of the DNA is shared with the progenitor, though over a wider and thinner section of the population. We often imagine our offspring and future generations in our own image, inheriting our perspectives and values. We see clones of ourselves continuing to work on the world vision that we had. That may be true in isolated societies, but situations like those are exceptionally rare. In most cases, the values and laws change completely after only a few generations. Another misconception we have about our biological legacies is in imagining ourselves as eternally Homo sapiens. At the moment, human evolution is accelerating exponentially. This may be one of the final generations to be considered Homo sapiens. We should understand that our DNA may eventually be unrecognizable. It may mesh with inorganic life or be replaced by something else completely. Perhaps we could clone ourselves in perpetuity, but we'd probably elect to improve all aspects of our being and become distorted in the process. Even the legacy of cellular life is limited.

Your perspective has the potential to create ripples well beyond your living years. Nonetheless, your true legacy is existence. All realities are imminent and each reality makes others possible. Having a lasting legacy is unavoidable in the realm of NE because you are the Creator and observer of all. Although it is an intriguing prospect to imagine something you've accomplished resonating timelessly, it needn't be a primary focus in life. The primary focus should be experiencing your unique perspective. Some of that experience may lead to a legacy, but that's not the goal. Legacies are simply traceable accounts of your actions, as Creator, you already know what you've accomplished. Legacies write themselves as we experience Everything in all its wonder and glory.

APPLIED TO GOVERNANCE

GOVERNMENT

Government is the foundation of civilization. Without it, people cannot interact peacefully or efficiently. Some essential services, like policing or public works, have obvious connections to a society's prosperity. In the business sector, however, government can seem like more of a hindrance than a facilitator of prosperity. The truth is that all prosperity (or lack thereof) can be traced directly to the government under which it transpires. Those who spray anarchy symbols on sidewalks and buildings do it compliments of the society that has provided them paint. Those in the West who yearn for socialism and communism do it from the cozy living spaces that their capitalist democratic republic has afforded them. Even smugglers, drug dealers and black markets owe their successes to governments that underpin the societies on which they prey. From time to time, we all find ourselves railing against government. It's hard to ignore some of the inept, corrupt and brutal things governments do in an effort to preserve their power. In that way, governments and businesses behave like living organisms. They protect themselves at all costs and grow whenever possible.

The key to understanding the organism of your government is to pan to its viewpoint. Governments, for better or worse, represent the people whom they govern. If those people are tyrannical and have slave mentalities, so too will their governments. If those people value their individual freedoms, their governments will follow suit. Your position as Creator and owner means that you define your government. Everything that society, and by extension, government does is at your will. If things aren't going your way, it's your job to improve them. As in other relationships, you must train it how to treat and handle you. That doesn't mean getting a free pass to behave any way you'd like. It means treating you fairly, responding to your inputs and representing your interests. To improve your government, you must change your mode from idle subject to active governor.

To govern is to lead. To govern is to judge. To govern is to manage. To govern is to protect. To govern is to build, fight, innovate, prosecute, regulate, tax, execute, legislate, communicate and provide. In governing, all of these tasks must be done while checking over our shoulder for those who would cut our reigns short. Detractors can be found in the media, political rivals, disgruntled constituents and even in our own staffs. To manage all the jobs of governing without getting de-throned or overthrown is a miracle. Governing in modern times is every bit as perilous as being at the top of an ancient tribal hierarchy, but without the advantage of knowing everyone in your tribe. Luckily, most people today abhor violence and the chances of governors being beheaded or flogged are slim. Still, it is possible that you may meet your end through the media in a sort of digital execution of your reputation. That shouldn't sway you from your duty to improve your government's perspective by contributing to it. MOE climbs to where the reins are and grabs them. Even if someone else holds them, he understands that they are his to hold. If you practice extreme ownership, you are probably participating in your government in some capacity.

When you ascend to a position from which you can see how things are being done, you will notice that some things should be done differently. But what's the best way to govern? Various forms of government have been tried over millennia. Kingdoms, republics, empires, dictatorships, democracies, theocracies, communism, socialism and oligarchies have all had their times in the sun. Each form of government reveals its weaknesses over time.

Your first inclination when considering the complexity of the system from which you project power might be to attempt to overthrow it and rule as a dictator. Single-minded leadership creates a streamlined path between goals and accomplishments. Ruthlessness causes subordinates to obey unquestionably out of fear. This may be necessary in the most war-torn or rudimentary startup societies, but it only works temporarily. Dictators rarely find proper heirs and frequently find themselves isolated while someone more ruthless lies in-wait. The other option might be a monarchy, but like dictatorship, heavy lies the crown when you have to protect it and modern societies no longer subscribe to the myth that DNA transfers the traits of good leaders to their kin. If a top-heavy government seems out of balance, perhaps you can decentralize a bit and try feudalism where lords and mercenaries rule over townships and report to you as king. Well, at least it would be a little decentralized as the noble class would absorb some of the burden governing and everyone would know their place in the hierarchy. Still, feudalism didn't succeed because of the vast inequality and smoldering distrust between hierarchal levels.

Now consider the most populist form of government: direct democracy. One person gets one vote and all the votes are counted equally. A system that operates like a business owned by its employees – fantastic. Everyone feels that they have a voice and some sway over the government. The direct democratic model works when the participating population is a basically homogeneous group. When the populace is diverse in culture and race, it becomes a competition to see who can get the most for their group in spite of the health of the group overall. The classical Greek model of democracy did not treat everyone equally. They limited the voting populace to men over thirty years of age who owned land. That meant to participate, you had to have a certain amount of experience in life, shown an ability to pay taxes and conduct business and have a financial stake in the outcome of the issues on the ballots. Those coupled with the relatively homogeneous citizenry of Greece, created a utopian model for democracy that withstood the test of time between the eighth and fourth centuries B.C. Subsequently, (the fifth through first centuries, B.C.), the Roman Republic became one of the earliest examples of representative democracy. Of all its classical periods (kingdom, republic, empire), Rome was most stable and prosperous as a republic. It's no wonder that when Western civilization re-awoke in the Renaissance, it took many queues from its Greek and Roman predecessors. England and the United States in particular have been compared to classical Greek and Roman empires.

Even the current vanguard of government models, representative democracy, shows signs of impending insolvency. Perhaps giving everyone a say in how things are done, regardless of track records, citizenship status, group affiliation or mental acuity isn't the best course of action. Another flaw being revealed in representative democracies is the failure to limit scopes of service. A resilient government is one limited to five fundamental responsibilities: taxation, creation of infrastructure, maintenance of a formidable military and the creation and enforcement of basic laws. As governments assume auxiliary roles in education, safety, healthcare and welfare, the fundamentals suffer. Western civilization is experiencing the consequences of such overreach. Inefficient school systems, muzzled police departments and government-subsidized medical insurance have ensured that the most vital services to citizens are shy of satisfactory. When democratic societies overfeed their governments, it ends in socialism. In socialist societies, all citizens (and in some instances, non-citizens) receive the same inferior government services, eventually leading to individual and national insolvency. Unchecked governments are rife with corruption, and corruption in a government leads to poverty and strife for all but a tiny sliver of its citizens. This can easily result in totalitarianism.

While there may not ever be a perfect form of government, we'll always strive to find one that better provides the experiences we desire. From the NE perspective, a better government would be similar to representative democracy in that its citizens would be represented, generally protected, able to create prosperity and free to believe what they want without persecution. A better government would differ in that it would reward only progress, swiftly punish criminality, have a fearsome reputation abroad, limit its range of services to the necessities, stick to a simplified and unwavering set of laws, expand globally, and limit human consumption to preserve the natural environment for future generations. Fortunately, the workings of the current world order aren't far off the mark. Nonetheless, the changes that must be made to keep it solvent and out of the hands of socialists, communists, masochists and anarchists are significant. The best policy in these instances is a shift in strategies from appeasement to provocation. Depending on the situation, you may have to become an oligarch, warlord or dictator. In other regions of the world, different circumstances require different measures, but in this case I'm referring to Western civilization. In a stable democracy, running for office might be the key. Whatever the situation, own it. Time is short. Take the reins and make your government more perfect from your perspective. Remember, government emanates from the superconscience. You must determine its makeup and its relationship to you.

EQUALITY

"We hold these Truths to be self-evident, that all Men are created equal, that they are endowed by their Creator with certain unalienable Rights, that among these are Life, Liberty, and the Pursuit of Happiness...." – Thomas Jefferson

No matter what your background or experience, all is equivalent. Superiority is impossible when all are one. Some of us may reside in more desirable places than others, but none is better than another. On the plane of NE, everything is universally equal. A foot is no more superior than the carpet it treads upon. Given that, why do some things seem better than others? Why are they so perceptibly unequal? The differences arise from our perspectives and what matters from them. The animal attached to said foot is interested in movement over a soft surface. Trading perspectives with the carpet would be an unimaginable prospect for a living creature. Yet the carpet, though not living, consists of millions of entangled molecules just bursting with potential energy. That potential energy is the same energy released during the Big Bang. Those molecules make up their own sub-universe with unique laws and varying states of charge. Perhaps being alive puts the animal in a superior position compared to that of the carpet, but only from the perspective of the animal.

When the most complex known living organisms on Earth capture, domesticate and even eat simpler life forms, does that make us superior to those lifeforms? When one nation conquers another, subjugates its population and confiscates its natural resources, does that make the people of the conquering nation superior or morally inferior for exploiting them? Now imagine the situations reversed. Would a dominant organism of lower intelligence treat one of higher intelligence humanely? Would nations of fewer means allow defeated peoples to live amongst them as equals had *they* prevailed? In all cases, the answer is no. Striving to survive is in every living organism's basic algorithm. Surviving means prevailing. It also means living a state of affairs that is desired by both the dominant and subjugated parties. Although absolute superiority is impossible, it is still possible for one to prevail over another from certain perspectives.

As we progress through spacetime, our fates are revealed to us. Much as one tectonic plate slides under another in a subduction zone, living creatures are the subjects of their unique circumstances. Our initial positions in the world depend on the occurrences around us. Sometimes we find ourselves charting our own paths and other times we find ourselves struggling for control. What we are, where we are born, what we look like and much of our persona are unchangeable. Historically, the definition of prevailing amongst Homo sapiens has been vastly different across continents and regions. The diversity of goals, resources and skills as well as the geographic separation of many populations resulted in the uniqueness of cultures, religions, architectures, languages, melodies, foods and artistic achievements around the world. Cultures clashed in major ways after Europeans discovered the Americas, but the differences between world cultures, even between cities and regions within the same countries, prevailed up to and through the industrial age and into the early twentieth century. That didn't mean life was peaceful by any means. Cultures have battled and blended throughout history. Empires colonized and influenced the places where they settled. Nonetheless, until the early twentieth century, there was no standard global view of how the world worked or what one should know or accomplish to succeed in it. Before the advent of radio and television, many cultures were largely mysterious to one another. Now, voices and images travel instantly across the world. Information, knowledge and products, so long the domains of advanced industrialized societies, are transferred, ingested and mimicked by previously exotic peoples. This has resulted in the convergence of visions and priorities between societies worldwide. On one hand, the unification of societies through technology is inevitable and should be applauded. On the other hand, as the global definition of success narrows, a great portion of the world population who once saw themselves as prosperous and fulfilled have been notified that there is a new standard of life to aspire to. The Western world enjoys a living standard that would be impossible to sustain globally. Meanwhile, the rest of the world has become interested in obtaining an equal standard of living. Many are willing to decimate their natural resources or even kill for a better life. This is due, in part, to television and the internet streaming glamorous depictions of Western lifestyles. Westerners are no more immune to the promotion of parasitic envy, but the third world has an appetite that would be impossible to satiate.

If any society has come close to uniting humanity, it is the United States of America. It's founding principles, built on the ideas of ancient Greek and Roman philosophies and structured after the constitutional laws of England, unleashed the powers of creativity and entrepreneurialism in its constituents. This has led to unprecedented innovations and progress in all categories of human endeavor. Because of the freedoms and access to opportunity offered to its citizens and even non-citizens, the US has become the center of world trade, military might and wealth around the world. It has also become a symbol of hope to all those oppressed outside its borders as it fought and won wars against brutal regimes and exported aide to countries in need. The US began promoting its imperfect, but broadly humanitarian values to the world in earnest in the early twentieth century. Those values would be tested and validated through two global wars and many other conflicts. In the 1950s, many European, Asian and South American countries adopted notionally similar forms of government and offerings of opportunity to their citizens. To this day, English is the international language spoken by most people because it's the language you must know to do business in the global economy. Throughout that time, one of the most recognized and repeated axioms when it came to the character of US has been an excerpt from the Declaration of Independence that, "All men are created equal". This, and the philanthropic actions of the US government and its citizens stand out as beacons of true equality and freedom in the world. For those who want what others have, the interpretation of Thomas Jefferson's declaration is interpreted as "We are all equal and therefore all of our outcomes should be equal". The original intent of Jefferson's wording was to say that everyone should be treated similarly under the law and that societal status doesn't change the way the law is applied, but original intent is difficult to defend across centuries and cultural transformations.

When people want what others have, yet lack the knowledge, clout or strength to obtain it, the only tool available to them is cunning. If those who have the prize are more virtuous, then those who covet the prize must appeal to the emotions, shame, or even socially divide the virtuous to get what they want. To an extent, that is what is occurring in the most compassionate nation ever to lead the world. Strong, courageous people have been held hostage by their emotions, divided, shamed and fleeced by hordes of the envious. The truth is, if the virtuous allow this to happen, they are indeed the weaker. The winner does what is necessary to gain or maintain a prize, even if it requires deception or brutality. One thing is certain. Between now and the emergence of an uncontested world order, there will be widespread international conflict. If the conflict spares Homo sapiens, hopefully the survivors will be governed by the following principles of NE.

All is equal. Each of us exist in infinite spacetime, experiencing all. Though all matter, and by extension, people, are intrinsically unified, no two events are ever the same. Different spacetime positions mean different experiences. None is better than the other, they're simply different. Equality in society means being treated similarly under the law despite immutable differences. A society can claim equality between people, but what people really want is fair treatment, not only from the government, but from other people. Then again, the definition of 'fair' can be subjective. To break out of the subjective nature of equality, one must acknowledge two things: 1) all is one and therefore equal and 2) no two perspectives ever experience the same thing. Never let guilt or shame subtract you from your rightful experience. Avoid jealously comparing yourself to others, and only make comparisons to gain perspective. Protect your perspective from those who would try to replace it with their own. If you veer from your chosen path, understand that there are infinite other options to consider and you will eventually experience each one. Everyone's struggles and triumphs are your own. See yourself in both.

JUSTICE

"Life isn't fair" is a good thing to tell someone who's in need of a little tough love. That said, it is patently incorrect. Life *is* fair. So fair, in fact, that there are scores being kept on micro levels that we cannot even fathom. Within Everything, no variable is neglected. Sometimes life is a little too fair for our liking. Still, when we don't get what we think should be coming our way, it's often perceived as unfair. Like good and evil, fairness is perspective dependent. Simply put, fairness is the perception of something going the way that it *should* go based on patterns or personal feelings. When something goes our way, we feel that we are receiving justice. When it doesn't go our way, we feel that we are being denied justice. When someone is striving for justice, they are really striving for something to go their way or retribution for something that didn't go their way. In its distilled form, justice is a sense of fairness and reciprocity.

Justice takes many forms but can be divided into two categories: natural and societal. Natural justice occurs in relation to objective laws of nature. When someone or something fails to adhere to a natural law, they suffer a consequence. The opposite when natural laws are followed in clever ways. Physics, chemistry, instinct and the laws of the wild are subject to this kind of reciprocity. Societal justice is devised around manmade laws which attempt to approximate fairness based on the values of the society or ruling classes administering them. Civil and criminal courts, parking tickets, taxes and social inclusion all fall under the jurisdiction of societal justice. Natural and societal justice differ in the same way that objective and manmade laws do. Natural justice is swift and irrefutable, societal justice is less direct and subject to the indecision, corruption and oversights of authority. The severity of societal justice can range from overly harsh to completely impotent, often leaving its subjects bewildered. For the most part, governments are interested in issues that impact the stability and longevity of their tenures. The primary goal of tribal councils is to keep other members of the tribe satisfied and obedient. It should be noted that societal and natural justice are often interwoven.

The reasons we want justice are the same reasons that we want money and success. Our biological algorithms seek survival and reproduction. Electrochemical signals in our brains create the sensations of either provision or denial. When we feel that we are being taken advantage of, it makes us anxious and react accordingly. When we feel that we have prevailed over would-be violators of our rights, we are rewarded psychologically. The word 'justice' implies not only prevailing but doing so righteously according to the laws of God, man and nature. The perception of justice as a state-supplied right is so ingrained into the fabric of Western civilization that many believe that it may be procured solely through systemic or legal means. The iconic image of a blindfolded woman holding a scale gives us the sense that we are in the halls of an ancient Greek court in which the wills of the Gods themselves are interpreted. That's true only if you consider the directives of politicians, lawyers and judges to be sacrosanct.

In truth only a small fraction of justice is provided though legal means. Most disputes are worked out between people who have their own ideas of fairness. Odds are, that's how you've resolved most of your disagreements. Justice is subjective. It's a concept that is heavily influenced by culture, chemistry and personal views. If given the chance to punish someone who robbed them, some victims would choose to have the thief keep what they took or give them the option of returning it. Others would have them pay a heavy fine or spend some time in jail for it. Still others would have them killed for breaking a pact with society and crossing them personally. When we do something that most members of our society deem wrong, we will most certainly face consequences. But wrong is in the eye of the beholder. If something has been done to hurt someone and it isn't condemned by society, then the burden of justice falls to the victim. There's also a question of whether or not one knows they're violating someone else's rights. Ignorance is a factor too.

From the NE perspective, all is one and our desire for justice is natural, but existentially illogical. MOE sees justice from the perspectives of both an animal and the Creator. From the animal's perspective, if someone or something endangers or harms MOE or those dear to him, he understands that he is an animal and entitled to react as an animal. From the Creator's perspective, MOE sees the assailant as himself in another spacetime location. Although he may react, he does so with love in his heart. In Everything, no wrongs are committed, only actions and reactions. Underreacting to offenses can cause feelings of victimization and weakness. Overreacting can lead to lasting remorse, especially if the assailant is unaware of their trespass. We share a special connection with all those who intersect with our worldlines. It is helpful to see justice as an emotion rather than a tangible goal to be obtained. The key to the perception of proper justice is a balanced perspective. Don't spend your life pursuing those who have wronged you, but don't allow them to get away without a fight. You are the owner of your experience and this experience includes conflict. Use the Creator to reason and the animal to execute and you will always have justice.

EDUCATION

What is education really? It's learning the patterns, skills and habits that are useful in life. Education is continually occurring at some level in our lives, whether formally or informally. We don't learn how to walk, use doorknobs or avoid dangerous creatures in a formal setting. Those are just skills that come with experience. In fact, only a small portion of what we know comes from formal education. The label 'uneducated' is humorous because it's so far off the mark. Modern society assumes that if someone doesn't graduate through the standard system of learning then they lack an education. While knowing a certain amount of language, history and math is crucial to functioning in society, knowing just the basics gives you the potential to learn anything. No matter who you are, you are constantly being educated. If you can read, write and do basic math, you are educated enough to advance your knowledge to any level. Advancing your knowledge of any subject provides a competitive edge, but even having multiple doctorate degrees ensures only a sliver of the knowledge called for in life. It is more important to have access to accurate knowledge and to deploy it quickly than to store entire semesters of generalized subjects in your mind. The information we need is stored in digital format available for immediate summoning via the internet.

Educated people spend the first quarter of their lives in schooling. All too often, even after completing their education they are just beginning their quest for the knowledge they'll need in life. You'd assume that twenty years of full-time education would foster more tangible abilities, but in most cases it doesn't. In the Western world, this is because the educational complex is tuned for maximum participation, outdated curricula, fiscal incompetence and the appeasement of special interest groups. For six decades, Western education has been dominated by idealists who looked down on vocational work and imagined their students in exclusively corporate or management positions. They've also integrated elements of social retribution into curricula, fomenting a hostile environment for the majority of students and detracting from the mission of teaching. Much of the time in school is spent learning subjects that have little to no real value to the student. Instead of streamlining the curricula and refocusing on more relevant subjects, the government throws more money at it. What use is a student who gets good grades if they're in subjects of little importance? This is not to say that history, art, music and sports have no value. They certainly do, but we're at a point in history where the educational system isn't providing enough technical knowledge and is pressuring students to adopt racially divisive and anti-Western political ideologies. The incipient demise of institutional education was accelerated by the coronavirus pandemic. Without notice, students around the world were forced to learn remotely though internet conferencing. Parents were simultaneously forced to give up the convenience of dropping their kids off for six hours of structured activity and catching glimpses of what and what their kids were being taught. As teachers' unions were directing teachers to strike for more pay and time off and staunchly defending the corrupt ideologies being forced upon students, the world was conducting a beta test for what was to come. With or without the input of educational bureaucrats, the die was cast in favor of a revolution in learning. Unfortunately for millions of other dutiful and passionate teachers, the thousands of cavernous buildings and billions of dollars in public funding, schools are going the way of retail stores. They're being replaced by more efficient means of information exchange.

It seems that our need to improve cerebral data storage will soon be met by neuroscience and microchip developers. Neural implants have been the subject of sci-fi fantasies since the advent of microprocessors, but their application was severely limited until recent advances in neurophysiology and processing power. Implants can now stimulate, block or record signals from neurons. They can also aid in sensory substitution by replacing signals from the damaged sensors in the eyes and ears of patients. Predictably, neural implants made their jump from animal and insect to human subjects via the desire to combat disability and disease. Research became focused on enabling paralyzed patients to move devices and communicate through thought-to-text. By 2012, a landmark study demonstrated that two people with tetraplegia were able to control robotic arms using direct thought. In 2020, two patients were able to wirelessly control a tablet to text, email, shop and bank, also using direct thought (26). This was the first time a brain-computer interface was implanted via the patient's blood vessels, eliminating the need for open brain surgery. In spite of the ethical questions raised by those who view the implants as unnatural, they have made their way into the human brain. It is difficult to stop progress in a field of research with so many valid reasons for continuance.

Soon, knowledge will be uploaded via neural links in our brains. It may be automatic and even free. In this way, we are approaching the line between Homo sapiens and the next evolution. As I've said, it is possible that we are one of the final generations of sapiens. Humanity is in the middle of a transfer of authority from humans to cyborgs and AI algorithms. The question we should be asking is what will become of humans without meaningful purposes. Will the cyborgs and AI look after and feed us or will we simply be pushed aside? When given the choice between evolution and resisting evolution, MOE chooses evolution every time. Until the day comes where we can upload knowledge, persistence and determination are the keys to our education. At the moment, hard-earned knowledge is still valuable it should be obtained in any way possible. We are in a golden age of education where, at least in free societies, knowledge can be gained just by buying a book or downloading a course. If we prefer to learn directly, schools are still an option for the time being. Educating our kids will require supplementation until neural links are safe enough for them. Knowledge is beneficial any way it is procured. If you desire knowledge, remember that it is yours to have. Whether it's enhanced technology or completely natural, your brain can learn an astonishing amount. Learning is just a way to remind yourself of the workings of your creation.

LAW ENFORCEMENT

"Every society gets the kind of criminal it deserves. What is equally true is that every community gets the kind of law enforcement it insists on." – Robert Kennedy

To be enforceable, manmade laws should be as close to natural as possible. Only laws that are understood can be obeyed. Only laws that can be obeyed can be enforced. Only laws that can be enforced should be written. Whereas the list of laws in most democratic societies is so vast and complex that one must hire an attorney to interpret them, the manmade laws of NE would fit in a small paperback book and be readily understood by everyone. Simplicity is key to a society's ability to adhere to laws. Consistency is also key. If laws change or are amended from year to year, they seem fleeting and malleable. Inconsistent enforcement leads to inconsistent compliance. Consistency should also apply to the enforcement of laws. There should never be an instance where the law is applied differently to two separate people. Instances where criminals walk free due to legal technicalities or mistrials give other criminals confidence that they might evade justice. Inconsistency shakes the public's confidence in law enforcement. Consistency of interpretation is also important. Laws shouldn't be open to interpretation. They should be spelled out clearly so that any enforcer or jury can apply them to the situation. Simplicity and consistency are the two requirements for effective laws and their enforcement. Now, let's have a look at how manmade laws would be implemented and enforced from the NE perspective.

Basic Rights – Just as in most democratic societies, every citizen in the NE empire would be born with basic rights. Many of these rights would mirror those in the US constitution but wouldn't be as vaguely worded or changeable. The rights to absolute self-expression, self-defense and activities that don't physically harm others would be guaranteed. Inquiries about what constitutes violations of these rights would be assigned to random juries who would decide the cases individually and on the spot. There would be no appealing of rulings.

Enforcer Rights – There's no doubt that law enforcement can get out of hand if given too much power. No one wants a roving gang of untouchable government wolves violating and extorting from the populace. On the other hand, enforcers must be intimidating to be effective. The truth is that we want to be protected by wolves. It should be understood that violating laws or associating with criminal elements might attract their attention. Enforcers need the leeway to be creative and build webs that criminals don't want to get tangled in. Law enforcement should be released of liability for all but the most brazen acts while on duty. The maximum penalty allowed for enforcers should be termination unless they commit an atrocity like mass murder or rape on the job. In order to enforce laws, enforcers must not fear reproach and must be defended by the communities they serve.

Right to Hurt Yourself, but Not Others – One area of law enforcement that most societies have wrong is the assumption that it's the government's duty to keep people from endangering or hurting themselves or *potentially* hurting others. Drug enforcement is a prime example of that crippling overreach, but examples abound from seatbelt fastening to blood alcohol testing. The government should not take the role of safety coordinator in personal danger or soberness. It undermines the intelligence of the citizen while creating fear of indirect consequences like speeding tickets rather than actual consequences like being injured or injuring others in crashes. Limiting driving speed, wearing seatbelts and staying sober should all be suggestions, but no one should suffer consequences for something unless it harms someone else or damages property. For instance, I should be able to drive as fast as I want with a martini in one hand but the minute I spin out and kill someone, justice should be swift whether or not I'm drinking. Similarly, a drug user should use as much as they want, but the minute they assault someone or leave their baby in a hot car to roast, they're subject to rigid NE law. The most dangerous thing about illicit drugs is the underworld that provides them. If the manufacture of drugs like cocaine and fentanyl were regulated and users could buy them affordably from pharmacies, they would be safer for consumption and the users wouldn't be drawn into an underworld to get them. All of the money saved and taxes collected could go to drug rehabilitation programs and psychiatric care. In the NE empire, only things that harm others or the property of others would be considered crimes. The most common argument I get regarding NE law is, "If you make everything legal, many will die, even innocent people." That may be the case initially. It would be difficult to stomach the initial spikes in drug and alcohol related deaths. However, as the system took hold, it would become apparent that the worst offenders would not be long for this world. They'd either die on their own or be *truly* processed by the NE law enforcement apparatus. Yes, some innocents would die, but it would be a sacrifice that society would have to weigh against the current drug/alcohol industrial complex that is crippling Western government and law enforcement.

Misfortune is Sad, but – Life must go on in greater society despite the misfortunes that many of us face, the foremost of which is cognitive malfunction. Senility, addiction, schizophrenia, bipolarism, psychopathy and general mental disability affect so many people in awful ways. Cognitive malfunctions also deeply affect those within a certain radius of the afflicted whether it's parents, children, spouses, friends, co-workers or the general public. Some of the afflicted are eventually abandoned by their closest contacts. This is absolutely heart-wrenching, but thankfully many charities, churches and volunteers are willing to pick up where they left off. In the NE empire, this is where the line of misfortune must be drawn. The most pitiful of us cannot be allowed to harm greater society. All advanced cultures are sympathetic to an extent, but to preserve civility, it is the job of government and law enforcement to uphold laws. Those who aren't able to live by the rules of society should be ushered into helping hands or, if too far gone, to a humane end. No one should be allowed to fester or harm others on the streets. In the NE empire, it wouldn't be tolerated more than any other infringement on human rights. This also goes for instances where people say they didn't know any better, were too young, inebriated or insane to tell right from wrong. Ignorance and insanity are not excuses to commit crimes. No matter the mental state of the assailant, physical harm to others should lead to penalties.

Prison and Other Punishments – The only thing that can reform someone is learning that wrongdoing leads to consequences. In Western society, some criminals are sentenced to decades or life in prison. Supposedly, that's more humane than killing them. Instead of ending an irredeemable life, society pays for an expensive residence in the prison system where they spend the rest of their days. Inmates are well-fed, watch television, pump iron, fight and network, and communicate with the outside world in today's prisons. They also retain most of their rights as citizens while in lockup. Contrarily in the NE empire, prison sentences would be shorter and much more intense. Basic rights would be suspended during sentences. Maximum sentences would be 10 years but after only a few months, inmates would be different people. After exiting the prison, their time would be done and their rights as a full citizen, including the right to work without the stigma of a crime on their record. As for recidivism, the mere thought of returning to prison would send urine streaming down an ex-con's leg. Three-time offenders would be given death sentences. If someone is convicted of a crime worthy of a death sentence, the sentence would be carried out within minutes of sentencing by firing squad. There are always shadows of doubt in criminal cases. Instead of allowing trials to last for years and rulings to be appealed, the following statement will herald each sentencing statement: "We understand that there is a chance you are innocent of this crime. Although we consider all the evidence and testimony available to us, no system is perfect. If you are innocent, our hearts are with you. Rare cases of wrongful conviction free our society from the perils of wrongfully exonerating the truly guilty."

Borders and Immigration – The NE empire would begin extending its borders as it gained wealth and influence. The eventual result would be borderless but until then, the empire would have to protect its sovereignty by upholding its boundaries. Empires, nations and countries are defined by their borders. If borders are not enforced, identity of the territory enclosed by them eventually ceases to be relevant. The NE empire would have an immigration system that would admit prospective citizens based on values and merits only. All who would cross the borders illegally would find themselves on the wrong side of a rigid law enforcement system and be treated as foreign invaders. The NE perspective allows for universal compassion while protecting one's own culture and national identity. To be a citizen of NE would be the greatest aspiration of many but to accomplish this, they would have to assimilate and represent the empire without question. Citizenship would not be obtainable just by being born within an NE territory. Those whose parents are not NE citizens would have to go through the same process as anyone else to be admitted as citizens, though pains would be taken to keep children with their parents. Citizenship could be revoked for treason, spying or similar infractions, but it would be more likely that such offenders would be disposed of in other ways.

Taxes and Finances – Taxes are unavoidable in society. In the NE empire, everyone would pay the same percentage, regardless of income. Cash and coin would be a thing of the past, replaced by digital currency. If it sounds a bit Orwellian or similar to the social credit system of the PRC, it might be, but it's the simplest way to manage finances in society and eliminate underground economies. Gone would be the days of keeping track of personal deductions and filing taxes. In this system, all citizens would receive a basic sustenance credit on a weekly basis and be able to build credit up to the equivalent of $10 million dollars in today's money. No single person would be allowed to own or consume more than that. Prices on commodities would be fixed and adjusted to match the demands of society. There would still be free market competition, but competitors would compete in terms of quality, not price. Hard assets like precious metals and gems would still hold value but would be accounted for in credit accounts. This would alleviate the tendency for people to horde material and promote workforce participation even after great success.

Personal Matters – Things like marriage, gender identity, ethnicity and religious beliefs should not be of concern to law enforcement. Any government under which its citizens are free should never inquire as to the status of any of those attributes unless it's to identify a suspect or missing person. If someone presents you with a survey asking your marital status, race, sex or age, rest assured that it matters to them. Sure, most of the time you can decline to answer but it should be very concerning if such things are being tallied because it is likely being used for something profoundly unfair. Things like religion are personal as well and not to be included in any legal language, currency or government statements. Yes, some natural and manmade laws coincide with religious doctrine, but religion should be fully filtered from government to maintain a neutral stance in legal matters.

<u>Anti-Corruption</u> – How does a government with highly enabled law enforcement avoid becoming corrupt? Through independent reviews conducted by citizens on a random basis. Every so often, citizens would be called upon to test the honesty and efficacy of a branch of law enforcement. This would pertain to the police, prisons, courts and executive offices that oversee them. The 'secret shopper' method is underutilized in society and business. Due to its unpredictability, corrupt officials wouldn't know who to bribe or intimidate. Random audits like these tend to keep people honest. The NE empire would have no tolerance for corruption and violators would be weeded out on a regular basis.

Manmade laws are highly subjective. Regardless of our current perspectives, we will eventually experience all aspects of them. We should keep this in mind as we consider ways to enforce them. We should also acknowledge that all realities are imminent while espousing the current one.

APPLIED TO CHALLENGES

HATRED

"As I walked out the door toward the gate that would lead to my freedom, I knew if I didn't leave my bitterness and hatred behind, I'd still be in prison." – Nelson Mandela

Hatred is evil. At least, that's what society wants you to believe. If you dislike something or someone, you are committing the sin of hatred. The word hate evokes images of atrocities committed by Hitler's 'Third Reich' in Germany or hooded Ku Klux Klan members burning crosses in the American South. Although those are poignant examples of atrocious acts, they are also the most overly publicized and rehashed representations of hate. Because of their sensational nature, Nazis and clansmen have been exhaustively delivered to society by media, cinema and educational institutions for eight decades. In the media, hate has a preferred face. The word 'hate' has become a tool of leverage against those who are deemed capable of it by politicians, government officials, bias organizations, the media and popular culture. Even voicing concern about crime or an injustice is considered hateful if, in the eyes of the enough people, it goes against an acceptable narrative. As provocative as the word 'hate' is, it's just an emotion. In reality, hate can be likened to an 'assault' rifle. When stripped of its intimidating-looking accessories, it's really just a rifle. Also like a rifle, hate has caused untold destruction and pain in the world because, in the wrong hands, its potential can be misdirected. Believe it or not, hatred, like rifles, has positive potential too. To harness that potential, you must learn to aim it only at the proper targets and deploy it with accuracy and discretion.

As disheartening as the word hate sounds, we should examine it from the NE lens. As MOE, we use all tools available to us and therefore view hate without predisposition. Deprived of all its stigma, what is hate? To understand what it means, we must examine the contexts in which it is applied. Universally, hate is dislike. But it's meaning varies depending on context. Expression of hate can range from polite interjection; "I hate to bother you", to strong aversion; "I hate spinach", to intense disdain and condemnation; "I hate those people" or active aggression; "We bashed their skulls in". The latter two levels are the ones that we're concerned with as the first two are really benign exaggerations for the sake of conversational potency. The hate that's considered evil is prejudiced hostility. Prejudice is the specific part of hate that repulses us, or so we say. According to many in today's society, it's even more despicable when disdain is applied to certain types and groups of people instead of giving each individual a clean slate to work from. Prejudice means that you are using preexisting bias to make decisions. Discrimination, prejudice and bias reside in the same boat as hatred – they're considered reprehensible by politicians, educators, the media and a majority of mainstream Western society. In all other areas of life, we are urged to use pattern recognition and discrimination to make good decisions. Data collection and analysis are key to survival and prosperity in all areas of technical and biological life. But according to the Western powers that be, we should turn a blind eye to characteristics and behavioral patterns of certain people yet amplify those in others. They'd be happy if we muted our instincts to see things as they've promoted them so that their vision of right and wrong can continue unchallenged. When someone tells you to ignore your instincts, beware of their agenda because it is either ignorant or malicious. Also beware of hatred that overstays its welcome.

At its core, hate is intense desire and is sometimes, but not always, unfounded. Some of us keep our desires to ourselves, some of us express them verbally, others actively work to implement them in society. Still others spend inordinate amounts of our lives serving very narrowly defined aspirations. In the case of MOE, there is a balance of desire and action. Desires guide our daily activities from the breakfast we eat to the music we listen to. As creatures driven by desire and repetition, we tend to stick with what works for us. That is how all species on Earth survive. As a highly intelligent species, we also have the ability to push the limits between what works for us and what could harm us. Blindly walking through life and ignoring red flags and warning signs has the potential to harm or kill us. On the other hand, becoming too complacent in our assumptions, even if they've been correct in the past, can stifle life's experiences. Those who want to experience life to the fullest push the boundaries and constantly re-evaluate routines and desires. If you have totally written off people due to the shades of their skin, their religion or country of origin, your life has been limited. If you dislike all people of a certain financial status, your life has been limited. If you think all dogs are bad because you were bitten once, your life has been limited. Hatred is an instinctual emotion that is sometimes uncontrollable. If it were to be separated into components it would be desire and frustration. The desire for the elimination of an irritant in your life is perfectly natural. Given the right direction, hate can yield positive results. For example, families stay together because the individual members hate being alone. Antibiotics and vaccines were developed because people hated losing their lives to diseases. Hitler was defeated because the Allied Nations hated the idea of Nazis ruling the world. In those examples, hate was motivation fueled by frustration and dire urgency. Understand, though, that when natural emotions are not acted on expediently and practically, they may devolve into excess baggage and wasted thought.

A JOURNEY THROUGH HATE

Like many young people, I carried the baggage of misdirected hatred from late childhood through early adulthood. From a young age, I felt like the world population needed a pruning. My early years had been spent in a neighborhood adjacent to open fields and farmland. All I had to do to find myself in a wide-open space was jump over my backyard fence. As I grew, I became accustomed to accessible wilderness where I could be alone if I wanted to. It's no wonder that when I was taken to public places like amusement parks or shopping malls, crowds had me feeling overwhelmed. Standing in long lines gave me lots of time to examine people and all their faults – skin blemishes, fat guts, crooked teeth and aromas. There were so many people that I wondered how there was enough food and oxygen on the planet to sustain them all. Everywhere I turned was another one... obnoxious and voracious. Each had their own agenda of exploiting and depleting the world's resources. Such thoughts from a boy you say? Yes, like many others, I had insecurities about people and their impact on *my* world. If it was up to me, I would have blended most of them into a pink purée and pumped them out into the ocean. Of course, this would have been done using a custom blender and an industrial pumping system.

On an individual basis, I cared for and respected people, but on a grand-scale, I felt that humans were overly prolific and destructive. In a way, I wanted to carve out a part of the world for myself and a few others. I had an intense case of rugged individualism so prevalent in North America. I thought I could do everything without help from greater society. You'd think a kid who had such thoughts wouldn't have any friends. To the contrary, I was a socially normal, well-liked kid with an average group of friends. They were usually with me on my excursions through the fields to ponds and over railroad tracks. In school, teachers usually had good things to report to my parents. No malaise was expressed except in the occasional playground scuffle. You wouldn't be able to detect it in me, nor was I able to qualify it until much later in life. It was more of a mode of discontent that I'd get into when considering a hectic world. I think it's fairly common in boys and I regulated it well. In all of this, I still had a deep need and value of camaraderie and community. I still appreciated friendly things like dancing, singing or exchanging gifts. Looking back at my developing mind, it's hard to believe the end result would be a relatively stable personality. Most of us have a contradicting an inner id, even as children. Perhaps mine was a bit callous, but I'm not ashamed of it.

After grade school, my family moved from Colorado to Tulsa, Oklahoma. There, I found plenty of fields and forests to explore. In my twelfth year, I was also getting a heavy dose of testosterone and pre-teen insecurity. In the crowded halls of the junior high, I encountered something as of yet unfamiliar – kids that didn't like me and weren't shy about letting me know it. Adding to it, one of my teachers was an angry woman who derided her students. The little voice of discontent had my ear. For the next few years, I was fighting in the hallways, visiting detention and being a mediocre student. During that time, the culture in America seemed to be changing as well. I watched the LA riots in horror. It looked as though the urban black population was out to kill everyone and no one was standing in their way. Oddly, around the same period, a small portion of white kids began to internally identify as black, fully enveloping themselves in the ridiculous charade by speaking in what is now known as Ebonics and wearing baggy sports attire. I'll always remember the first time I heard a boy call another boy a bitch. It was such a backwards violation of heterosexual norms that I vowed to punch anyone who ever referred to me in that way. It also became fashionable to openly ridicule European and white culture in music, movies and TV shows. Even mainstream music was making a shift from rock to rap and R&B. It seemed like Western culture was being hijacked and most people were in denial and the rest were welcoming of it.

There were more black people in Tulsa than in Colorado, but not in numbers large enough to be a problem if entanglement with them was avoided. Socially, this was an incredibly lonely time for me. In Colorado, I was born with friends and never had to pursue friendships. It seemed like everyone in Tulsa was already paired up or in a tight-knit group. After a year of complete isolation, I met a boy in my neighborhood, we were good friends for a year, but his family eventually moved to Texas. Surprisingly, we'd find ourselves reunited in a few years but at the time, I was once again starved for friendship. The next year, a black family moved into the neighborhood. They were unpacking in the driveway. As we drove past, I rolled my eyes and declared what everyone else in the neighborhood was thinking, "There goes the neighborhood!"

One day my younger sister and I were walking down the sidewalk and the man of the house was spraying off his driveway. My sister instinctively crossed the street to avoid the spray, the man or both. I felt obligated, not only to show I wasn't scared of him, but also to introduce myself. As it turned out, his oldest son, Anthony, was my age. He would go on to be my friend for the rest of my days in Tulsa. He didn't go to public school. After a harrowing year in mainstream high school, his parents enrolled him in Catholic school, presumably to keep him away from the negative influences so prevalent in public schools. They were from St. Louis and knew what they didn't want Anthony involved in. In his company, I resisted the internal defense mechanisms of changing how I spoke or going out of my way to prove myself as a non-racist. Of course, he was living in a white neighborhood and had much more incentive to adapt to me than I did to him. Our relationship worked because we wanted it to. We met each other halfway and it was a wonderful couple of years. Knowing Anthony proved something I already suspected; on an individual basis, I wasn't concerned with race. I could have just as good a relationship with a black or brown kid as any other.

Three years later, my family moved again to an area just north of Houston, Texas. My dad was following the path of an executive petroleum engineer and had to go where the corporate headquarters were. Houston is a hub destination for many in the oil industry. By then, I was sixteen and my spirit was as restless as ever, informed by the music of Nine Inch Nails and Alice in Chains. My years in Tulsa had toughened me and taught me to pursue relationships instead of waiting for them. It also taught me to decide to embrace my circumstances instead of picking out the flaws in them. Houston was bigger, hotter and more crowded than any other place I had lived prior to that. Nonetheless, with a driver's license, moving was an adventure. The population was also browner and blacker than any previous location I'd lived in. The area we lived in was generally insulated from all the violence and crime in and around Houston. At school, I was still fighting in the halls occasionally, but more in defense of others. The Western cultural transformation was in full swing and OJ Simpson was on trial for double murder of his ex-wife and her friend. Our school had about the same number of black students as the one in Tulsa. Much as in Tulsa, they were generally self-segregated, and weren't a factor in my daily life. That doesn't mean they weren't belligerent. Once one of them made a comment about my sister's legs as she walked by. She didn't notice and it just wasn't enough for me to confront him and risk getting pummeled by his group. The typical scenario when black students fought with white students, male or female, was the white student being outnumbered and absolutely pummeled while the rest of the bewildered (and cowardly) student body looked on in horror and intrigue. I'd witnessed a couple of those incidents in both Tulsa and Houson, and each time it was shocking to see. Many times, it seemed that the victims were just as bewildered, having crossed some arbitrary line set by the aggressors and pulled into a severe beating. Not many would, nor still will, admit that the feeling was as though you had found yourself in state prison and the guards were telling you to "avoid eye contact and you'll be just fine". The advantage the black (and to some extent, Hispanic) kids had was the collective will to join in the conflicts of their racial brethren. They could gang up on others where white kids usually wouldn't help each other in such perilous confrontations. Their racial loyalty made up for their small numbers. I admired it, yet understood that most of the incidents were predatory, cruel and lacked any strategy other than the law of the wild – might makes right.

When OJ was acquitted, one black student wrote "Not Guilty" on a piece of posterboard and paraded down the hallways, forcing it into the faces of white students. I took pause and thought about how asinine and openly racist he could be without repercussion. I also thought about how ludicrous it would be if a white student had done the same if the situation were inverted. I must acknowledge the total difference in mindset between the groups. The sign holder lived with the perception of isolation due to his being surrounded by students of another race. The surrounding culture was suspicious of him but frightened of confrontation with him, so he could plow into it without fear of retribution. There was no incentive for him to be mindful. He wasn't interested in winning hearts or minds. He was interested in the one thing hate promises us – release. The world was going his way on that day. Eventually, life goes back to normal and people go on with their lives, but that memory stuck with me.

News reels provided an ever-growing trove of exemplary material to replay in my head and my disdain grew. Still, I had many things on my mind like graduating high school, part time jobs and getting into college. I could see what had occurred in Los Angeles, Rwanda, Somalia, Haiti, in the media and in parts of nearly every American city and metropolitan area. Although I felt my culture was being assaulted while it toiled, I knew it was a big world and couldn't let racial skirmishes divert attention from my goals. I didn't want race to define me or my actions. My observations didn't stop me from watching sports, laughing at black comedy, or listening to hip-hop. It didn't stop me from visiting my old friend Anthony in Tulsa either. Nevertheless, if given the option I would've ground most black people into a mocha shake and pumped it to the ocean. Even if there was collateral damage like losing Stevie Wonder, Oprah, Eddie Murphy or even my friend Anthony, I would've elected to go forward with it. It is interesting how one can respect and appreciate individuals but still long for the overall eradication of their kind.

While I was busy with my life, I didn't take much notice of my sister's social situation. In Tulsa, she had entered and won a modelling competition at fourteen years old. She had been active in modeling since then. As I was in my senior year, she was participating in modeling shoots and even got a bit part in a holiday add for our local mall. Despite her success she was becoming more isolated in school. She had dated a friend of mine, but they broke up. He told me it was because she didn't want him hanging out with me while they were dating. Upon hearing that, I felt perfectly fine letting her go her own way. I didn't disown her, but I was relieved when she voluntarily exited my social circle. I went on with my busy life for another summer and then went to college in northern Texas. For a year, the voice of racial discontent was muffled by difficult classwork and living in a dormitory near some of my friends from high school. I was unaware that the year I graduated high school, my sister had begun using drugs. While I was in my first year of engineering school, she was frequenting crack houses. It wasn't until the next year that my parents started acting strangely. They had solemn demeanors on the phone. I could tell they were keeping something from me. Perhaps it had something to do with my grandfather's cancer or the failing health of our family dog. My mom mentioned something about my younger sister "jumping out of windows". I figured it was a stupid party incident or a bout of recklessness like some of the wild nights I'd had in high school. It turned out to be something darker than I was prepared to imagine. She had broken a window out of a house to escape a man who had beaten her nearly to death. She was picked up by an ambulance a few houses down, covered in a shirt lent by whoever found her. Later, I was to learn that she was addicted to drugs and likely selling herself for them.

Not much is ever said about what happens to the men and boys in the lives of women and girls violated so heinously. Well, I'll tell you. Aside from being falsely accused of such depravity, it's the worst thing that can happen to a man. The part of you that gave a damn about peace and humanity dies. It puts an unspeakable incident into your mind and presses "replay" for years. If you succeed in not going to jail for murdering the perpetrator, you are still a prisoner of your regrets, hatred and rage. No posse comes to your door with torches vowing revenge, no marches or riots occur in the victim's name. The only guarantee is excruciating mental agony. The one hint of justice that materialized was a call to our house from the local district attorney. He was ready to press charges. The answer from my father was, "No, my daughter doesn't want to press charges and I want to do what's right for her." Upon hearing that, my blood crystallized. In his mind, he was looking out for the wishes of his daughter, the victim. It's also likely that he didn't want her activities laid bare publicly. In my mind, he had put a scared, drug-addicted minor in a position to deny herself long-term justice and a violent predator back into society to prey on other young women. For many years, I didn't see my father or anything he did regarding my sister as legitimate. The strain it put on our relationship was immense. Upon recovery, my sister let me know the basics of what happened. I asked if she wanted me to kill the guy who did it. Her response put a pin-point focus on the subject of my hatred for years to come, "No, he'll just find another white girl to hurt". In retrospect, her assertion that she didn't care about the potential next victim was cold beyond belief. From the perspective of a crack addicted girl, she was terrified of the caged animal, needed to keep her drug sources intact and didn't want her family mixed up in it (though that ship had already sailed).

I finally had a picture of the demon that had violated my sister and it was exactly who I'd presumed it would be. I wasn't given a location, name or police report and had to return to college the following day. I was supportive as I could be but my rage was intense. With justice denied from multiple angles, the need for vengeance had been seared into my soul.

That same semester, my childhood dog and grandfather also died. Not only was my mental acuity on trial in engineering school, but my family was beginning a long descent into darkness. I thought the best thing I could do was to stay out of trouble, stay in school and do well in life. What I didn't know was how consumed with rage I would become. My grades slipped and the only thing I wanted was the slow and methodical torture of a deserving beast. The family I was so close to had become a shell of itself as my sister's continued addictions and her resulting mental deterioration taxed them emotionally and financially. My anger would shift between the animal who'd violated her to society's tolerance of such atrocities to what I viewed as my parents' complete miscarriage of the situation. I did some detective work and came up with a possible location of the incident. I would make the ten-hour drive one weekend, do some reconnaissance and track down my prized game. Still, I knew that I didn't have enough information, had no money to spare for the trip, didn't own a gun and dreaded the possibility of being caught. The trip never materialized. I told myself that revenge would come after I achieved success in the world of accountability and calculation. I would then exact revenge on many people, starting with those who had wronged my family. I felt that while I was a vulnerable young man, they had the upper hand, but they had no idea who they had crossed.

Holding it together with that much anger and proved nearly impossible. Drinking became a risky endeavor as with just a small amount of alcohol would dull my inhibitions and bring my hate to the surface for all to behold. Relationships were lost and strained due to my invisible wounds. Anthony somehow found my phone number and contacted me to catch up. We talked briefly, but I wasn't interested in reconnecting. I was a different person. Back home, the pain in my family life proved hard to shake, especially during holiday visits. My sister had become an unbearably offensive and cynical presence. In their attempt to keep her from running away in search of drugs, my parents would endure her abuse and satisfy her demands, no matter how ridiculous. If she would wreck a car, they'd buy her a new one. If she was pulled over drunk, my dad would take care of all the legal legwork. She was never made to face up to any consequences and because of it, she had become a menace to society in her own right, especially while driving. My refusal to take her verbal abuse lying down left me out in the cold during visits. I was generally pushed away because I was a threat to the "safe space" my parents were trying to cocoon her in. In a strange way, she had become our family's own tyrannical dictator. My parents showed all the hallmarks of oppression, denial being the most insidious of them. Visits were hard and frequently traumatic. That's the road I took to intense, crushing hatred. Hatred can come from anywhere or anything. Like success, it gains momentum from one incidence to another. From the disfunction of one person came a domino-like effect of collisions between cultures and worlds.

On the verge of surrendering my previous goals and becoming someone else, I found myself at a crossroads. I could see the promise and opportunities before me. On one hand, I had set myself up for a great life and it had just begun. On the other, I felt that my family had abandoned me to chase the fires of addiction, a man who deserved to die a violent death was amongst the living and a spoiled academic semester had dashed any hopes of me getting a decent job after school (or so I thought). The reasons for hatred were clear and simple to me. There were people in the world that would oppress, abuse or even kill me and my loved ones if allowed. In turn, I would do the same to them with great zeal, whether or not it was sanctioned by law. Society and government do their best to signal that hatred is wrong but false virtues are easily discernible. At the peak of my frustration, the idea of a justice-starved existence was unbearable. In my mind, the best way to improve society would be to kill some people. I began to imagine a scenario where I would begin to hunt, punishing and harvesting as many malignant souls as I could until I was caught. I'm sure many other parents, siblings and children of victimized people imagine similar scenarios. When one reaches the conclusion that society is incompatible with their values or is outright hostile to them, potential hatred can become kinetic. In some cases, people decide to end lives in massive shows of discontent. Some want the post-mortem fame, and some could care less. I liked the ideas of both raw justice and notoriety. My circumstances had me enraged, yet powerless both personally and socially. During that time, I fit the profile of a mass killer.

So, what stopped me? The same thing that stops other would-be killers: self-preservation and perspective alteration. I couldn't hand over the life that I so carefully crafted to the misery of a drug addict or the underworld that preyed upon her. I'd seen pictures of people with head wounds and couldn't imagine a piece of lead ripping through my brain because I'd put myself on a rampage. I had to zoom out to a bigger picture of life. What had occurred didn't remove the opportunities before me. My best years were just starting and I wanted to see them through. I knew I'd have to carry the hatred with me because I didn't know how to rid myself of it other than through the expression of vengeance. I thought, if anything, I could live to fight another day and make a bigger splash if I ever decided to do anything murderous. Within all that pain, something life-changing occurred. I went to such a dark mental space that I had no choice but to interrogate the idea of existence itself. I wasn't sure I could live in a world with no justice. I had to know the workings behind evil and its presence in our lives. I had to deconstruct everything from the universe to spirituality to society and reconstruct it from the beginning. In so doing, I had to derive the foundation of existence itself. It was in this crucible of anguish that the Paradox revealed itself to me. I can't give total credit for my realization of NE to those events, but it definitely provided a catalyst for the deep thought that brought me there. I continued to bear the burden of parasitic hatred for many years, but the revelation of NE was the beginning of the end of its grip on my life.

It isn't lost on me that before the tragedies that befell my sister, I viewed people, especially blacks and those of the third world, as a toxic mess that had to be dealt with. Within that perspective, the law of attraction showed its dark side. I had spent time in the realm of negative thought and it led to my entanglement with a negative reality. What's the worst possible outcome a man can imagine in the realm of racial animus and conflict? Well, it happened. I wasn't involved materially in any hostilities, but I was involved psychologically. If you have a strong image in your mind of something that you don't want to happen, it's as powerful as imagining something that you do want to happen. Via the law of attraction, I literally conjured the situation in the superconscience by entangling my thoughts with it. I not only created the monster who preyed on my little sister, I also created an unstable and addiction-prone sister. It would take several years for me to realize this but once I did, I had to take stock of all the negative people and interactions I had in my life and ask, "Why did I create them?" In realizing I had created not only the people in my life, but reality itself, I knew I had great control over my experience. I began to see my sister as a character I had written into a play. I chose to reinvent her character as a creative and independent person. I also recognized that my parents saw her only as a drug addict who would never gain control over her life. After another dark incident involving my sister, I asked my mother to imagine a new version of her daughter. I wasn't sure my request was truly heard, but things began to improve in the next few years. Several years later, she had moved out of my parents' house. She began to teach painting to groups. It appeared that her condition had improved. Over the phone, my mother told me she had imagined a new version of my sister and I should do the same. She didn't remember that I had suggested that to her, but I didn't care. It worked for a few years and my parents got to experience genuine retirement for a while. Nevertheless, memories leave ruts and old characters tend to re-emerge. For reinvention to be successful, you must keep believing in the new character or risk them slipping back into their old scripts.

After my journey, I know hate for what it is – a strong aversion to something. We all hate something. It can't be eradicated nor should it be. Hate has a purpose, and just like a knife or a gun, it can be turned on its owner. Hate is useful only in creating traction for worthwhile causes. Absent of timely or meaningful action, hate is destructive only to its beholder. Hating someone for prolonged periods is like drinking poison and hoping they die. So, how do we rid ourselves of hatred that has overstayed its welcome? As you might have guessed, the secret resides in the oneness of NE. In our experience of Everything, we will see, do and be all. We are the brothers whose hearts are crushed and full of rage. We are the addicts bouncing through life, on our paths of destruction, sorrow, shame and redemption. We are the drug dealers and pimps, feeding on naivety and innocence on our hellish tours of the damned. We are characters in a show that we produce and direct. Once we understand that we're looking at ourselves at different points in spacetime, we can let go of hate for good.

Remember that hate saves lives as well as takes them. The key to harnessing its power is in knowing when and how to deactivate it. Go through your rolodex of hate. Find the people and things that have overstayed their welcome and tear the page out. They're not worth your mental exertion. They were put in your life for a reason, but when your interaction with them is complete, you can move on. Take time to examine how they have changed your path and how different your life would be without your interaction with them. If necessary, create an alternate vision of them. As MOE, you needn't be bothered by those who accuse you of hatred, for you are the most peacefully inclined, open-minded being there is. For you, parasitic hatred is an impossibility. You can't truly hate your own embodiment. You can show disgust for it, try to banish aspects of it or even grind it up and pump it into the ocean, but you can't hate it eternally. Those who may accuse you of the 'evil' of hatred are only doing it out of their own ignorance or prejudice. Follow your instincts and do what must be done from your perspective. By all means, rid yourself of parasitic hatred, but don't discount the motivational power of your emotions. The forces of hate require direction to do good, just like any other implement. Others may not understand your motivations or methods now, but your positive intentions will be revealed in the end.

JEALOUSY

Everyone envies and likes to be envied, but envy can become parasitic. Envy can be positive or negative. When envy becomes tainted by negative emotions, it's jealousy. We've all been jealous of someone or the target of someone else's negative envy. Like hatred, it's an emotion that is deeply engrained in the human psyche and linked to our social pecking order. It's often hard to discern between envy and jealousy. Sometimes, the only one who knows whether it's one or the other is its beholder. Some conceal their jealousy out of politeness, to avoid conflict or to gain an opportunity. We like to see those who we believe deserve success obtain it, and those who don't to eat crow. Who hasn't felt a bit of *shadenfreude* at the news of an 'undeserving' party's misfortune? Some of the jealous feel that their own potential is stolen or overshadowed when someone else is successful. Others feel that someone else is winning more than their 'fair share' and would like to see them lose for once. Still others harbor preexisting negative feelings toward the victor and any success they have enrages them. In any case jealousy, like misguided hatred, can have terrible effects on the jealous as well as the envied. In fact, a great deal of hatred is rooted in jealousy. Friends envy us while our enemies are jealous of us and our enemies might be closer than we think. Success, real or perceived, may stir up jealousy regardless of your intentions and the best policy is to know how to handle it when it emerges.

Through the NE lens, jealousy is an immutable trait in primates and is not easily subdued. However, it can be turned into an asset. One way it can be used is in exacting retribution. Have you ever heard that the best revenge is living well? Success in life can fan the flames of jealousy in your detractors. Letting those who've wronged you smolder in jealousy can be a very satisfying way to get even. Jealousy can also reveal the true intentions and deepest desires of its percipients. If someone is irked about your happy marriage, job promotion or other life adventures, you can be sure that they desire something similar or are insecure in those areas. Be aware of your own tendencies to lash out at the enviable circumstances of others, as you may be revealing your own insecurities. Also be aware that stoking jealousy in others won't win them over. Although you can't help it if your successes and exploits make others jealous, no one likes a braggart. Just as jealousy can be an asset, it can be detrimental to its subject.

As MOE you'll have little use for jealousy other than its revealing characteristics. Some satisfaction may come through seeing others envy you, but negative envy isn't what you should strive for. Jealousy is suffering and, although inevitable, is something to be avoided. The reason we achieve goals, have adventures, foster good relationships and gather possessions is to cultivate positive experiences. Yes, being envied can enhance your experience, but it shouldn't be mistaken for a long-term goal. We should be sharing our experiences with others in ways that they can easily digest and get behind. Nevertheless, humans are a jealous bunch and some are intolerant of even slightly positive traits or successes in others. Be ready to redirect the focus of the jealous from your wealth and exploits to your character. When focused on one's character, jealousy may be converted into a more positive form of envy. In Everything, there is no need for jealousy because all realities are imminent. By existing, we will see, do and be all. Everyone's time for greatness will come, guaranteed.

KILLING

"It's a hell of a thing, killing a man. You take away everything he's got and everything he's ever gonna have." –
Clint Eastwood as William Munny in 'The Unforgiven'

During our time as organic lifeforms, Earth's conditions necessitate a long list of actions. Unfortunately, killing is one of those actions. Killing provides food, pest control, landscaping, clothing and building materials. Despite the wars and murders happening at any given time, it is still exceedingly rare for humans to intentionally kill other humans. The act of saving another person from harm is much more desirable for the vast majority of us. Sympathy for others is one of the reasons Homo sapiens have risen to the dominant Earth species. Within our societies, homicide is the ultimate offense. As opposed to killing insects or animals, killing other humans is much more personal. The food, fur and leather killing occur behind closed doors, out of sight and out of mind. Pest, landscaping and lumber killing involves species so removed from us that we don't identify them as sentient.

The reasons for homicide are wide-ranging. Uncontrolled rage, revenge, jealously, conflicting ideology, obsession, hatred, insanity, opportunity, notoriety, material gain, sadistic cruelty and even reasonable fear are all causes for murder. While less than one tenth of one percent of us will ever commit homicide, the popular media makes homicidal tendencies seem a bit more commonplace. Is it evil, or just an action with more serious consequences than we're comfortable with? To answer this, examine killing through the NE lens. Most of us agree that conventional killing isn't evil. Workers who slaughter animals, kill bugs and cut down trees do it to provide for themselves and others. In those cases, the killing is an obvious part of the cycle of life. There are instances when poachers overhunt or go after endangered species, but they are also providers, however misguided. Conventional killing is no more evil than a fox eating a mouse or a jaybird plucking a worm from the ground. It's a necessary part of life.

How does homicide differ from conventional killing? The difference is in the status of *Homo* sapiens. Humans are endowed with rights and protected by law. We have possessions and vast networks of societal connections. The idea that we'd kill something of similar intelligence is both unsettling and intimidating. Many of us believe that humans are the only creatures with souls and that killing another person will leave one disturbed, haunted or even damned. Due to our conditioning by society, humans occupy a pedestal of universal superiority and pseudo-equality under the law. This disposition gives us the confidence to lead relatively worry-free lives. I say *relatively* because there are still homicidal people among us. We lock our doors, carry weapons, study self-defense techniques and keep our children under close watch in case we cross paths with them.

In homicide, there are three motives. The first is gain. By removing someone from the equation, the killer might gain property, opportunity, notoriety or any number of things at the expense of the victim. The second is gratification. In the case of revenge, sadism, hatred and perversion, the killer isn't interested in gaining anything but gratification by harming or killing the victim. The third motive is defense. Sometimes the prospective victim(s) is a perceived threat and the killer feels they have no choice but to eliminate the threat. Defense is understandable because, even in cases of paranoia, the killer does not want to kill yet feels threatened. Still, whatever the reasons for killing, there may be consequences beyond those you were trying to avoid.

The most troubling cases of homicide indicate a lack of emotional reasoning that we call 'having a conscience'. Those who harm or kill without conscience are considered especially vile, but are they evil? In the *Good and Evil* section, we discussed the line drawn between good and evil and how it limits our options for reasoning with violence. The idea that you are either good or evil leaves many on one side of an arbitrary boundary. Once we are given our identities, we tend to play our roles. Often, a killer's perception of themselves is informed by what society tells them and their answer becomes, "yes, I'm evil". Some will even smirk when they say it because they would like people to believe they possess some sort of dark or demonic power. Others will tell you that they aren't evil, just sinners or powerless to stop themselves. This is closer to the truth but shouldn't lead to being relieved of consequences. Through the NE lens, no one is evil. Those who commit homicide are immersed in one combination of reality, however unfortunate. No evil person has ever existed. Still, actions have repercussions. If you kill someone, prepare for consequences. Whether the consequences stem from societal laws or the victim's own clan, killing a human is a dangerous proposition. In the same way that killers aren't evil, society's reaction to them isn't evil either.

In fact, societies everywhere seem to have lost their capacity to address infractions against them. A balanced society meets actions with comparable punishments. The prison systems in the Western world are much too kind to those who have violated their citizens. Should someone who dismembered or tortured innocent people receive decades of fame on death row, select a delicious final meal and be gently put to sleep? Through the NE lens, properly addressing frightening people is to match them with frightening repercussions. That would address some of what is called evil and quell many an observer's need to see requisite justice. It would draw society closer to natural laws and do away with those who brazenly violate them. The key to society obtaining satisfactory justice lies in rejecting any notions of evil in either the perpetrator or the system that processes them. By utilizing the NE principle of rejecting the notion of evil, we'd have the will to single out terrorizers and declare, "No more. You're done here." and go on with universal love in our hearts.

So far, we've addressed intentional killing. In cases of accidental killing, there is a potential for immense suffering on the part of both parties. Accidental killers are often emotionally damaged or suicidal due to their guilt. Having been negligent or ignorant only increases the guilt and its possible repercussions. It is important for those who have ended a life to understand that their worldline intersects others in unavoidable and sometimes tragic ways. Ending the life of another doesn't end their existence in spacetime. For a life to end, it must have been. If something was, it always will be. Existence has no beginning or end. There will come a time when you kill another person, intentionally or not. There will also come a time when you are killed by another. Understanding the inevitability of all occurrences, the absence of evil and the permanence of existence should help you come to terms with it. Though poignantly cathartic, William Munny's statement about killing a man is actually wrong from the NE perspective. If he was MOE, his statement would read more like, "It's a hell of a thing, killing a man. You change a perspective and its influence, but nothing can be removed from existence."

WAR

"A conqueror is always a lover of peace."
-Carl von Clausewitz

War is sometimes required of us. In its throws, there are moral quandaries, not the least of which is taking life. From the NE perspective, death is an illusion while, from a human's perspective, it is something to be avoided at all costs. War isn't always a fight to the death. Put simply, war is an intense effort to achieve an objective. The definition of war we're most familiar with is, *"armed conflict between states, societies or other groups"*. The word war itself has German and Saxon roots meaning *"to bring into confusion"*. Although it brings to mind an archetypal image of helmeted, camouflaged troops, firing guns and sheltering behind embankments, war is actually much more multifaceted. In addition to conventional war, where combatants have organized militaries, wear distinctive uniforms and abide by select rules of engagement, other possible variations include cold, cyber, germ, guerilla, terror, psychological, nuclear and total war. War can be confusing, uncertain and destructive, but from the perspective of MOE, it can also be useful and fascinating.

Cold wars, like that observed between the US and Russia from the end of WWII until 1991, employ weapons development, espionage, digital attacks, psychology and propaganda to obtain an advantage over an adversary without officially declaring war on them. The development of thermonuclear weapons throughout the 1950's assured mutual destruction of all humanity if two or more major military powers became engaged in a direct conflict, so indirect "cold" war became the only way for major powers to skirmish without declaring war and destroying each other and the rest of the world in the process. Cold wars are wars of attrition as the less economically stable will either have to surrender due to collapse or declare suicidal all-out war on the more stable adversary.

This was seen when the Soviet Union declared insolvency and disbanded. Although the US vs. USSR cold war was the first and most notable between nations, it was the start of a trend. In an age of nuclear and biological weaponry with the potential to wipe humanity off the map, wars between nations with nuclear capabilities are best served cold. Much like total war, the goal of cold war is to weaken or divide the adversary, making it possible to overcome them, ideally without a single battle.

Cyberwar is a favorite tactic of both cold and total warriors, as it is hard to defend against, destructive, semi-anonymous and thus far hasn't risen to the prerequisite threat level required to justify a declaration of conventional war. Germ warfare shares similarities to cyberwar in that it is destructive and difficult to prove or trace. Countries that initiate biological warfare assume the risk of the act of war being revealed and being drawn into a hot war, but possibly by a weakened opponent. Cyber and germ warfare are relatively inexpensive, decentralized and can be disguised as business or research. Given those attractive qualities and potentials for destruction, germ and cyber warfare are the weapons of choice for countries like China who lag in the realm of conventional weaponry but excel in the concept of total war.

Terror and guerilla warfare look similar at first glance, but guerilla fighters generally target the military personnel and facilities of their adversaries while terrorists intentionally target civilians and other 'soft targets' to achieve their political aims. The line between guerilla fighter and terrorist can blur if the guerilla fighter becomes desperate or depraved enough. Once the line between guerilla and terrorist is crossed, reconciliation is unlikely. Many times, terror is done for terror's sake as a final suicidal act of retribution on a society. Terrorism and guerilla warfare are the tools of outnumbered, out resourced, yet determined underdogs. War tactics blend. For instance, terrorism is a type of psychological war. Striking fear and disturbing the continuity of peace is psychological.

Propaganda, threats, misinformation and social pressure also fall into the category of psychological warfare.

For centuries, war tacticians have reverted to two great texts of wartime strategists, *On War*, by Prussian general Carl von Clausewitz (1780-1831) and *The Art of War* by Chinese general Sun Tzu (544-496 BC) for insight into the nature and conduct of war. Both generals advocated the broad use of psychological, economic and diplomatic tactics to bend the will of their opponents. Clausewitz's view of war is more applicable to modern nation states in that it is limited in context to commanders on battlefields; acting within the resources and circumstances granted by states and subordinate to politicians. His insightful argument that war is not an end in itself, but an extension of politics through other means has made him one of the eminent masters of modern warfighting strategy. He stressed winning the minds and hearts of allies and opponents because, according to Clausewitz, the side who wins the will of the people is most likely to prevail overall. He also stressed the complex and dynamic nature of war, the danger of overly complex planning and the virtue of plasticity under tremendous pressure. Clausewitz would agree that war is nothing more than an intense effort to achieve a goal. To him, it was paramount to start with a well-defined goal and stay the course during and after war. He acknowledged that war changes internally over its duration, often confusing the participants into fighting battles that do not serve its original purpose. To Clausewitz, those who are victorious remember the specific reason for which they are fighting.

Both Clausewitz and Sun Tzu believed in the integration of political, economic and social measures to win the overall war over discrete battles. Where Clausewitz's stratagems were rooted in the world of a nation state, Sun Tzu's apply more broadly. Operating an era thousands of years before Clausewitz, his freedom to conduct diplomacy and war without as many political hindrances allowed him to advocate a method of full-spectrum warfare that he called "total war". Total war, in the eyes of Sun Tzu, allows one to defeat the enemy by fully analyzing the situation and attacking all aspects of the enemy's opposition to their cause. This means understanding the real reasons they are fighting, their sources of strength and how to deactivate both. In his eyes, the perfect war was one in which the objective was met without a fight. Sun Tzu reminds us that there are effective alternatives to battle. He also stressed that the morale of your own army as well as your opponents is key. Other takeaways from the Art of War include appearing strong when weak and vice versa, leaving your opponent a way to exit a conflict on your terms, avoiding prolonged conflicts, choosing your battles wisely and dividing the enemy from within.

Today, many study Sun Tzu and Clausewitz's war strategies and apply them in non-military arenas including business, government and personal relationships. In all its forms, war remains an intense effort to achieve an aim. The aim may be destruction. It may be unification. It may be emotional balance. It may even be peace. That's right, if the stars are aligned and one waring party is both strong and benevolent, war brings peace and prosperity. Still realize that peace is also perspective dependent. One man's peace can be another's trauma.

War, its nature and how to conduct yourself in various scenarios of battle on Earth is well understood through the NE perspective. The most successful warriors have the presence of mind to apply knowledge from history and their own previous battles to the current battle. They also have great desire and incentive to fight for their causes. They become so focused and convinced of victory that fear and doubt are pushed aside. They utilize the entire spectrum of tools at their disposal and do whatever is necessary for a positive outcome. Most importantly, they know why they are fighting and have a plan for after the war is won.

In matters of intense effort, MOE is a total warrior and student of all tactics and means available for success. MOE are students of history, psychology and technology, as are other successful warriors. Where MOE differs is in understanding the phrase, *"I am you at a different spacetime position"*. From that standpoint, MOE has a markedly enhanced perspective over even the most skilled tacticians. There are several aspects of NE that offer advantages:

- The reduction or elimination of fear through understanding the inevitability of all experiences.

- The gain in efficiency realized by observing true oneness and reduction of psychological hindrances such as parasitic hatred, vengeance and remorse.

- The ability to see the "biggest picture" afforded only to those who have deciphered the Paradox. Having a view from this perspective makes your actions, goals and methods enigmatic to your opponents.

There are more commonalities than differences between the methods of MOE and traditional war tacticians. To understand the most important of the traditional tactics, *On War* and a good interpretation of *The Art of War* are recommended reading. Some of these principles are referenced and ingrained in the MOE principles of warfighting. Both of Sun Tzu and Clausewitz had actual combat experience and orchestrated strategies and tactics unlike me, whose battle experience is limited to civilian and interpersonal experiences. MOE warfighting principles are their principles, but with the addition of the NE perspective. The most important of them are the following:

In Offensive War

1. Know your objective and its consequences. Consider where the objective fits into the big picture. Is a war necessary, or just a diversion from something else you should be doing to obtain the objective?

2. Remember your original intent but keep an open mind for information that may change your intent.

3. Know yourself and declare war on anything that needs improvement. Health, public speaking, strength, knowledge, mental acuity and skill are good examples.

4. Know your opponent well. Learn about their motivations, strengths, weaknesses and center of gravity. It is their center of gravity you must attack.

5. Avoid projecting your values onto your opponent. They do not necessarily share your values.

6. Transform your war into a cause. Align it with a progressive new feeling and play to people's emotions. Willpower is proportionate to the belief in possibility.

7. Avoid hating your enemy or believing they are evil. Such emotions can cause brain fog, hasty decisions, reduce the chance for peace, increase the probability of unnecessary destruction. Remember that they are you at a different spacetime position. Use your opponent's hatred to unmask their intentions and push them into hasty action.

8. Once committed, use all resources and advantages available to you. Perception is an important and underutilized asset in war.

9. Appear indifferent and harmless. Keep your intentions mysterious until the time of attack. Surprise your opponent. Don't give them any sense of your schedule.

10. When you attack, do it quickly with overwhelming force.

11. Leave your opponent a way to exit the war on your terms. An opponent who feels cornered will give you a vicious fight.

12. Be as brutal as necessary. Although you have no hatred for your opponent, the urgency of the situation has necessitated war. War, as life, can be brutal. During war, all of your actions are a product of the war. Remorse should be discarded along with hatred and fear.

13. Avoid drawn-out struggles. Either fight fully for your objective or focus your resources elsewhere. Brutality and quickness of action are useful here.

14. Win or lose, forgive your opponent. If you are victorious, your objective is complete. You may fight another day but simmering anger and contempt poison only the beholders.

In Defensive War

1. Explore all the options for peace. Play to your opponent's emotions and state your case for alliance. Highlight your similarities. Notify them of the Paradox and your true oneness.

2. Trade space for time. Time is more important than space in defensive war. Retreat to advance. Negotiate while advancing. Use the dynamic of the situation to move unpredictably fast here or slow there.

3. Get your opponent to battle on your terms. Control the dynamic by holding back and forcing them to make the first move.

4. Create an unpredictable and threatening presence. Appear strong when you are weak and vice versa.

5. Know your opponent's gnawing insecurities. Find something about them that deserves ridicule and make them a clown for it. If they hate you, all the easier to trigger hasty maneuvers.

6. Use reverse psychology to get your opponent to make false moves.

7. Expose your enemy's soft flank and attack it relentlessly.

8. Defeat your opponent in detail. Separate and conquer small groups or aspects of them individually.

9. Occupy the moral high ground. Set a good example. Combat falsely moral warriors by exposing their hypocrisies.

10. Give your opponent enough rope to hang themselves. If your opponent is insecure or belligerent, deny them targets long enough to let them self-destruct. Never interrupt an opponent in the act of self-destruction.

11. Create alliances with common goals. Beware of allies that may overpower you after the objective is met.

12. Penetrate their minds by any means necessary. Send messages across enemy lines, use media, propaganda and scare tactics to demoralize your opponent.

13. If faced with an enemy who wishes to absorb you, join their ranks and destroy them from within.

14. Forgive your opponent. They are you at a different spacetime position. If you are victorious, be happy. If they are victorious, be happy for them.

The word war evokes images, both heroic and horrific. It is one of the most destructive endeavors we undertake. Yet, much is constructed in its wake. War is tragic, but it is also part and parcel of being a human on planet Earth. Without war, Homo sapiens would stagnate as a species. In times of relative peace, like the one this book was written in, war continues as politics. Our intense efforts to achieve objectives continue to elevate us to new heights as we begin to see the reality of our existence more clearly. Perhaps the oneness of NE will be universally realized and war will be directed to preservation and advancement over destruction. Well, certainly.

CRUELTY

Like many other emotionally driven behaviors, cruelty resides on a spectrum. It can range in severity from a social slight to boundless torture. Cruelty can transcend species and range from unintentional and ignorant to premeditated and ingenious. What makes an action cruel? Cruelty has qualifying and aggravating factors. The two factors that qualify an action as cruel are 1) the action causes harm to someone or something and 2) the action has no purpose other than the suffering of the recipient. Aggravating factors include 3) the recipient is undeserving of the action and 4) the recipient is defenseless against or vulnerable to the action. The first two factors are necessary for the action to be considered cruel. The third and fourth aggravating factors add to the severity of the act either individually or as a pair. Now we have a designation for cruelty. It's interesting that our reaction to cruelty depends on aggravating factors. Aggravation can potentially change the nature and results of a cruel act. When the someone is finally punished for especially 'evil' deeds, the general public delights in their anguish. The understanding that cruelty is well deserved gives it license. This allows it to be administered without reprisal. The same goes for the aggravating element of vulnerability. No one with a functional conscience likes to see helpless people or creatures subjected to cruelty. To prey on the helpless, even if it's out of opportunity, is depraved. It also reveals weakness in the perpetrator. Factors like these add to the perceived severity of cruelty and give license for it to be reflected back upon its initiator(s). This emphasizes the perspective dependence of cruelty. Where and how it is justified depends on your viewpoint.

At some point or another, we all fantasize about wielding the power of cruelty. As bad as it sounds, this is quite normal. Take the representation of villains in books and movies. Often, the primary villain in a fictional story is given a dark demeanor, but also enviable characteristics like chiseled features, special powers or a form of shadowy charisma. Villains frequently begin as high achievers or underdogs that become disillusioned. Their disillusionment leads them to defy the status quo and embrace negativity, in so finding their evil identities. Look no further than the legend of Lucifer as God's fallen angel for such a storyline. While we are obligated by these narratives to despise the villains, we are entertained by the prospect of their allure and forbidden powers. Most viewers are drawn to the villain as much as the heroin despite the fact that the most brutal end is usually reserved for the villains. Without the characteristic of dominating power, the disposition of the villain would be much less attractive. Just as we seek significance through notoriety and permission through wealth, dominance is what we seek from cruelty. Cruelty is the desire to control another's fate, even against their wishes and unload our frustrations onto a captive audience. In short, cruelty is an expression of domination.

If there was one human trait that most would like to see eradicated, it's cruelty. Cruelty puts many in difficult and horrific positions and others in positions of perceived power. The cruel often revel in their actions, making them especially vile and dark-natured. So, is cruelty evil? No, although it may appear as such from many perspectives. Recall that in Everything, all actions are imminent and therefore good. Nearly all primates take part in cruelty, knowingly or unknowingly, at some point in our lives. Small children discover the joys of stomping insects, terrorizing animals and picking on anyone more vulnerable than themselves. Kids are cruel, in part because they haven't learned otherwise and also because they haven't learned how to disguise their intentions. The normal trend as we age is that the emergence of empathy reduces or eliminates our tendencies for cruel behavior. Unfortunately, this isn't the case for everyone. While most of us tend towards the kind side of the cruelty spectrum, some of us refine our skills in intimidation and wrath on the other side.

So, how can cruelty be stopped? Unfortunately, it's a hard-wired trait in humans. Sometimes the only answer to cruelty, especially the aggravated variety, is to return it to the purveyor in an overwhelming and unforgettable way. However, unchecked exchanges of cruelty can escalate and spread like wildfire as seen in tribal and gang conflicts. Cruelty evokes feelings of vengeance in people, regardless of the reasoning behind it. If your goal is to reduce the effects of cruelty in your life, the primary aim should be to stay vigilant and protect yourself and defend others from it when possible. Avoid those who signal cruelty, even if they are attractive or charismatic. The other action you can take is to learn to recognize your own tendencies to be cruel. Remember, cruelty doesn't equivalate to evil. It's a natural expression of domination. If you feel a sense of domination of someone or something, ask yourself if you ever jerk the leash emotionally or physically. Even if it's subtle or in a playful manner, it could harm the recipient. Over time, this can wear on relationships and create bad vibes in your perspective. Most of us won't reach the intensity of cruelty as an Albert Fish or Josef Mengele, but we're all on the spectrum. The further we move toward kindness, the more rewarding our perspectives become. Keep in mind that all realities are imminent and although some may be terrible, none are evil.

VENGEANCE

What's the difference between justice and revenge? That's a trick question because there is none. Both are forms of retribution that depend on perspective. One could say that justice is more fairly estimated and rendered, but it's retribution all the same. The word 'revenge' has a distinctly different connotation. It's often used as an intensifier as in the phrase 'with a vengeance'. It's seen as emotionally driven, unsanctioned and even cruel. Conversely, 'justice' implies legitimacy and adherence to manmade laws. The vengeful are vigilantes while the police are purveyors of justice. If law enforcement is unbiased and free of corruption, then the laws it upholds are likely legitimate. As we know, those instances are rare. If the laws where you live stray too far from those of nature, odds are that they are corrupt and illegitimate. Society's goal is to keep the peace, not necessarily to deliver justice, despite what they may advertise. If justice is accomplished in the process of keeping the peace, then all the better. Revenge is often born when the burden of delivering justice falls to the individual.

Revenge, like justice, is only worthwhile if it yields a positive result. If the only aim of your revenge is to make your adversary suffer, then you've veered from the path of NE into parasitic hatred and cruelty. Perhaps the aim is to teach your adversary a lesson or to reclaim something that is rightfully yours. In those cases, revenge should be swift. Prolonged quests for revenge tend to damage the seeker as well as the recipient. If the need for revenge is left to fester for too long, it will devolve into a mental blockage and aimless rage. If revenge is justifiable from a panned and zoomed perspective, fast action is key. No threats should be made, no journal entries made and no gloating after the fact. Complete the revenge with stealth and expediency and move on with your life, emotional baggage dropped. Not all revenge is kinetic. To seek it passively, you could befriend your adversary's contacts and tell lies about them. Revenge can also manifest positively. Living well, knowing your adversary will learn of your success is a positive form of revenge. That's one of my favorites because it promotes positive action. Another form of positive revenge can be found in disproving your adversary's assumptions or declarations about you and turning them into a fool and a liar. Sometimes revenge eludes us altogether. If it can't be had or its window is missed, drop the baggage and move on knowing that all realities are imminent and revenge is only perceived.

What if someone is attempting to exact revenge on you? What if they are pursuing your demise around every turn? Luckily, very few have the calm demeanor or presence of mind of MOE. If you notice someone attempting revenge, they're likely doing it with little regard to the vulnerability and exposure that vengeance can bring them. Their efforts, whether passive or direct can be easily led to dead ends. If they harbor hatred for you, their emotions can be used to trigger hasty maneuvers or expose their conniving intentions. You could also deny them the conflict they seek and wear them down over time. The best scenario, though, is to remember that all who intersect with your worldline are part of an incredibly rare and implausible existence. Your interactions in this life are to be cherished. If someone is vengeful towards you, it's because they perceive that you've violated or taken something from them. The same applies if you are vengeful toward others. When all is one, this can't be. We owe it to one another to acknowledge our oneness and convey it to others. Through the NE lens, all spacetime positions and perspectives are sacred. Peace is always the first choice if possible.

DECEIT

What's one of the worst things someone can do to you? I guarantee it's not to deceive you. In connotation, the word 'deceit' is right up there with 'hatred' and 'cruelty'. From the Ten Commandments on, deceit has been considered one of the great evils that man is capable of, bestowed on us by Satan himself. There are countless cautionary tales about lying and many manmade laws against it. It has certainly led to the demise of untold relationships and to the end of many lives. Still, deceit is one of those words with a more complex meaning than its connotation suggests. On one hand, it's used for nefarious purposes without regard for the pain it causes. On the other hand, it's used as a defense strategy and a way to protect others. The result of your deceit depends on who you lie to and why.

Like many other despised human traits, deceit is deeply engrained in our subconscious. We lie on a daily basis to avoid unwanted solicitations, unnecessary interactions and to comfort others. We lie to keep our emotions in check and to present a consistent persona to the world. We even lie for recreation when playing card and board games. We're all liars. If one never lied, they would find themselves isolated, just as those who lie compulsively often do. The motivation for a lie is as important as confirming its presence. It's important to see beyond the negative reputation of deceit and embrace it as a vital implement of navigation. Deception is a tool available only to the most advanced species. It requires the ability to both comprehend the possible ramifications of the truth and to imagine an alternative set of facts that would mitigate or eliminate negative reactions to it. Like all advanced tools, deception can cause severe harm if aimed improperly.

So why does lying cause so much harm? Being lied to is insulting, but it also compromises trust. Exposed deceptions cast doubt on all areas of life of the deceiver, not just the subject of the deception. It causes people to doubt the very foundations of their relationships. Lying to cover up negative actions is perilous, but the negative action is the real culprit. The subsequent lie is just a last-ditch effort to save face or keep things going as usual. If you unsuccessfully lie to cover up a wrong that you committed, then don't be surprised if the lie itself is added to the list of offenses credited to you. Not enough credit is appointed for good intentions in lies.

Like cruelty, deceit lands on a spectrum ranging from positive benevolence to wanton malice. Those who deceive also range from bumbling to masterful and from compulsive to highly reserved. The corner of the spectrum which produces the most positive results is the benevolent, masterful and reserved one. Diagonal to it is the malignant, bumbling and compulsive liar. Habitual lying is similar to a mental disorder or addiction where the liar experiences a temporary high and suffers the inevitable consequences for it later on. In those cases, the well-being of the victim is secondary or completely unaccounted for. Some even get a rush when being deceitful. The possibility of being caught raises their endorphins, producing a 'liar's high'. Other lies are just poorly executed. Whether it's to protect the feelings of someone or out of malice, bad lies are quickly discovered. Once the deception is exposed, the deceived begin a journey of confusion, anger and, if the liar is lucky, forgiveness. Forgiveness is one thing, but trust is another. Trust takes time and testing to rebuild. Doubt is a frustrating element that destroys relationships.

We began this discussion describing deception as an implement of navigation and it certainly is. To use it as an implement, understand that deceit may be achieved actively or passively. Active deceit, otherwise known as lying, requires formulating alternative accounts of what has occurred or is occurring. Lying for positive results requires more than just being dishonest. It requires a comprehensive reforming of reality. A careful liar takes all variables into account, leaving no stone unturned. Lying with care requires an understanding of the psychology and patterns of all parties involved. It also requires an off ramp whereon the deceit can be terminated and life can return to normal. Every added variable and person engaged tangles the web further and makes the off ramp less plausible. This is why so few of the wise are inclined to actively deceive. The safer form of deceit is passive. It's less risky because it can easily be disguised as discretion. This is where the expression, "they're on a need-to-know basis" comes from. Though some wince at the idea of withholding the truth, others view it as simply not providing unnecessary or unrequested information. Passive deceit isn't lying, but rather avoidance of volunteering information that otherwise would not have emerged. Why give info that otherwise would've been hidden from those who don't need to know it? Too many lies are uncovered simply because the deceiver couldn't keep a secret or their ego got the best of them. This has compromised militaries, business deals, criminal organizations, relationships, etc. Even passive deceit can prove difficult for those with average impulse control. Just because deceit is passive doesn't mean it's benign.

It's one thing to deceive, but what if you're the one being deceived? We all like to consider ourselves impervious to tricksters, but at some point everyone finds themselves at the business end of a lie. Think of some of the memorable lies you've fallen victim to. Now try to imagine the motives behind them. Were they malicious? Though malevolent lies certainly occur, most lies are enacted out of preservation either of self, a relationship or a situation. In other words, most people lie to save their own skin and not necessarily to hurt others. Yes, lies still cause damage and hurt the recipients but it helps to put them into context. Most liars lie out of fear and insecurity. In fact, many compulsive liars are shown to have had insecure childhoods and feel compelled to compensate for fear of abandonment. So, what should you do when you realize you've been deceived? If the deception is out of preservation, let the liar confess. Let them know the gig is up and demand the whole truth. Let them know how it affected you. Then let them know that you understand the context and that they are forgiven. Never hold a lie over someone's head for too long. Unless it's compulsive, permanently labeling someone a 'liar' is a disservice to both parties. Most liars are worthy and capable of redemption. In the case of malicious lies, identify and disprove them whenever possible. Offer the liar an exit ramp but make it clear that their mission has failed.

From the NE perspective, there are no lies, only perspectives. All is true and all will be revealed. For MOE, the primary implement of deceit is in discretion. Information is powerful because it alters perspectives. It's important to regulate and direct it whenever possible. Though passive deceit can be used to harm, our intentions are benevolent. Consequently, our management of information is masterful and reserved. MOE uses direct deceit only when necessary and with extreme discretion and care for the recipient. Our goal is to transform perspectives to obtain positive results. In the event of malicious deceit, the rules of defensive warfare apply but with the knowledge of universal oneness within reach.

FAILURE

"But, on the whole, tho' I never arrived at the perfection I had been so ambitious of obtaining, but fell short of it, yet I was, by the endeavor, a better and a happier man than I otherwise should have been if I had not attempted it." - *Benjamin Franklin*

Existence is the ultimate, all-encompassing achievement, though sometimes our senses tell us otherwise. As you know, Everything is complete and no further achievement is necessary. The same applies to failure. As defined, failure is the inability to meet an expectation or objective. Whether or not we fail depends on the expectations we set for ourselves. If our expectations are lofty, we might find ourselves failing more often and more dramatically than if our objectives are more practically conceived. The realization of failure can induce emotions ranging from slight annoyance to complete devastation. It can cause one to reflexively retry or to walk off a bridge. Just as in the case of achievement, experiencing failure is part of existence. In our interactions with the limitless perspectives and quests within Contemplation, we'll experience many perceived failures. Although failure is virtual, it's as real as anything gets. Perception is the only differentiator between failure and success.

Is failure avoidable? Yes and no. It is avoidable in the sense that you may experience something that you interpret as success. Part of life is the experience of creating outcomes. If the eventual destination is one of success, you will have the full experience of achieving that success, including failures along the way. If it's one of failure, you'll have the experience the shortcomings that lead to it. In his quest to improve in thirteen self-defined virtues, Benjamin Franklin discovered that, although we may fail to meet an exclusive standard, many auxiliary objectives may be met in the process of trying. If you grasp the meaning of the saying, "within the journey lies the reward", then you are halfway to ridding your vocabulary of the 'f' word altogether. Even though it can't be avoided, failure is not always a given. In our quests to achieve, we go on journeys that take us through much more than our narrowly defined objectives. Those "auxiliary" experiences often times become little victories in their own right. Several unforeseen experiences can be had during a long, hard-fought journey for an intended experience. If the main objective isn't met, it can sometimes be offset by other adventures along the way. We can't fully avoid failure, but we can offset it when it happens with other victories. This doesn't mean living in denial but learning from unmet expectations and continuing forward in the most efficient way possible.

Of course, we're not always trying to succeed for ourselves. Our achievements affect those around us. They shape the opinions others have about you and the prosperity of your loved ones. As mentioned in the preface, the animal part of your being strives to further your causes and those of your kin. Every perspective that intersects our worldline reacts and adapts to our experiences. The worldlines which track ours are special in that they experience many of the triumphs and tragedies that we do. Loving and appreciating other perspectives makes failure an unwanted prospect and gives us impetus to strive for other outcomes. Although our perspectives are divided across spacetime and between universes, the Paradox dictates singularity. Other perspectives are really our own at different spacetime locations. It's important to know that when you fail, you are not failing those whom you love but rather experiencing an unmet expectation in their presence. The failure is seen and experienced differently from different perspectives but is part of a shared reality.

Understand that those whom you compete with are also you at different spacetime locations. When you fail and they succeed, their success is yours to relish. All occurrences are ours to appreciate or abhor. When goals are lofty, failure is an ever-present possibility. The ability to pan to other perspectives and truly appreciate them is the key to managing it. In the event of a massive, crushing failure, the best way to deal with it is to alter your perspective of it and turn it into a victory. Understand that Everything happens and that all occurrences are imminent. In the realm of NE, all experiences are successful. The ultimate achievement is the contemplation of existence.

DESTRUCTION

Things come together and they come apart. That's the nature of mass in the universe. At the point of conception, all mass and energy occupied the same nonexistent position and it will always occupy it, at least conceptually. From the NE perspective, nothing is created nor destroyed. Nevertheless, in the current embodiment of possibility, destruction is perceived in many different ways. Our common understanding is that when something that is meaningful to us is unraveled to the point that it is no longer relevant, it's been destroyed. Destruction can apply to social structures, relationships, physical objects, celestial objects, ideas, and other states of being. The biggest destroyers in the eyes of humans are natural disasters, conflict, disease and scarcity. Most of the time, destruction has a very negative connotation. The word conjures visions of smashing, exploding, shredding or otherwise obliterating something that was once nicely organized and, in our minds, 'whole'. Destruction shares a commonality with achievement and failure in that it is perspective dependent. One person's destruction may be another's achievement, but in any case, things are merely reconfigured or dispersed, never absolutely eliminated. We may try to avoid 'destruction', but when it is inevitable, all we can do is appreciate it as a reconfiguration. No organization of matter is ever permanent.

Organisms need organization. The more complex the organism, the more arrangement it requires to be successful. As the most complex organism known to exist, humans happen to organize and construct more than any other. When we 'create' something, we're really just reorganizing it, though sometimes in ingenious ways. The majority of our lives are spent organizing matter and bringing it to its highest purpose from our perspectives. In society, wealth is created by creating arrangements that can be reproduced on a grand scale. The closer to 'perfect' the arrangements, the better. Take automobile manufacturing for example. Over time, car makers have become aware that consistency in production leads to satisfaction for the consumer. It's very satisfying to enter an enclosure designed for comfort and aesthetics but also guaranteed functionality. The same applies to all constructive endeavors. Our species craves and thrives on well-organized structures. Compared to the fertile realm of life and organization, the chaotic landscape of destruction feels baron to us.

If we're so bent on organization, then why does destruction sometimes please us? Most of our time and energy is spent organizing and building, but some deep-set part of our mind appreciates destruction. Destruction can be viewed as an achievement as well as an infraction. Great construction projects require a fair bit of destruction. The felling of trees, digging of trenches, routing of pipes and cable are all activities that necessitate destruction. When major buildings in Las Vegas are imploded, crowds stand and cheer from a safe distance as old buildings fall in on themselves, are replaced momentarily by plumes of dust, and emerge as piles of rubble. When we're confident that the result will be something bigger, better and more organized, we're happy to usher out the old. The dichotomy is also apparent when examining the results of wartime innovations. The development and deployment of atomic weapons during World War II is the most vividly stunning example of the usefulness of destructive force in generating a positive outcome. While many argue that it was a naive and cruel action to take, the result was that it saved many more lives than it took. It hastened Japan's surrender thus preventing an invasion of mainland Japan. The study of atomic energy also led to medical breakthroughs and treatments for cancer. The passage from the Hindu scripture 'Bhagavad Gita' where the god Vishnu states, "Now I am become death, destroyer of worlds." was recollected by the physicist J. Robert Oppenheimer upon the first successful test of an atomic bomb in 1945. He and many others knew they were using the most powerful weapon yet wielded by mankind as a means to procure America's victory. Beneath his purported emotional anguish over the development of nuclear weapons and their deployment in Japan, Oppenheimer most certainly understood the principle of using destruction to a positive end. He would've been pleased to see Japan's miraculous recovery and conversion to a capitalist powerhouse in the 1970's. Total destruction like that seen in nuclear annihilation brings with it a sense of catharsis and purification. What better way to wipe the slate clean than to sterilize a conflict with a decisive blast? Destruction is the ultimate release of pent-up rage. As long as it is occurring somewhere or to someone who 'deserves it', it can be very satisfying.

Through the NE lens, destruction is a fact of existence and depends upon perspective. If used as a means to further our causes, it can be an enjoyable task that promotes discovery and healthy release. If aimed in the 'wrong' direction, it can be devastating and painful. In either case, it's inevitable so observe it in all its magnificence.

DISABILITY

Living as an animal on a terrestrial planet requires many incredible abilities. Surviving and thriving as a human requires more ability than that of any other animal. Though we are blessed with an abundance of talents, some of the thousands of systems which propel us through life are subject to malfunction or fail to develop altogether. The fact that we can go on despite the malfunction or absence of these systems is testimony to our adaptability as a species. In the wild, if an animal breaks a limb or is born lame, the odds of its survival are nil. Humanity takes care of its own and even provides tools like crutches, wheelchairs and artificial limbs to aid the disabled. Still, having a disability and being surrounded by so many of the able-bodied can feel like a loss. Disability affects those closest to the disabled as they share the burden of making up for a lost system. The situation is worse when someone or something with special needs receives no help or is exploited due to their vulnerability. The fate of the disabled rests in the hands of the societies in which they live. Disability is an imminent experience that we will all face.

So, how can we reconcile this ominous presence in our reality? From the NE perspective, ability is relative. Although one may be blind, deaf or crippled, they still possess much more ability than any other lifeform on the planet. Unless someone is totally disabled, it doesn't serve them to define them based on their broken system(s). One of the top-voiced aggravating aspects of having a disability is the hyper-focus that people have on their malady. They are labeled 'disabled' in spite of their thousands of intact abilities and talents. A certain segment of the population thinks that it helps people to be globally defined by their challenges, or things they perceive as challenges. This is preferred by some because it provides recognition to receive special treatment from society, but the long-term effect is branding and isolation. The key to becoming less defined by your immutable characteristics is to amplify something else about yourself and reject the labels people try to append to you, regardless of their intents. Notable examples of successful amplifications include Franklin Delano Roosevelt, Stephen Hawking, Sudha Chandran, Lou Ferrigno, Stevie Wonder and Marlee Matlin. All had disabilities and all found ways to be defined otherwise. Another aggravating aspect of disability according to the chronically disabled is how sad it makes other people. When we see others with obvious disabilities, we tend to feel sadness for and empathy towards them. Whether you know or care for someone with a disability or are disabled yourself, disabilities are heart-wrenching challenges but are usually under control at some point. It might be a shocking contrast compared to able-bodied life, but disabled life doesn't equivalate to continual sorrow. Once disabilities are managed to some degree, the lives of the disabled have immense potential for fullness. In the worst cases of disability where the afflicted is suffering, no haste should be made in alleviating that suffering, though it is one of infinite possible experiences.

PHYSICAL ILLNESS

"Everyone who is born holds a dual citizenship in the kingdom of the well and the kingdom of the sick. Although we prefer to use only the good passport, sooner or later, each of us is obliged, at least for a spell, to identify as citizens of that other place." – Susan Sontag

Complex organisms face a continual onslaught on our systems from our environment and our own physical makeup. Bacterial and viral infection, poisoning, cellular abnormalities, genetic mutations and aging can all lead to physical illnesses. Illness is one thing that every animal experiences in its lifetime. Some illnesses come and go, some are chronic and some are fatal. When illness strikes, it's as if you're being assailed by nature and there's some truth to that assumption. Our living bodies are massively powerful and complex systems which displace, consume and expend thousands of calories a day. We live in an ocean of cells and broken bits of DNA. Our immune systems do an untold amount of molecule sorting in defense of our bodies from bacterial and viral infections. Thankfully, even the infections that slip by aren't typically death sentences or the causes of chronic problems. Our bodies do a stellar job fighting and healing from the onslaught. Humans are the only Earth species capable of treating the sick. We possess powerful knowledge which allows us to manufacture and distribute lifesaving and therapeutic medicines and vaccines. These drugs and remedies cure illnesses that decimated and rankled the human population only a century ago. Still, being human comes with the possibility of becoming ill. Though we outrun many illnesses, it still catches up with us at some point and exercises its ancient right to alter our fates. From the NE perspective, we should experience each day, sick or not. All is imminent and time is sacred.

MENTAL ILLNESS

While technically a physical ailment, mental illness occupies a different category because it takes place in the mysterious catacombs of the brain. It can be caused by things including viruses and infections, emotional or physical trauma, drugs, genetic mutations or developmental issues. Mental illness is harsh on the afflicted and those who care for them. Not only are the mentally ill vulnerable, but their behaviors are often misinterpreted as mean, crude, disrespectful or disobedient. They're often unsavory characters due to the torment their conditions cause them. Most are tortured souls. It's often said that our bodies are the only places we have to live. That's doubly true for our minds. As with other illnesses, there are many medications and treatment options for mental illnesses. Often, the mentally ill must choose between going through life in a medicated state or risk getting hurt in an unhinged episode. If you're mentally ill and fortunate, someone is looking out for your best interests. All too often though, the instability and outright danger posed by the mentally ill leaves them susceptible to homelessness and other bleak realities. Like other ailments, mental illness is usually an unavoidable kink in development of the world's most complex creature.

From the NE perspective, some things should be recognized about mental illness. Firstly, it is one of the infinite possibilities that will be experienced. We may see it from a distance now, but we'll get our turns eventually. Second, illness is relative. One person's illness could be another's Valhalla, or at least not as bad as it appears from a 'normal' perspective. Third, a life lived with an illness is *still* a life lived. A lot of experiences, good and bad, can be had through a mentally ill perspective. Lastly, the ill may have rights, goals and vocalized opinions yet, due to their malfunctioning brains, they mustn't be allowed to control or to harm others. Those with dysfunctional minds should garner our sympathies be treated humanely and with as much dignity as possible, especially since they're one with us. Nevertheless, a burden of the able-minded is to guide those who've lost their natural bearings while upholding the values and rights of those who haven't. If you care about someone with mental illness, show them in the ways that you can, but put your well-being first. It's important that you maintain your longevity to care another day.

ADDICTION

Mental illness has many offshoots, but there's one that has been the scourge of mankind in the last few centuries, it's addiction. It's been over sixty years since it was recognized as a mental disorder yet it's likeness to a sinful disposition and weakness of spirit is too much for most to disregard. The truth is that our personalities are connected to our brain chemistries and all personality flaws are mental in nature. Addiction is especially insidious in that it can be concealed, at least for a time, by the afflicted. Unless they're in the advanced stages of dependence or showing other signs of illness, addicts can be hard to spot. Sometimes the ingested substances or insidious activities can work to enhance their personalities and performances, at least temporarily. Some observers may point to the fact that many great works of art, entertainment, music, literature and business have been accomplished under the influence of addictive substances, and they'd be right. Nevertheless, addiction involves more than just cigarettes, alcohol and cocaine. People can become addicted to food, sex, internet surfing, working, gaming, television, shopping and a long list of other activities that trigger the reward centers in our brains. Some of the things we're addicted to are considered normal in moderation which makes them incredibly difficult to regulate. It's hard to reduce television time when almost every room in your home has a TV in it. It's hard to stop overeating when eating is an essential part of daily life. Alcohol is a requirement at most adult gatherings and nicotine, though in decline, is still front and center at every quickie mart checkout counter. Whether we know it or not, most of us are addicted to something in some capacity. Humans reside on an addiction spectrum. It takes an almost supernatural level of awareness and discipline to break free of addiction but before anything can be done it must first be recognized by the addict.

Addiction can be seen as a series of loops with four stages: desire, consumption, satiation and despair. The desire stage is possibly the most exhilarating and hopeful of the stages. In the desire state of mind, a mental trigger has caused the addict to want something appealing, new or possibly dangerous. It is at this stage that the prospective addict has the greatest chance of escaping the loop. If you or an advocate of yours can convince yourself to avoid the addictive substance or activity, then you can avoid the powerful undertow of an addiction loop. With each cycle of the loop, the pull of desire strengthens as despair precedes it where it once emanated from a less desperate psyche. During consumption of the addictive substance or participation in an addictive activity, all is mechanical and automated. At this point, the addiction is being fulfilled, leaving the addicted at the mercy of the impending results. It is at this point that the most damage is possible and any sliver of self-preservation the addict has can mean the difference between life and death.

Usually, but not always, consumption is followed by satiation. By then, the falsely positive results of the addictive activity are working in the brain, rewarding it with positive chemistry (or death in the cases of an overdose or suicide). Though the addict may feel satisfied, their bodies or surrounding circumstances might beg to differ. After satiation of a parasitic addiction, the physical and psychological tolls become apparent either to the addict or the people surrounding them. This is when despair sets in and the addicted are left with two options: go for another loop or try to overcome the addiction. Unfortunately, most addicts go for hundreds of loops before their choices change for the better. Many never fully emerge from the cycle.

Addiction is a condition of existence and it will be visited upon all of us at some point. As in other mental ailments, similar observations should apply; some addicts may be perfectly happy in their states, a life lived as an addict is *still* a life lived and the chronically addicted should not be allowed to harm others without repercussions. For now, the power and vastness of NE has me in a position of ownership and control. A true MOE has the best defense against the pull of addiction. No single activity, feeling or deed can change your outlook to one of despair. You can try it, set it down and break free of it at any time because you write the script.

DEATH AND DYING

Death looms at the end of every worldline, promising an abrupt change in the realities we're accustomed to. At any time, we could be struck by a mortal injury and be forced to succumb to it. Death haunts us daily, forcing vigilance in most of our activities. It's an overwhelming prospect. Throughout our lives, we avoid it at all costs. If we show signs of expiring, our loved ones, friends, brethren and medics gather around us and attempt to keep us alive or say goodbye. Staying alive is the most critical prerequisite of our experience. Even when our lives end in homicide or suicide, we are protective of ourselves and others up to our final moments. If there's a golden rule to life, it's 'don't die'. Most societies also employ another rule; 'Don't let anyone you care for or are responsible for die'. This second rule makes sense in the context of survival and common decency but, like any doctrine, can be taken beyond its helpfulness. In some instances, we are kept alive against our own will, while suffering or even when it's obvious our body has exceeded its serviceability or capacity to heal. These misunderstandings are usually rooted in good intentions, but they underscore the extreme aversion to death that most of us have.

Aversion to death is natural. All lifeforms have evolved various methods of self-preservation. Survival is engraved into the DNA of every species, but in the last century humans have extended the average life expectancy from sixty to eighty years. Before modern medicine was widely available, we were assailed by disease and death just as other animals. Prior to the medical advancements of the twentieth century, even elites and royals had to rely on superstition, folk medicine, herbs and bloodletting to cope with ailments. Death hounded the living continuously from birth onward without relent. In the ancient and even post-Renaissance eras, people lived with the knowledge that they, or a loved one may suddenly fall ill and die. The demise of babies and children was commonplace. In the ancient world, those in their forties were considered senior and respected though the label 'old' was applied to the loss of ability to perform useful tasks, not necessarily to age (27). That's an alien concept when compared to our forties as a halfway point in life today.

In advanced modern societies, the amount of attention paid to the life quality and ultimate survivability of individuals is inspiring. Never before have our chances of death been so well-defined, categorized and quantified. Thanks to good record-keeping the average person can simply look up their activity on the internet and get an idea of how likely it is to affect their mortality. Smoke cigarettes and ride motorcycles? Here's your likelihood of surviving. Eat healthy and drive an SUV? Here's how you can expect your chances to improve. From airbags in vehicles and helmets on skate boarders to advanced medications and organ transplants, people around the world strive to evade mortality in all its forms. Though some may delay it, the irony is that no one escapes it.

With death around every corner, it's not surprising that our ancestors presumed that immortality was reserved for the afterlife. Pharos, Vikings, Mayan Priests and Christians have all asserted that, upon death, the worthy would enter a kingdom of peace and abundance where they would reside, unchanged, for eternity. Offerings, prayers and sacrifices had to be made to the correct deities to ensure that when the time came, the admission would have been paid and they would be granted passage into the kingdom. Meanwhile on Earth, suffering and death were ubiquitous parts of everyday life. Today, we've become somewhat insulated from the reality of death. That's not to say that mortality isn't present, but rather that it has been cleverly shrouded in an attempt to protect our sensibilities. What was once a straightforward reality is now a more distant realm and death is neither seen nor acknowledged until it affects our lives directly or we stumble upon it unexpectedly. Death arrives as a dark stranger and leaves a deep impression in our psyche. It has always left voids in the lives of those left behind, but today it's a foreign and ominous subject.

When we die, all our plans, possessions and accounts are suddenly cancelled. Death takes everything from us. This, combined with the mystery of what, if anything, survives beyond the body can make it a frightening prospect. We can't help but be troubled by the idea of being reduced to ash or decomposing flesh and mixed in with the dirt and mud that we've clomped off our shoes all our lives.

Amid all this, there are glimmers of hope that we may learn what awaits us in the afterlife. So, where are *you* once your body has died? A popular belief is that a tangible bit of celestial energy that encapsulates our earthy human perspective continues through the ages, overseeing the living and watching over those whom we cared for. As comforting and beautiful as that idea is, it's more of a keepsake thought for coping with the void left by someone who is gone. Imagine how limiting it would be if after dying you were tasked with solving the earthly problems of the living. One might surmise that if a spirit is unable to ascend to heaven or is stuck in purgatory, it might attempt to complete unfinished business or right a wrong. All realities are imminent, but from the NE perspective, there are other possibilities worth considering.

Explanations of the dying experience are sharply divided between the known biological processes and the possible spiritual transcendences taking place. Through the NE lens, spirituality and biology are part of the same system. Biologically, death is the expiration of the system of cells that hosted a perspective. Since its conception, your body has been the origin of this unique outlook. It has carried you everywhere and is your primary vehicle in navigating the superconscience. But cells have finite life spans, so the question becomes, "Are *we* systems of cells or are we hitching rides in them?" To understand death from the NE perspective, you must get comfortable with the fact that you *are* your surroundings. Again, it's a very foreign concept to be put in the same category as non-living matter like rocks, water and foliage. The truth is that we're comprised of the same elements, just organized differently. From our highly coordinated structures, perspectives are experienced both locally within the body and remotely by particles in the universe entangled with it from the time of Contemplation. When we die, the cellular systems which keep the body functioning cease to operate in a closed loop, individual cells disassociate and movement ceases. This could be compared to an electrical circuit opening and losing its charge. When circuits are opened, the energy once conducted through them returns to the surrounding environment and the circuit is 'dead'. Once closed, the circuit can accept a charge and continue working. When a living 'circuit' is opened, it's difficult, if not impossible to close because the components are more complex and less durably associated. The energy (and perspective) conducted through a living organism also returns to the environment when the circuit is opened and the collective experience of the cellular systems (or soul) is dispersed within the superconscience.

We assume that perspectives are experienced exclusively by cellular associations, but the Paradox dictates that we are all matter, space, time and occurrence in all dimensions. This means that *all* spacetime locations have perspectives, not just those contained within living beings. While alive, we are an integral part of a cellular system and play the part of a living creature. We meticulously maintain our systems, keeping them running and happy. Still, our perspectives are linked to the universal consciousness of existence which permeates the multiverse and compels us to experience all possibility. It shines through the fabric of spacetime like a flashlight through a sheet. When your body dies, a tiny speck of light (your perspective) is obstructed but the light behind the fabric is not extinguished. It radiates through the fabric as innumerable other perspectives become illuminated. When your body dies your experience remains part of an infinite continuum. The vessel that hosted your most recent perspective remains organic matter, absent of centralized command and free to react naturally with the environment without regeneration. It would be as if it was a fingernail clipping. You are, and will always be, in the vast and boundless realm of the Everything. Our lives leave imprints in the fabric of spacetime. Those imprints, when paired with the ongoing experiences retained in the superconscience manifest in what we refer to as souls. Ultimately, you are the Creator. You generate forces and occurrences both seen and unseen, hence you are experiencing *your* manifestation, living and otherwise.

Hundreds of thousands have died and were subsequently revived. The vast majority of them say their perspective (or spirit) continued beyond the death of their body. Their time spent in the realm of the physically dead ranges from seconds to hours. Many claim to have had wonderful and enlightening experiences while dead. Some of their accounts offer fascinating and comforting glimpses into the afterlife. Although skeptics have dismissed near-death experiences as the oxygen-deprived brain experiencing its final neuroelectric pulses, the vivid and detailed memories brought back by some defy that logic. In many cases, the subjects' brains were technically dead and would not have had the ability to perform complex thinking or to create the purported memories. Within those thousands of documented experiences, there are several recurring themes: A column or tunnel of light, the life of the deceased 'passes before their eyes' in a very detailed replay or 'life review', there seems to be a turning point between hellish, desolate darkness and light, an angel or deceased relatives await to greet the deceased in the afterlife and finally, nearly everyone returns with a feeling of jubilation that the light is awesomely comforting and death is not to be feared. One of the most remarkable cases of near-death recollection was that of Mellen-Thomas Benedict who died for an hour and a half while in hospice for terminal brain cancer in 1982. His account is as follows:

"The life review is a very important natural phase of both living and dying. Mine started the second of my death and repeated backwards. I got to see why I had gotten sick. It started in the womb prenatally. My biological father, who is now dead, was beating my mother while she was carrying. When he was punching her, I was inside her belly hearing the thunder. I was feeling her pain because I was wired to her nervous system. Every time he hit her, I felt her pain, her fear and her depression. These things may affect different people in different ways, but it pissed me off. I was born angry. That led to a life of being a joker at the parties, but never really trusting people and never getting close to people. And I never understood

this till I had my life review. I also saw that there was a moment I gave myself brain cancer. As children we were being shown films of "Duck and Cover" and nuclear weapons at school and that cockroaches would be the only thing left. Then by the time I was in my 20s, the ecology thing was happening and they were all saying we were going to blow up the world 500 times and we were going to overpopulate and overgraze. The pivotal moment which I saw in my life review was this ecology group put out this photo that's quite famous. It was an aerial photograph of Los Angeles compared to a microscope picture of a cancer cell and they looked very similar. The minute I saw that photograph, I had the thought in my head that nature had gone wrong and created a cancer called humanity and humanity was going to kill this planet. I lived with that belief in my head from that moment on and guess what? I'm a human. I created a brain cancer. So, your world belief, how you see the world, the lens you look through can be devastating or rejuvenating. One morning while in hospice, I felt this blast of light coming in the window. I woke up for a split second and fell back to sleep and the next thing I know, I was outside my body looking at my body and there was a light leaving my body and I said, sort of, "I must be dead". That was what I thought to myself. I tried to wake up my hospice caretaker who was down the hall, but of course, not having a body I could not. The minute I realized I couldn't wake up my caretaker, I ended up back in the room that my body was in and suddenly darkness closed in all around me. I tell you that was the scariest feeling in the world. It felt like hell. I fell into a deep, dark hole as it were almost like a black hole. It seemed like there were many others in this same hole with me. I saw a thin line of light. It was almost like a little star in the blackness, but it was so far away. But almost immediately my life review began, almost like a holographic movie in this darkness all around me. Once I got out of what I call, you know, the hell hole or the black hole I was stuck in and did make my way to the light, it was an amazing experience because something very similar to a guardian angel appeared to me as I called out. I was calling out desperately for help and I realize now that this was the metaphor for my own higher self that was reaching out to me. The only thing I could relate it to at the time was an angel because of my upbringing. As I went to the light or the long tunnel, a part of it was going to the light and the other part of it was coming from the light. As I was moving up, I sort of realized that the light going up was all the people that were dying at that time and the other side of the same light column was all the souls coming in and being born. I was rescued by the light, taken to the light and like any good atheist that stands before the light, I immediately knew it was God. My first big question to the light that I perceived as God was, "Why is humanity so dark and doomed? Why was this ever created?". At that moment, the light breathed me into it and suddenly I found myself in a mandala. It's the only way I can describe it, was an endless mandala of all the human souls that have ever existed. In that mandala of human souls, I could look into every human soul and you may not believe this, but I had a look into all of your souls too. All of you were there. Every human soul that had ever been. In that, I could see no evil, no darkness whatsoever. Then I was shown my soul and again, there was no darkness. Nothing I suspected; it was not there. It was all an illusion. In that moment, it was like an atom bomb went off and everything that I ever knew was obliterated. Then these souls – and it was all of you too – gave me life again. These souls gave my soul life again and, in that moment, my soul was reborn. I had never received such love in my life as I received in the mandala of human souls with the light. I keep that love alive in my heart forever. There's nothing in this world that you could do to taint your soul. Not even Adolf Hitler was tainted once he went through the light. That's why the more you resist giving up the darkness, the harder it is to get to the light. I know because I was one of those. I was stuck to my darkness until I learned to forgive myself and forgive my life and love my life. When my caretaker found me on the floor, she said, "You were talking low so I put my ear to your lips and you were saying, 'I love my life, I love my life'."

Within a couple months after my experience, the light would just come and get me and take me out of my body and every time it happened, I thought I was dying again. It took me about a year to get comfortable with these experiences. Basically, what I learned was that creation has just begun. We've just begun our journey and the future is so bright for humanity. I know people can't see it now because it's been a long, hard path coming up the evolutionary chain and building civilizations as we have known them. I was shown that human beings are one of the most graceful things ever on this planet, believe it or not. Hardship and conflict are simple metaphors for something that's a little more complex in the universe. Stars create and destroy each other, so there's a give and take happening. I got a glimpse into the souls of humans and there was no evil whatsoever. At that moment, I fell in love with humanity. There's always much more good happening than evil, but we haven't transcended survival yet, so we're constantly on the lookout for what we call evil. I got to see what is called a mass potential of humanity. The mass potential of humanity is looking into the heart of humans. There is goodness in every human heart that has ever been. Once you go to the light, you are purified of any darkness, disease or anything you might call evil. I was shown that our minds are at such a young state at this time that it's like that of a child who thinks they are the center of the universe. We're not actually the center of God's eye. We are a part of a whole beautiful system and we're about to mature as a species, which is very important to the survival of the species and the planet. I was shown this in these great – I guess you would call them movies. I was also shown that the whole Earth is actually one living being and the human part is an incredibly special part. Every human alive today has worked their way up from primordial into being the top of the DNA chain. Our DNA is really the book of life on the planet. Every human being alive today has been everything this planet has been so far. On this particular planet, with the type of star we have and the gravity and all of that, we are the sum total of everything that has happened on this planet. We're just learning now not to separate ourselves from nature and the planet. As we mature within a couple of hundred years, maybe a little sooner, we start having true contact. True contact, not mysterious fuzzy pictures. What we learn speeds us along so quickly that it is astounding what comes to us. We're like Noah's Ark. There will be a period for humanity when we start star-seeding that will be phenomenal. You remember all the wagons going out west? Going to new worlds will be a fantastic period of human history. The Earth itself will become more like a natural park. It will be like Mecca, the mother planet that everyone should return to at least once in their lives. Our ascension, as I learned on the other side, is a very natural evolution of dense being in the more subtle being. No two atoms even touch. We are more spirit than flesh. What's interesting is, when I was looking at my body, this light was leaving my body. Many years later, I am studying the field of bio photonics. You hear people say that they see a light leave the body when a person dies, well now that is proven scientifically. When your cells start dying, they give up their biophotons and you are emitting light until every single cell in your body has completely deteriorated. You are giving off quantum material that goes into the subtle energy realm, which we call the 'other side'. There is no beginning or end to our journey. Life does not begin or end here. The journey from anywhere to here is an impossible journey that happens every day in everything, everywhere. The journey is not linear or time restricted. Die then when or where you choose. The end of the spacetime illusion is near. We are all here together right now. In reality, there never was a past. There is no future. It is always now." (28)

Mellon-Thomas's experience and the conclusions he drew from it are breathtaking, but also key in the mastery of time on Earth as a human. His observations fall perfectly in line with the principles of NE. An additional thought I would add is that the column of light and photonic 'souls' within it are not exclusively human, but particles of the consciousness of Everything. When your body dies, you are brought back to the realization that you are one with all, one with Everything. That realization must feel like the warmth and unconditional love that so many describe. My kids are five years old at the time of this writing. My mother passed away in the fall of 2020 and it triggered their curiosity about death. With them being so young, I try to keep it lighthearted while being honest. "Everything was fine before you were born and everything will be fine after you die. When you die, you are still *you*, but you will be focused elsewhere. Everyone's body eventually dies, but *we* continue infinitely." My son, with a bit of lingering concern in his voice asked, "What happens to our bodies then?" I replied, "You know when we cut your hair? Your hair was part of your body. After it was cut, it was no longer a concern of yours. While your hair is swept up and thrown away, you continue on. The same is true for the rest of your body when you continue on." Though full comprehension of death is years away, children can find comfort in knowing that they exist infinitely, even after their bodies expire.

SUICIDE

Some of us find ourselves in bad enough circumstances or states of mind that death is preferable to experiencing what remains of our lives. Contrary to what many believe, these people are often justified in their decisions. When we die, no matter the cause, that's when it was fated to happen. Sometimes life presents us with situations that are truly hopeless. Consider someone in a burning building who has to choose between burning alive or falling to their death, or someone with terminal cancer that has spread to their brain. These are situations where suicide, or assisted suicide are understandable choices. In those circumstances, it's commendable and brave to end your life on your own terms. There are also those of us who feel hopeless but aren't in truly hopeless situations. Someone who's had a bad divorce, the death of a loved one or is socially outcast may feel that all is lost and there is no way out of the darkness that has descended upon their minds. In a way, that too is an illness from which there may be no escape. For those genuinely seeking survival from their hopelessness or suicidal thoughts, the keys to survival are perspective alteration, honesty and consideration of others. Sometimes changing your perspective is all it takes to get over the despair caused by grief or loss. Other times, opening up can cause an intervention and save your life. Consideration of others may also help you climb out of your predicament. Those who commit or attempt suicide aren't the only victims of their actions. We think of those who've wronged us or relationships that have crumbled but what about all the children who know you? Would you want them to be traumatized by your untimely exit? Senseless suicide leaves an indelible scar on everyone even remotely connected to those who commit it. Every memory of that person's time on Earth becomes tainted by their final decision. I suspect that some who commit suicide would like others to ponder their reasoning for the rest of *their* lives. Though it may seem otherwise from the suicidal one's perspective, unwarranted suicide is as selfish an act as murdering an entire family. Still, suicide doesn't warrant a trip to hell or purgatory. Suicide may not be your proximate fate, but it is as imminent as any other. What you end up doing is imminent. Just know that all perspectives are special, even if they meet tragic ends.

REGARDING THE PARANORMAL

I f the NE perspective can be applied to so many other areas of life, perhaps it can be used to interpret some of the unexplained phenomena that we can't yet confirm as real or unreal. With the proliferation of personal and surveillance cameras recording our every move, our dwellings, empty streets, warehouses, wilderness and the skies, visual evidence of the paranormal is becoming commonplace. There are simply too many recorded anomalies for all of them to be hoaxes or hallucinations. Objects can be seen moving and flying through the air with no explainable motivations. Disembodied voices can be heard speaking full, relevant and intelligible sentences. Craft-like objects in the sky demonstrate capabilities that defy the known laws of physics. Strange humanoid creatures can be seen roaming the countryside and retreating into the wilderness. Although it's a broad topic, let's review the most common subjects of paranormal intrigue and consider them from the NE perspective.

THE OCCULT LABEL

What comes to mind when you think of the occult? Witches, fairies, spells, tarot cards, crystal balls, rituals and…cults? The word occult is derived from the Latin word *occultus*, meaning "clandestine or secret" but in modern usage it means "interest in or knowledge of the paranormal". The word, "occult" was originally used in sixteenth-century Europe in reference to astrology, alchemy and natural magic as the "occult sciences", now considered pseudosciences. Although esoteric practices had long been performed, it was during the renaissance following the Middle Ages that the word *occult* was used to describe them. Its connotation had more to do with the small number of people knowledgeable in the subjects than their eccentricities. Over the next centuries, as empirical science became more important, occultism came to be seen as incompatible with the concepts of science (29). The word "occult" began to be associated with irrationality and the rejection of science and modernity. Meanwhile, qualities that had no rational explanation, such as magnetism, were labeled occult. Isaac Newton's contemporaries disparaged his theory that gravity acted through "action at a distance" as occult (30). In the nineteenth century, proponents of occultism, also known as esotericism, began to argue that occultism doesn't mean the rejection of scientific progress or modernity. French esotericist, Eliphas Levi, stressed the need to solve the conflict between science and religion with the wisdom found in esoteric principles (31). Scholar Antione Faivre noted that, rather than outright acceptance of "the triumph of scientism", occultists sought an alternative solution, integrating scientific progress with "a global vision that will serve to make the vacuousness of materialism more apparent" (32). The German historian Julian Strube argued that occultists wished for a synthesis of science, religion and philosophy and that occultism was concerned with the formation of new "scientific religions" while propagating the return of ancient forms of "true religion" (33). By the late 19th and early 20th centuries, some European and American occultists began to distance themselves from Christianity in favor of pre-Christian belief systems and modern paganism while others took influence from Buddhism and Hinduism. Another characteristic realized in occultists was an emphasis placed on the "spiritual realization of the individual" (31) which would strongly influence the New Age, Human Potential and, most recently, the NE movements.

Modern usage of the term *occult* isn't typically in the context of official esotericism or occultism, but rather a catch-all basket for anything that doesn't readily fit into the categories of science or religion (29). Due to its treatment by journalists, sociologists, cinema and the media, *"the occult"* has connotations that range from irrational and illegitimate to satanic and demonic. However, thanks also to cinema and the media, some topics that were once "occult" have become popularized and, in some ways, destigmatized.

When we think of the occult today, all of the first topics listed come to mind, but other topics still technically fit the definition of occult as well. The belief in otherworldly life, unsanctioned spiritual contact, numerology, herbal and homeopathic therapies, hypnosis, NLP, cryptozoology, scribing and unproven scientific and social theories qualify. Thankfully, many of them have come to command the respect they deserve. Most new concepts in human thought have spent time in the realm of the occult. Religions, technologies, small businesses, social clubs and political concepts have all been there. Many eventually shed the stigma, but some have no intentions of shedding the "occult" badge. Secret societies, dark magicians, satanists and fortune tellers thrive on it because the label brings with it the luster of the forbidden. The important thing to understand is that "occult" is just a label meaning "exclusive and understood by few". It's inevitable that you will come across or even participate in the occult in your lifetime. Have no fear if you find your activities labeled as such because one day you may be considered an early adopter of something that transforms the world.

SOURCERY AND WITCHCRAFT

The use of superstitions and rituals to summon supernatural powers or to control people and events is alive and well today. It's expressed in Voodoo, Wicca, Santeria, Brujeria and various other traditions. In Europe during much of the Middle Ages, it was common for magic to be practiced alongside Christianity. Witchcraft was widespread in the cultures of the ancient Middle East and still exists there today. Those accused of witchcraft in

Saudi Arabia are beheaded if found guilty. In South Africa, they are burned alive. The Bible strongly condemns sorcery and verses such as "Thou shalt not suffer a witch to live" in Deuteronomy and Exodus provided justification for witch hunts in the early modern period (34). The main source of contention for the mainstream religions is that the worship of other gods and powers threatens their own religions and traditions. Some sorcery is well-intended and some ill. Many rituals, salvos and caricatures are meant to heal and increase the prosperity of both the sorcerer and the subject. Still, even a skeptic would be a bit nervous if they knew a powerful druid or shaman had a doll made in their image or had put a hex on them. The power of superstition and suggestion lends itself to sorcery, but its real power lies in intent. Sorcerers are very well-practiced in the art of projecting their intentions and some are skilled at messaging the superconscience. The same applies to pastors, clerics, mullahs and monks. The key from the NE perspective is in understanding that you are the source of all intent. If your worldline intersects with that of a sorcerer, you have written them into the script. It's your choice to either observe and appreciate their eccentricities, use their abilities to your advantage, succumb to their power or write them out of the script altogether. As MOE, the power is in your hands, just don't try to beat them at their own game. Your game is existence and you are its Creator.

EXTRASENSORY PERCEPTION (ESP)

There are many well-documented and compelling cases supporting the validity of ESP, but the lack of repeatable results leaves it scientifically unacceptable. Though parapsychology is considered a pseudoscience, plenty of people, including crime detectives, the military and private citizens seek assistance from psychic mediums. Just because we don't understand some functions of the human mind doesn't mean we can't use them to benefit society. Perhaps humans will learn techniques or configure our neuropathways to bypass the mechanism which makes us perceive ourselves as residing in discrete spacetime locations. This might allow us to see other locations as if we were there. My personal experiences with premonition provided exciting glimpses into ESP. My conclusion was that ESP is an interaction between the mind and the superconscience. Though thrilling, on-demand viewing across spacetime would be overwhelming and is unnecessary for Homo sapiens. Consciously observing the future or past could provide advantages but, once we realize others *are* us at different spacetime locations, the value of "advantage" fades. Moreover, no amount of foresight can exempt one from experiencing all realities. The way in which we perceive time and space is a gift. It allows us to focus on one discrete area of possibility and move on to the next without pulling the whole veil off at once. Premonitions and psychic visions happen, and when they do, it's miraculous. However, we should be wary of endangering our orientation to the present. Psychic ability may also be viewed as the superconscience "glitching", but we know that there are no errors in the superconscience, just experiences to be had. We're always traveling time. We can take it moment by moment or open up a wormhole and jump in like whitewater rafters. Luckily for most of us, we don't have to decide just yet.

HAUNTINGS

The effects hauntings have on us vary from positive surprise and benevolence to insidious oppression and possession. It's obvious that something beyond our grasp is occurring, but what and why? If dying means becoming one with Everything and releasing the perspective hosted by our cellular systems and spacetime locations, then why does it seem that some spirits remain engaged and even covet our existence? Shouldn't the dissolution of one perspective immediately lead to the realization of others and the complete release of the past? To get a better idea for what might be happening, it's helpful to characterize the observable patterns of hauntings. They can be separated into four main categories: residual, intelligent, poltergeist and inhuman. In each of these categories, there are positive and negative examples. Strangely, we rarely account for the spirits of animals. We tend to view ourselves as the only earthly species inhabited by spirits, or at least spirits that matter. Yet, some very convincing surveillance footage shows shadow-like ghost pets walking with their oblivious former owners and the spirits of deer leaping and running from their bodies after being struck by vehicles. Although we tend toward apprehension at the word 'ghost', hauntings have as much positive as negative potential. When considering ghostly phenomena, remember that good and evil are relative. Now, let's consider the main categories of hauntings:

Residual – As the name suggests, when an event creates energetic residue or an imprint on an environment, it can act like a recording playing in a loop. Residual hauntings are considered unintelligent and don't consciously interact with observers. It is theorized that traumatic events cause most residual activity and that it can be triggered by objects and actions related to the events. Places like battlegrounds, crime scenes, hospitals, asylums, jails and schools are often the subjects of residual hauntings. It is also thought that foundational materials like stone and wood can absorb energy from such events. This is known as the Stone Tape theory. Reports of activity starting during construction or renovation of old structures are common. It's also commonly reported that residual activities stop after demolishing or burning the affected items. This thinking makes physical sense because all matter is energy and it's certainly possible for energy to be transferred between masses. Residual hauntings don't affect us other than by the occasional scare and increased awareness of the ethereal plane.

Intelligent – Unlike residual hauntings, intelligent hauntings seem to be driven by the conscious spirits of deceased individuals. Both residual and intelligent hauntings can be attached to locations, materials and objects, but intelligent spirits can roam without the need for a host. Intelligent hauntings are sought after by paranormal investigators because they can offer answers to questions posed. They also have more potential for fright and danger because negative conscious energy has been known to attach to people and cause harmful thoughts and actions. Still, there have been plenty of reports of benevolent spirits warning people away from danger or providing comfort to those who need it.

Poltergeist – The German word, approximately interpreted as 'rumbling ghost', is believed to be caused by a living person who is moving physical objects and creating other phenomena telekinetically. Usually, the person is unaware that they're the source of the mysterious activity. Sources are typically young females and going through puberty or other psychological stresses, but older women and males have also been sources of poltergeist activity. The activity, which can also include the emergence of foul odors, voices, shadows and intricately stacked furniture resembles a taunting, malicious haunting. This has led to poltergeist activity being associated with spiritual activity. There have been very few officially studied cases, but the unofficial consensus is that poltergeists are caused by conflicts within the subconscious mind. This puts them in the category of superhuman abilities, but it's important to consider them when it comes to hauntings. Through the NE lens all hauntings are real, but reality is an extension of the superconscience. As with premonition and psychic ability, poltergeist activity reveals a connection between our subconscious minds and the realities we experience.

Inhuman – Often referred to as demonic hauntings, spiritualists assert that the entities behind these hauntings never existed in human form. Inhuman hauntings are credited for some of the most insidious activities including oppression, possession, terror and bodily harm. If we're to believe Christian lore, many angels are pure spirits and haven't existed in human form either. Therefore, inhuman hauntings can also be extremely positive and protective. Most of us are more intrigued with the dark side of hauntings, but it's comforting to know that there are angels waiting to guide us to the positive side of existence.

Have you ever watched the popular cable TV shows that feature paranormal investigators spending the night in purportedly haunted places to pursue evidence of the paranormal? They're entertaining and sometimes frightening to watch. The investigators use audio recorders, modified radios, electromagnetic field (EMF) detectors, and thermal imagery to search for and communicate with ghostly presences. The evidence captured over the past thirty years with enhanced technology is remarkable. In some cases, investigators claim to be pushed, punched and scratched by malevolent spirits. These occurrences are increasingly credible, as they are backed by environmental measurements, real-time audio and visual footage from multiple camera angles and countless recordings of electronic voice phenomena (EVPs). There are several recurrent themes observed before, after and during spiritual contact. One is a sudden, measurable drop in temperature around the activity. Temperatures have also been known to rise in the presence of 'evil' manifestations. Another theme is the sudden draining or discharge of energy from storage devices like camera batteries. There's often an appearance of glowing orbs, anywhere from marble to basketball-sized, gliding through the air near or around the activity. It's speculated that these 'orbs' might be the visible manifestations of spiritual energy transferred from the environment or the storage devices previously mentioned. As in many other earthly phenomena, modern physics and electronics are helping us look beyond the veil at possible truths behind many paranormal occurrences. The toolkits used during investigations give us a window into how paranormal activity affects the environment and how it's detected. EMF meters are used because it's believed that spirits, or the portals they travel through, cause electromagnetic fields similar to those in appliances and electrical wiring. Thermal imaging cameras are used to capture temperature changes and to spot volumes that aren't the same temperature as their surroundings. 'Ghost box' radios broadcast white noise while sweeping across multiple frequencies. Although it would be impossible for a human to say anything over multiple frequencies, spirits seem to be able to. The replies that come from those radios are usually relevant and consistent in vocal tone. Structured light sensor (SLS) cameras have been employed to work similarly to interactive video game systems where the user's body movements are sensed. The sensors 'map in' stick figure-like structures of the investigators and unseen entities. The footage captured on SLS cameras offers more insight into how spirits manifest and move. Strange stick figures, not of the investigators, can be seen appearing on command, touching and climbing onto investigators, appearing to attack them or following simple commands and blinking out of existence.

The segments that give me the biggest chills are the ones where the investigators replay enhanced EVP recordings of guttural growls, screams or angry voices that seem malevolent. It's unsettling that something from a different dimension could invisibly and maliciously pursue us. Some accounts describe 'attachments', wherein a spirit will follow them home from a haunted location and harass or terrify them for days or even years after an investigation. But what could cause an attachment? Perhaps the investigator was vulnerable to it or an object was taken from the location and it transferred energy from that location. Maybe the investigator simply forgot to request that the spirits not follow them home. Or they didn't properly cleanse themselves of the foreign energy. Either way, the message conveyed is that it can be hazardous to delve into the paranormal. Most paranormal experiences are by chance and witnesses don't have the luxury of foresight or preparation. The encounters can be doubly terrifying when the witness isn't prepared for what they experience. Remember, not all encounters are negative or scary. One could argue that witnessing the embodiment of the Virgin Mary, Buddha or Mohammed are paranormal events. Seeing or feeling a loved one who has passed is paranormal. Hauntings can be positive if we are pragmatic and open to them. The reason TV shows focus on the negative hauntings is because fear sells. That's why you never see ghost hunting crews visit locations with positive reputations.

When asked about their experiences, many paranormal investigators will tell you, "You had to be there to understand the feeling". The feeling is of witnessing something that shouldn't logically be part of our objective reality. When asked about their motivations, many say they want to learn about the afterlife. Others say they want to help the dead find peace or move on. Still others say it's just fun to explore historic or abandoned places with the added thrill of possible contact with the paranormal. Two emotions experienced by investigators are excitement and fear. The fear is real, especially since many have reportedly had objects thrown at them, received bruises and scratch marks, and have experienced possessions by malevolent spirits. The excitement is palpable, as many say communicating with the dead is the definition of a spiritual experience. As for myself, I am a member and advocate of the positive existence but remain inexplicably drawn to the excitement of being scared and am therefore intrigued by negative hauntings.

One of the more harrowing examples of an inhuman haunting can be found in Annabelle, the Raggedy Anne doll that was given to a nursing student in 1970. After exhibiting strange behavior, a psychic medium told the owner that the doll was inhabited by the spirit of a dead seven-year-old girl named Annabelle. Once the owner and her roommate accepted the doll and its supposed inhabitant, Annabelle became more troubling and sinister. She began moving inexplicably and writing notes that said, "Help Us", and "Help Lou". Astonishingly, the owner's roommate had a fiancé named Lou. He would later be attacked by Annabelle, first by attempted strangulation, then by slashing with a knife. When the famous paranormal investigators Ed and Lorraine Warren examined Annabelle, they deemed her demonically possessed and took ownership of her. On the way to the Warren's Occult Museum in Monroe, Connecticut, Ed experienced an unexplained loss of control of his car and nearly crashed into a tree. Once at the museum, Annabelle was put in a box to keep visitors from making physical contact with her. On one occasion, a boisterous young man mockingly banged the glass of Annabelle's case. He died in a motorcycle crash later that day. For the remainder of the doll's residence at the museum, signs were placed on the box stating, "Warning: Positively do not Open" and "Do not Touch Anything".

There's also the ongoing saga of the 'Dybbuk Box'. In 2001, an antiques dealer based in Portland, Oregon bought a small rectangular wine cabinet at an estate sale. Its previous owner was a holocaust survivor from Poland. The woman's granddaughter told him that the box had been kept in her sewing room and never opened it because a dybbuk (malicious clinging soul) lived inside. The box contained ritual items such as locks of hair, pennies, a rose bud and a wine goblet. After gifting the box to his mother for her birthday, she had a stroke, scratching out the words, "No gift!" on a sheet of paper as the stroke overcame her. An employee at the antique shop had also witnessed breaking items and profanity coming from the basement of the store where the box was previously stored. The owner wrote that he experienced horrific nightmares involving an old hag that would "beat the living daylights out of him". He also said the box seemed to have an aroma of cat urine around it. Subsequent owners reported similar nightmares and smells including a college student who bought the Dybbuk box from the second owner and resold it on eBay soon after. He had experienced bloodshot eyes, insect infestations, nightmares and hair loss after buying the box. The winning bidder was a skeptical museum director in Kirksville, Missouri. Again, the box preyed upon its owner, causing him to cough up blood, and wake up with welts over his entire body. Fearing that the box had some radioactive or bacterial element, he had it tested for both and came up with nothing. He finally consulted with a rabbi who instructed him to put the box inside a gold-plated wooden box and bury it. Apparently, that worked as he reported his symptoms immediately stopped upon burying the box. Although he vowed to keep it buried, he later sold the box to Zak Bagans of the popular History Channel show *Ghost Adventures* to display in his museum of haunted, cursed, morbid and disturbing oddities in Las Vegas.

Skeptics might be quick to point out that the owners or investigators of allegedly haunted places or objects are experiencing confirmation bias. If one believes something is haunted by a malevolent spirit, then it will inevitably provide an explanation for the bad things that happen to them. With so many individual instances of consistent and unexplainable phenomenon, it's hard to dismiss them all as coincidence. Assuming that Annabelle and the Dybbuk box are possessed, the question is how and by what or whom? Most believe they're possessed by demons or malevolent human spirits. A common viewpoint is that Earth is between spiritual realms. The realms are divided into good, evil and limbo or Purgatory. In this view, the malleable character of humans subjects us to an eternal custody battle between the kingdom of God (good) and the kingdom of Satan (evil) pending final judgement. During the time spent waiting for a final judgement or for fear of judgement, spirits can be left between worlds or in limbo. Due to the timeless nature of spiritual existence, the unjudged can be trapped in limbo for many years. This, according to the classic view, is the source of intelligent hauntings by human spirits. From that standpoint, both angels and demons may influence us and draw us in their directions and dead relatives, friends and ancestors may also reach out to us to warn, protect or even harm us.

If you were to ask a religious cleric about paranormal investigations, they would warn you against opening lines of communication with spirits without the protections afforded by their dogma. We're most familiar with the Catholic forms of spiritual protection due to their frequent appearances in movies and television shows. In the West, if you find yourself pursued by an unwelcome spirit or demon, it is common that one presents a crucifix, applies holy water to their surroundings and reads The Lord's Prayer to deter it or cast it out. These rituals are so deeply engrained in Western culture that when frightened, paranormal investigators invoke them regardless of their religious beliefs. It must be entertaining for Catholics that when most people are up against a wall spiritually, they turn to Catholicism for a solution. Other religious protections are used throughout the world to varying degrees. Verses from the Koran are used similarly when Muslims encounter dark spirits. The customary solution in most of the world is to call upon God's help in the event of an encounter with perceived evil, but ancient indigenous smudging ceremonies are gaining popularity and are widely perceived as effective.

What we're talking about is the possibility that there are passages, portals and other connections between the realm of the living and non-living. We understand all realities to be imminent and therefore true. There are definitely residual energies, pathways, alternative universes, angels, demons and lost relatives guiding us through life. Strictly defining and deciphering the exact methods of opening and closing those passages is beyond the scope of most of our objective realities. Just as our worldly realities are of our own creation, so too are the paranormal. Communication with the spirit world is possible because all realities are connected to the superconscience. Spirits can do everything we imagine they can. It is not only in the case of poltergeist activity that we are the source of hauntings. We are the source of all spiritual activity. We can get as creative as we want with the nature of spirits, angels and demons. As with so many aspects of existence, realizing ownership causes dramatic results. It also means that we must accept all realities. As they come to pass, remember that some may frighten and trouble as well as amaze and encourage you. Clairvoyants and paranormal investigators tap into the superconscience when they use their techniques to communicate with other realms. It may seem that entities are reaching out to us from unknown realms, but in reality, we are creating them in the superconscience. The silver lining to hauntings is the knowledge that some of who we were will be retained in the minds of others when we die. As you know, death is only the expiration of the vessel from which a perspective emits. True death is impossible in a cycle that has no beginning or end. The afterlife is virtual as is existence.

ALIENS AND UFOS

Do aliens exist? You know the answer to that. The possibilities of life are endless in a universe containing billions of galaxies. Thanks to the Hubble and James Webb telescopes, we know what's out there is more wonderous than we can fathom. More than 100 billion stars with an estimated 300 million potentially habitable planets reside in the Milky Way alone. Some of those possibly habitable planets are as close as 30 light years from our Sun. (35) Extraterrestrials wouldn't have to travel intergalactically to visit Earth. They could travel here from inside the galaxy. Beyond its existence, there are much more exciting questions to ask about extraterrestrial life. We'll get to them shortly. UFOs and encounters with extraterrestrials have been formally reported since the years of the Roman Republic, but the recent ones are the most poignant because they're backed by visual evidence. Over the last several decades, recordings of unexplainable phenomenon in the skies and reports of encounters with alien-like beings has increased dramatically. As with other paranormal phenomena, this is certainly linked to the availability of personal camcorders and smart phones to capture sightings at the touch of a button. It could also be due in part to the reduction of stigma attached to those who report the incidents and the plausibility of extraterrestrial life entering the mainstream conversation through the media and cinema. Many recent sightings are from such credible sources that officials are perplexed and sometimes alarmed by them. Here are just a few compelling examples referenced from modern accounts of UFO and ET encounters:

November 23, 1953 - USAF 1st Lt. Felix Moncla, Jr., who, together with his fellow crew member, 2nd Lt. Robert Wilson, disappeared over Lake Superior on November 23, 1953, while pursuing a UFO which was seen on radar in their F-89C "Scorpion". Data at the time of the incident suggested to radar operators involved in the pursuit that the object being pursued by Lts. Moncla and Wilson had suddenly reversed its course, approached the aircraft, and merged with it. No trace was ever found of the missing men, the F-89 - or the unknown machine. (36)

November 5, 1975 – Travis Walton was working with a timber crew in a national forest near Snowflake, Arizona. While riding in a truck with six of his coworkers, they encountered a saucer-shaped object hovering over the ground, making a high-pitched buzz. Walton claims that as he left the truck and approached the object, a beam of light suddenly appeared from the craft and knocked him unconscious. The other six men were frightened and drove away. Walton claimed that he awoke in a hospital-like room, being observed by three short, bald creatures. He claimed that he fought with them until a humanoid wearing a helmet led Walton to another room, where he blacked out as three other humanoids put a clear plastic mask over his face. Walton has claimed he remembers nothing else until he found himself walking along a highway five days later, with the flying saucer departing above him. His story was the basis of the biopic science fiction film *Fire in the Sky* and has been a popular example of a compelling abduction story since its release. (37)

November 7, 2006 – At approximately 4:30 pm, close to a dozen employees, including pilots, ramp workers and airport managers, at Chicago O'Hare International Airport witnessed a silent, disk-shaped object up to 24 feet in diameter and dark gray in color hovering in plain sight above United Flight 446 departing from Gate C-17. Several independent witnesses outside the airport also saw the object. The disc was visible for approximately five minutes. One described a disc-shaped craft, stating that it was "obviously not clouds." According to this witness, the object then shot vertically through the clouds at high velocity, leaving a clear hole in the cloud layer. The hole reportedly closed itself shortly afterward. (38)

2004, 2014 and 2015 – The "FLIR", "GIMBAL" and "GOFAST" video recordings of cockpit instrumentation displays via infrared gun-camera pods on US Navy fighter jets are widely characterized as official documentation of UFOs. The leaked videos were the subject of intense media coverage in 2017 and later declassified by the Pentagon in 2020. The Navy confirmed their authenticity in 2019. The FLIR, or "Tic Tac" incident was observed off the coast of San Diego. The pilot who had been sent to track mysterious movements observed on the radar in the previous days, made visual confirmation of an estimated 40-foot-long, white oblong shape (hence "Tic Tac"), hovering somewhere between 15,000 and 24,000 feet and exhibiting no notable exhaust from conventional propulsion sources. Another crew member with 17 years' experience would later observe that the object would dart from altitudes of 50 feet to upwards of 60,000 feet in seconds. This incident and others were factors in the creation of the Unidentified Aerial Phenomena (UAP) Task Force, created to hunt down any relevant encounters service members may have had with aerial objects that pose a threat to national security. The GIMBAL and GOFAST incidents took place over the east coast in 2015. In both, similar videos were shot of objects exhibiting maneuvers that seemingly defied the laws of physics in speed and trajectory. (39)

An increase in UAP sightings during arial training exercises like the ones which yielded FLIR, GIMBAL and GOFAST has been acknowledged by the US government. In 2020, congress introduced legislation to declassify reports of UAPs and findings of military investigations in another effort to decode the origins and intentions of UAPs. Following the declassification of 144 different observations in June of 2021, a congressional hearing was held on the subject in May of 2022. This was the second hearing of this kind. The first was held in 1970 to discuss the findings of Project Blue Book, a 22-year investigation into UFO activity. In his opening statements, Congressman Andre Carson noted that "This hearing and our oversight work has a simple idea at its core: unidentified arial phenomena are a potential national security threat. And they need to be treated that way." He also said that "UAPs are unexplained, it's true. But they are real." Scott Bray, deputy director of naval intelligence noted that "While there haven't been any collisions between UAPs and pilots, there have been at least 11 near-misses." (40) While the declassified videos and the subsequent hearing show an attempt to be more open about UAP sightings, many ufologists and interested viewers couldn't help but yawn at the typically bureaucratic proposed solutions: to increase sensors, reporting and staff. This all but ensures that real answers won't be coming from the US government any time soon. Given the military's reaction to the hundreds of sightings and multiple near-miss incidents, it is evident that something beyond the general public's knowledge is occurring. There is speculation that an intelligence-based deep state may be promoting UFOs as an extraplanetary security threat in order to promote a form of one-world government.

One outspoken skeptic of the intelligence state's objectives regarding ET activity is Dr. Steven Greer. He founded the Center for the Study of Extraterrestrial Intelligence (CSETI) in 1990 to promote a diplomatic initiative to contact advanced ET civilizations. Dr. Greer and a number of those in his network claim to have the ability to initiate UFOs to appear in the skies using their "cosmic consciousness". According to Greer, his first encounter occurred in the Appalachian mountains when he was 18 years old. Six months prior, he had a near-death experience that gave him a glimpse into universal consciousness. *"The experience taught me that there's nothing to be afraid of and there's nowhere to go because you're already there. You just have to open up to what's already there. After that experience, I thought of ways to get back to that state without being deathly ill. I began to learn how to do meditation. There's a whole universe folded within every conscious being, which is why in these quiet, deep meditative states you can obtain knowledge, see places and communicate. In reality, it's always there and you just have to learn to communicate with it. There's this deeper aspect of ourselves that is simultaneously interwoven and when we go deep into meditation and connect to that, then we have reached the point where we can be ambassadors to the universe."*

Greer has been hosting events where groups of participants attempt to contact ETs using meditation and invite them to show their presence. This has led to multiple recorded mass sightings of what appear to be lights from intelligent sources glowing, zipping by, stopping and reversing, performing coordinated maneuvers and even reacting to verbal requests. These are called CE5 (Close Encounters of the fifth Kind) events. The fifth is the highest recognized kind of ET encounter and is characterized by direct and intelligent communication between humans and ETs. According to Dr. Greer, before holding CE5 events he'd had several of his own experiences wherein he was able to summon ET craft to appear. One purported summoning incidence took place in 1977 over his birthplace in Charlotte, NC. Air traffic control and commercial pilots witnessed the appearance of two UFOs circling above the area. The experience led him to limit his requests and to realize the potential for others to witness them as well. He then formulated a simple protocol to summon ETs. It consisted of entering a state of quiet universal consciousness by meditating, locating the ETs in the universe and vectoring them to his location (41). Dr. Greer and Mellen-Thomas Benedict, whose near-death experience was described previously, share a commonality in that their experiences allowed them to see beyond material consciousness into universal consciousness, otherwise known as the superconscience. Both were also able to access that state on a fairly regular basis after their experiences. They, the CE5 participants, military aviators and countless others who've had ET, near-death and paranormal experiences are describing interactions with the superconscience. When removed from our physical conscience, we remain within the superconscience – the consciousness of Everything.

Now for some questions beyond whether or not ETs exist:

Are they accessible and, if so, will we ever be able to open a dialog with them? Earthlings and lifeforms from all other locations in the universe are part of Everything. As components of Everything, they are one with us. At some point, their perspectives will be ours. At this point, their perspectives are beyond our comprehension. If they're extradimensional beings that happen to be passing through our dimension by chance, then they might be unaware of or indifferent to us. If they're intentionally hopping into our spacetime vicinities to interact, then they will communicate when and to whom they decide to. Some claim to have communicated with aliens and even had follow-up visits or abductions. Those are isolated and rare incidents and likely not attempts to open up a dialog with the entirety of humankind. Crop circles, if genuine, seem to be an earnest attempt to communicate. However, lifeforms intelligent enough to travel between stars would communicate in an Earthly language if they were trying to get a point across. Maybe the markings are signals to humans that can decode them or to other ETs. Or maybe it's just artists or pranksters making their marks. For the time being, it appears that ETs are avoiding broad contact. Perhaps it would be fruitless or endanger their missions. Still, it is peculiar that they would allow themselves to be seen, which in itself could be interpreted as a form of communication. All they would have to do is avoid emitting light. As our understanding of the universe and our technology grow exponentially, so do our sightings and encounters with ETs. It's possible that a dialog is forming between them and those who understand communication with the superconscience. A broader dialogue will likely form once humanity's cosmic intelligence reaches a critical point. Perhaps by then we'll have evolved into Homo deus.

Do they manipulate, or even genetically alter us? By merely appearing in the superconscience, they manipulate us. We are intrigued, frightened and divided by the possibility of extraterrestrial life. We have created civilian and military organizations such as the National UFO Reporting Center and the Mutual UFO Network, and most recently the US department of defense's Unidentified Aerial Phenomena Task Force to share experiences and gather data. The US government has even enacted legislation to make government findings on encounters and sightings more transparent. Whether we believe their existence or not, they have an impact on our reality. The more poignant question is if they interfere with our lives. If some abductees are to be believed, then the answer is yes. There are recurring themes to many abduction stories. In the majority of cases, it is reported that the aliens study us or even take tissue samples. In some of the cases, abductees claim to have found foreign objects implanted into their skin. Some claim to have been in telepathic communication with the aliens during the abduction. Others claim to have seen a mix of full aliens and partially alien humanoids. If they are to be believed, then the aliens are either taking our DNA to blend it with something else or modifying it to change our species. Given humanity's significantly higher intelligence over the other creatures of Earth, it's possible that we are a closely monitored genetic engineering project. Livestock mutilations or, more accurately put, surgeries point to more direct manipulation of Earth creatures. It is peculiar that livestock are dismembered, but few if any humans turn up in similar condition. If the aliens wanted absolute silence, they could presumably purge their subjects into space. If we are being studied or altered, there's nothing we can do but accept our fate as less-intelligent beings. Whatever they're doing seems to be to our advantage.

Do they interfere in or even dictate world events? Two of the examples given are from official US military archives. There have been many more similar encounters with the US and other militaries and police forces around the world. Sightings around nuclear weapon storage sites and warfighter planes suggest that they are interested in the outcomes of our conflicts. More likely, they would be trying to help us avoid self-destruction. In that case, it's no wonder that with the advent of nuclear weaponry at the end of WWII, the modern age of alien encounters began. Perhaps they've already helped us avoid a nuclear catastrophe. The proliferation and poor handling of nuclear weapons around the world was very precarious during the cold war (and even afterward). If ETs are so much more advanced than us, why do they allow us to exist? The answer to that is that they probably *do* want us to exist. If they didn't, it wouldn't be difficult for them to annihilate us or sterilize the entire planet.

What are their intentions? Given their apparent advanced intelligence, our own thoughts, wants and emotions cannot be projected onto them. Anger and malice, for instance, are unlikely traits for space travelers to have. They have transcended much of the rationale we have as humans; therefore, we cannot decipher their intentions. We need not be worried about them, though. If they wanted to harm or control us, they'd already be doing it. If they're already interacting with or manipulating us, we have no say in the matter. It is a good sign that we've been allowed to live. If one were to speculate on their main objective regarding Earthlings, more evidence points to helping us survive than anything else. It is likely that they are welcoming us into the cosmic community as we transcend material survival and move towards universal consciousness.

Are there multiple kinds from multiple locations? Undoubtedly. Again, if abductees are to be believed, aliens range from the familiar, gray-skinned humanoids with large heads and black eyes to tall 'space brothers' with Nordic features to scaly reptiloids. Life in the universe is likely vast beyond what we can imagine.

Are they us in the future, time traveling? Many UFO sightings appear to show objects pulsating from visible to invisible, almost as if they're blinking into and out of existence. It suggests that they are not fully in this plane or perhaps passing through dimensions. Their silent jumps from point to point demonstrate a mastery of spacetime navigation. Humanity is on track to crack the code of spacetime navigation. Given this, there should be no doubt that we will see our future selves visiting or even altering the course of history from time to time. As mentioned however, we cannot project our thoughts and emotions onto them. It would be impossible to understand them due to the chasm between their intelligences and ours. The best we could hope for is for a voluntary dialog. So far, it doesn't look like they feel the need to explain themselves. By the time we discover the keys to extraluminal travel, we'll probably be evolved beyond Homo sapiens. Time travel for Homo sapiens is as futile as rearranging grains of sand in a desert. To transit between distant stars and galaxies, one must also have the ability to comprehend the complexities that result from those travels. If all realities are imminent, then you may as well effect what you can in the time that you have. Currently, most humans have very small spheres of influence. Interstellar or intergalactic travel would vastly increase the size of those spheres. Though, it seems like more than the current human psyche is ready to manage. Yes, it may be us from the future, but highly evolved versions beyond our patterns of thought.

CRIPTIDS

Since zoological discovery began in earnest during the Age of Enlightenment, man has discovered millions of species of plants, insects and animals. Thousands of new species are discovered and classified each year, though that number can be a bit misleading because many "discoveries" are corrections of past misclassifications aided by molecular biology. Most new discoveries are invertebrates including insects, worms, sponges and crustaceans. Another large portion of discoveries is in plant species, many on the verge of extinction. Reptiles, amphibians and fish make up the balance. As for mammals and birds, it is estimated there are less than a dozen yet to be classified (42). So, although there are many discoveries and corrections each year, the discovery of a large mammal like a Yeti or Bigfoot would be historical. Creatures such as these are called cryptids, originating from the Greek word, "krypto", meaning hidden. The capture or discovery of the corpse of any legendary cryptid would be cause for celebration in both zoological and paranormal circles. Imagine the worldwide commotion if the carcass of a recently deceased plesiosaur was tugged onto shore of the Loch Ness or a small cage containing a Chupacabra is brought into a zoo for observation. Imagine standing across the glass from a family of huge Florida Skunk Apes. As saddening as it would be for such rare and majestic creatures to be in temporary captivity, it would reawaken the sense of wonder and mystery people once had about the natural world.

Cryptids are surging in popularity for the same reason that ghosts and UFOs are. The proliferation of cameras capturing everything has left few places to hide. Most of the time, they're caught unexpectedly in the background, but in some instances, the creatures notice the camera and even interact with those filming. That said, it's also become easier to simulate and fake encounters with video editing software and improved makeup and costume designs. Still, there are too many compelling instances to call them all hoaxes. Often, those providing footage of encounters have nothing to gain from the exposure and even risk being ridiculed for it. One cryptid in particular, the Yeti, seems to be appearing more often. If environmental change is any indication, it could be following the pattern of other wildlife as civilization encroaches further into its habitat and as droughts, fires and floods become more extreme.

But it gets even stranger. The definition of a cryptid has expanded to the non-animal, paranormal realm. Now count Dracula or Frankenstein's monster could be considered cryptids. Some are even suspected to have manifested via the power of popular belief. Terrifying concepts like "The Rake", "Indrid Cold" and "Slenderman" originated as fictional internet memes that went viral. Most of the short videos and stories featuring them are obviously fabrications, but those who post them aim to introduce them into the collective consciousness of viewers. Some very creepy videos have been captured of a "Slenderman" about nine feet tall, stick-figure thin with impossibly long arms and wearing a suit topped by an elongated head with a featureless face. The sightings mostly feature him (or it) appearing in the backgrounds of innocuous home videos. He's said to stalk humans and bring their lives to an early end. It's mostly innocent fun. Those involved, usually adolescents and teenagers, appear to be entertaining themselves in a post-Freddy Krueger world. It's as if they want to be scared of something and have to resort to seeking it out on everyone's favorite portal – the internet. In 2014, it took a negative turn when two 12-year-old girls in Waukesha, WI lured a friend into a forest and stabbed her 19 times in an attempt to appease Slenderman, who they feared would otherwise harm them or their families (43). Luckily the victim survived. In a strange way, the girls *had* become proxies of Slenderman, at least the one conjured within the darkest corners of the superconscience. The rise of cryptids summoned via the internet is an example of what can be rendered through group thought. When we consciously focus on something, whether positive or disturbing, the image can be implanted mentally and hold our focus until it manifests in our intentions or actions.

Like ETs and ghosts, cryptids demonstrate the far reaches of our imagination. The prospect of encountering something unknown and frightening, yet still a resident of our landscape stokes our sense of wonder about the world and our place in it. All too often, we lose sight of how amazing "conventional" existence is. Just because something is unexplained doesn't mean it's false, nor does it mean that an explanation is necessitated. If you were to see a bulb-headed, black-eyed gray alien walking around in plain sight, most of us would shriek in amazement and never forget the moment. But if you were to see something just as incredible, like a giraffe or koala bear at the zoo, it would barely register on the excitement scale. Heck, you might not even mention it to anyone or remember it happening. That's because these things have been fully defined, documented and studied by people. We become numb to things you've been conditioned to. Our own human form is another example of an unappreciated marvel. We're definitely on par with alien life in strangeness and magnificence. In addition to our physical form and abilities, our creations are unparalleled. Yet, we're jaded. When something becomes commonplace it loses its intrigue. Although everyday life on this planet is a mind-blowing experience, unknown phenomena keep their intrigue because they remain mysterious and rare. We daydream about what it would be like to live on another planet as an alien, discovering true cryptids or living in ancient or futuristic worlds. What we really desire is a change of perspective. We want to be diverted from our state of mind and shown an alternative existence, even if it's a disturbing one.

We should also address the fact that the vast majority of cryptids and ETs are configured similarly to humans. For the most part, they have human characteristics like two eyes, a nose and mouth (Slenderman excepting), two arms, a torso, two legs and stand upright (Nessie excepting). While many cryptids were supposedly once human, most other paranormal figures are also humanoid. This is probably because we relate to the humanoid form much more readily than others. When something is created in our image, it's easier to imagine its perspective, intentions and ferocity. Even without encountering the paranormal, we're in the midst of the grand playground of reality. That's the real cause for wonder. There's no need for an aliens, ghosts or cryptids to rouse us from boredom. All we have to do is look at it from a different angle. We should be able to fully embrace our adventure, knowing we've existed for billions of years, will continue to exist for billions more, are in the midst of a unicorn life cycle and have the means to affect our environments and outcomes. Just living is a ticket to the front row of the most awe-inspiring and incredible show imaginable. If you happen upon something paranormal, enjoy it and pay it the respect it deserves. It may have its own set of laws to be adhered to. All realities are imminent.

FINAL THOUGHTS

You now have the power to see existence from the NE perspective. This is the first time this information has been offered to the public. I'm not sure how you will apply it nor if its revelation will cause an immediate reaction, gradually work itself into the collective consciousness of humanity or lie dormant for decades or even centuries. I *am* sure that it's been installed and is reconfiguring reality as we know it. Only time can unveil the results of such transformational notions. If you are a Master of Existence, all that you can see, think and contemplate is yours. The NE perspective can be used to overcome challenges, solve problems and answer questions. It can also provide a sense of calm within chaos and love in the face of the challenges posed by terrestrial living. Though many of its applications have been outlined in the preceding chapters, many others remain unaddressed. It's up to the individual to apply the Paradox where and how it is needed to optimize their perspective. If you find yourself in pain, in need, denied, delayed or in other ways burdened, recall the Paradox. The oneness and ownership that it offers will set you back on the path of happiness. If you love your existence and long for its permanence, understand that it had no beginning and will have no end. Existence is an infinite contemplation and you are doing the contemplating. If you have loved ones whom you can't imagine living without or have searched fruitlessly for companionship, know that all is one and we are never alone. If you want more out of life than what you think you've been allotted, understand that existence is an unfathomably heroic voyage and you'll eventually experience all.

THE TENETS OF NE

To understand these principles is to master existence.

1. Everything is possibility contemplated within Nothing. It is what *would* be.

2. Though Nothing is, our proximate reality is Everything. Within this contemplation, all is included and experienced.

3. Everything is virtual and instantaneous.

4. Though Everything is virtual, unknown paths unfold before us, providing infinite experiences from infinite perspectives.

5. Though Everything is instantaneous, the perception of time allows us to navigate through discrete possibilities and experience them individually.

6. Right, wrong, good and evil are perspective dependent. Regardless of our decisions, all occurrences will come to pass.

7. You are the one who contemplates existence, the Creator. Understanding this makes you a Master of Existence (MOE).

8. MOE acknowledges ownership and practices perspective alteration to achieve peace, happiness and success.

9. Existence is the ultimate commitment and adventure.

10. It doesn't happen. Take it as seriously as you want, but more importantly, experience it.

FURTHER GUIDANCE

NE has given me the ability to evaluate situations, no matter how complex or difficult, and formulate shockingly direct ways to understand and improve them. For those struggling for answers or applying the Paradox, I have set up a discussion forum where an experienced and certified MOE can offer clarifications on NE principles and provide helpful suggestions in harnessing existence. To inquire, please visit: ***https://www.neparadox.com***. In addition to the forum, you will find an official NE registry where you can claim your spot in history as having officially received the Paradox. For those who'd like to join our team of certified MOEs, a training program is available. Those who become certified will be called upon to help spread and clarify the message of NE both locally and globally.

CITATIONS

1. Staff, History. History.com. *Who Invented Zero?* [Online] August 22, 2018. http://history.com/news/who-invented-the-zero.

2. Mathematics in the Near and Far East. [Online] grmath4.phpnet.us.

3. Struik, Dirk J. A Concise History of Mathematics. s.l. : Dover Publications.

4. Wallin, Nils-Bertil. The History of Zero. *YaleGlobal Online.* [Online] November 19, 2002. https://yaleglobal.yale.edu/history-zero.

5. Kaplan, Robert. *The Nothing That Is - The Natural History of Zero.* New York, New York : Oxford University Press, 1999.

6. Odenwald, Sten. Why the Big Bang is not an Explosion. *The Washington Post.* 1997.

7. Stacey, Nic. *Everything and Nothing: The Amazing Science of Empty Space.* Furnace Limited MMXI, 2016.

8. Natalie Wolchover. Quantam Magazine. *What Shape is the Universe? A New Study Suggests We've Got It All Wrong.* [Online] November 4, 2019. https://www.quantamagazine.org/what-shape-is-the-universe-closed-or-flat-20191104/.

9. [Video] Survived Pilot Told What He Experienced in the Bermuda Triangle. [Online] https://youtu.be/pTCwAn3MEBk.

10. Vishvas, Maitrey. The Best Way to Travel Through Space - Wormholes! [Online] May 16, 2021. https://maitreyvish115.medium.com/the-best-way-to-travel-through-space-wormholes-a43873bf2f28.

11. Kurzgesagt. *[Video] What is Dark Matter and Dark Energy? https://youtu.be/QAa2O_8wBUQ.* 2015.

12. The Theory of Everything: The Quest to Explain All Reality. *Wondrium.* [Online] 2017. www.wondrium.com.

13. *[Video] Parallel Worlds Probably Exist. Here's Why [https://youtu.be/kTXTPe3wahc].* s.l. : Veritasium, 2020.

14. Harari, Yuval Noah. *Sapiens: A Brief History of Humankind.* Israel : Divir Publishing House, 2011.

15. Wrangham, Richard. *Catching Fire: How Cooking Made Us Human.* UK : Profile Books, 2009.

16. Neimark, Jill. How We Won the Hominid Wars, and All the Others Died Out. *Discover.* 2012.

17. Tollefson, Jeff. nature.com. *COVID Curbed Carbon Emissions in 2020 - but not by Much.* [Online] Jan 15, 2021. https://www.nature.com/articles/d41586-021-00090-3.

18. [Video] Jack Ma and Elon Musk hold debate in Shanghai. *YouTube.* [Online] https://youtu.be/XI5fXp0uDEE.

19. Harari, Yuval. *Homo Deus: A Brief History of Tomorrow.* 2015.

20. Nilsen, Rita Elmkvist. How Your Brain Experiences Time. *Norwegian University of Science and Technology.* [Online] NTNU, August 29, 2018. https://www.ntnu.edu/how-your-brain-experiences-time.

21. The Ten Longest Races in the World. *Sports Management Degree Hub.* [Online] 2022. https://www.sportsmanagementdegreehub.com/10-longest-races-world/.

22. Reber, Paul. What is the Memory Capacity of the Human Brain? *Scientific American.* 2010.

23. O'Neill. Life Expectancy (from birth) in the United States, From 1860 to 2020. *Statista.* [Online] June 21, 2022. [Cited: July 22, 2022.] https://www.statista.com/statistics/1040079/life-expectancy-united-states-all-time/.

24. Emerhoff, Dr. Stewart. Is There Life After Death? *Through the Wormhole.* s.l. : Sci, 2012.

25. Brodd, Jeffrey. *World Religions.* Winona, MN : St. Mary's Press, 2003. 978-0-88489-725-5.

26. Abbott, A. Mind-controlled robot arms show promise. *Nature.* [Online] May 16, 2012. https://doi.org/10.1038/nature.2012.10652.

27. Hillier, Susan M and Barrow, Georgia M. *Aging, the Individual and Society (10th ed.).* 2014. ISBN 978-1305176935.

28. Benedict, Mellen-Thomas. Mellen Thomas Benedict on Coast to Coast am (2009 Audio). AM 1450, St. Cloud, MN : Leighton Broadcasting, 2009.

29. Hanegraaff, Woulter. *Occult/Occultism In Dictionary of Gnosis and Western Esotericism.* s.l. : Brill Publishers, 2006. ISBN 978-90-04-15231-1.

30. Buchdahl, Gerd. *History of Science and Criteria of Choice p. 232 In Historical and Philosophical Perspectives of Science v. 5.*

31. Pasi, Marco. *"Occultism" In von Stuckrad, Kocku (ed.) The Brill Dictionary of Religion pp. 1364-1368.* s.l. : Brill Publishers, 2006. ISBN 9789004124332.

32. Faivre, Antoine. *Access to Western Esotericism.* Albany, NY : SUNY Press, 1994. ISBN 0-7914-2178-3.

33. Strube, Julian. *Sozialismus, Katholizisimus und Okkultismus im Frankreich des 19.* Berlin : De Gruyter, 2016. ISBN 978-3-11-047810-5.

34. Witchcraft Across the World - Near and Middle East. *Witchcraft - A Guide to the Misunderstood and Maligned.* [Online] 2009. [Cited: June 16, 2022.] http://www.lukemastin.com/witchcraft/world_near_east.html.

35. How Many Habitable Planets are Out There? *SETI Institute.* [Online] October 29, 2020. [Cited: June 24, 2022.] https://www.seti.org/press-release/how-many-habitable-planets-are-out-there.

36. Keyhoe, Donald. Disappearance of Two Pilots. *UFO Casebook.* [Online] https://www.ufocasebook.com/twopilots.html.

37. Travis Walton UFO Incident. *Wikipedia.* [Online] [Cited: June 21, 2020.] https://en.wikipedia.org/wiki/Travis_Walton_UFO_incident.

38. Haines, Richard F. *Report of an Unidentified Aerial Phenomenon and Its Safety Implications at O'Hare International Airport on November 7, 2006.* Oak Harbor, WA : NARCAP, 2007.

39. Pentagon UFO Videos. *Wikipedia.* [Online] 2021. https://en.wikipedia.org/wiki/Pentagon_UFO_videos.

40. Kluger, Jeffrey. Congress is Finally Taking UFOs Seriously, 50 Years After Its Last Hearing on the Mysterious Subject. *Time.* June, 2022.

41. Mazzola, Michael. *Close Encounters of the Fifth Kind: Contact Has Begun.* Star Contact LLC, 2020.

42. Chapman, Arthur D. *Numbers of Living Species in Australia and the World.* Canberra, AU : Australian Government, Department of the Environment, 2009.

43. Moreno, Ivan. Wisconsin Girl Gets Maximum 40 Years in Mental Hospital for Slender Man Stabbing. *Chicago Tribune.* 2018.

44. Benedict, Mellen-Thomas. *Journey Through the Light and Back.* Naples, FL : Purple Haze Press, 2009.

45. Sabrina Stierwalt, PhD. Why Do We Laugh? *Scientific American.* [Online] Feb 9, 2020. [Cited: May 11, 2022.] https://www.scientificamerican.com/article/why-do-we-laugh/.

46. Crabb, G. *English Synonyms Explained.* New York : Thomas Y. Crowell Co., 1927.